WITHDRAWN

The Miner

Natsume Sōseki

THE MINER

Translated, with an Afterword, by
Jay Rubin

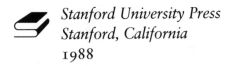

Stanford University Press
Stanford, California
1988

Stanford University Press
Stanford, California
© 1988 by the Board of Trustees of the
Leland Stanford Junior University
Printed in the United States of America

CIP data appear at the end of the book

This translation
is for Raku
who knew

Acknowledgments

THIS TRANSLATION would not have appeared without a good deal of moral and financial support at crucial points along the way. My colleagues at the University of Washington Fred Brandauer, David Knechtges, and John Treat encouraged me with their interest early on, and Andrew Markus and Ching-Hsien Wang provided some timely information and opinions in the later stages. My thanks are due also to Professors Yasuko Imai of Shizuoka Prefectural University, Toshio Ohki of Hamamatsu University School of Medicine, and Edward Fowler of Duke University. None of the people named here should be associated with whatever flaws may remain in the book. The only people to read the entire manuscript were two anonymous readers for Stanford University Press, who provided some excellent suggestions for revision, and my mother, Frances, who surprised and encouraged me by enjoying it, and *not* just because her son was the translator.

Uninterrupted work on the translation was made possible by a grant from the Division of Research Programs of the National Endowment for the Humanities, an independent federal agency, with additional support from the University of Washington's Japan Foundation Endowment and from the university itself. An earlier version of the Translator's Afterword appeared in the *Harvard Journal of Asiatic Studies*.

None of the above would have been true or possible without my wife, Rakuko.

J.R.

Contents

Translator's Note

THE MINER (*Kōfu*) was originally serialized in a Tokyo newspaper, the *Asahi Shimbun*, in 1908.

Few personal names appear in the text, and only one of them includes the surname in addition to the given name. This name appears in the Japanese order, surname first, the practice adopted in the Afterword. The author's surname is Natsume, but in the Afterword he is referred to by his pen name, Sōseki, following Japanese custom.

All monetary sums mentioned are minuscule. A *rin* was a tenth of a *sen*, which was one hundredth of a *yen*, which was worth about a thousand times more than the yen we hear so much about today.

Most of the smoking done in the book employs the traditional *kiseru* pipe with its slim bamboo stem and tiny metal bowl. The "tobacco tray" mentioned at one point was actually a small box. It held such utensils as a tinder cup for repeated relightings and a cylindrical (usually bamboo) receptacle, into which the spent shreds of tobacco were energetically knocked.

THE MINER

$\mathbb{B}$EEN WALKING through this pine grove for a long time now. These places are way longer than they look in pictures. Just pine trees and pine trees and more pine trees that don't add up to anything. No point walking if the trees aren't going to develop. Better stay put and try to outstare a tree, see who laughs first.

Left Tokyo at nine last night, walked like mad straight north. Exhausted, no place to stay, no money. Crawled onto a Kagura stage* in the dark for a little sleep. Hachiman shrine, probably. Woke up cold. Still pretty dark. Been walking ever since without a break, but who feels like walking when there's no end to these damned trees!

Legs weigh a ton. Every step is torture. Like having little iron hammers strapped to my calves. Kimono tail tucked up for hiking, legs bare. Anywhere else, I'd be set to run a race. But not here. Not with these pine trees.

Here's a tea stand. Through the reed blinds I see a rusty kettle on a big clay stove. A bench out front sticking a couple feet into the road. A few straw sandals hanging over it. A man in a kimono— a *hanten* or *dotera*† or something—sitting there with his back this way.

I was moving past and peeking from the corner of my eye and wondering whether I should stop and rest or forget it when this fellow somewhere halfway between a hanten and a dotera spun around in my direction. He had these teeth black with tobacco stains and fat lips and he was smiling. I started feeling weird but then he turned serious. I saw that he had been having fun talking to

*A roofed, open-air stage in the precincts of a Shintō shrine for the performance of sacred Kagura dances. Here, the shrine belongs to the cult of Hachiman, the god of war.

†Two kinds of thickly padded cloaks worn in cold weather. The *hanten* is a short jacket, the *dotera* a full-length kimono normally used for lounging at home or sleeping.

3

the old lady in the tea stand and for no good reason swung around to the road where that smile of his landed smack on me. So he turned serious and I relaxed. I relaxed and then I felt weird again. His face was serious and he kept it sitting there in a serious position, but damned if the whites of his eyes didn't start creeping up my face—mouth to nose, nose to forehead, over the visor and up to the crown of my cap. Then they started creeping down again. This time they went past the face to the chest, to the navel, and came to a stop. Wallet in there. Thirty-two sen inside. Eyes locked onto it right through my blue-and-white kimono. Still focused on the wallet, they crossed my cotton sash and arrived at my crotch. Below that, only bare legs, and no amount of looking was going to find anything to see on them. They were just feeling a little heavier than usual. After a long, careful look at the heaviness, the eyes finally arrived at the black marks my big toes had rubbed onto the platforms of my *geta.**

When I write it out like this, it sounds as if I was standing there in the one spot for a long time practically inviting him to look me over, but that wasn't it at all. In fact, the second the whites of his eyes started moving, I knew I wanted to get out of there. But knowing what I wanted to do wasn't enough, I suppose. By the time I had my toes scrunched up and was ready to turn my geta, the whites of his eyes had stopped moving. I hate to say it, but he was *fast.* If you think it took a long time for his eyes to creep all over me like that, you're wrong. Sure, they were creeping, and they were calm as could be. But they were fast, too. Damned fast. Here I was, trying to walk past this place, and all I could think of was how strangely a pair of eyes can move. If only I could have managed to turn away before he had finished looking me over! I was like somebody who announces that he's leaving a place *after* he's been ordered to get out. You feel like a fool. The other fellow's got the upper hand.

Once I started walking, I had a strange, angry feeling for the first ten or twelve yards. But those ten or twelve yards were all it took for the feeling to disappear—and for my legs to grow heavy again. I've still got the same legs, don't I, and the same iron hammers strapped to them? Of *course* I can't move quickly. Maybe I was born slow, but

---

*Flat wooden footwear raised about one-and-a-half inches off the ground by two horizontal "teeth" and held onto the feet (normally bare) by cloth thongs.

that can't be the reason those eye whites crawled all over me. When I think about it like this, my anger begins to seem pointless.

Besides, I'm not in any position to let little things bother me. I've run away and I'm never going home again. I can't even stay in Tokyo. I'm not planning to settle in the country, either. They're after me. They'll catch me if I stop. Once my troubles start running around my brain, there's no place far enough out for me to relax. So I keep walking. But since I'm walking with no particular goal in mind, I feel as if a big, blurry photograph is hanging in the air in front of my face. Everything's out of focus, and there's no telling when it might come clear. It stretches off ahead of me into infinity. And it'll be there as long as I live—fifty years, sixty—stretching out in front of me no matter how much I walk, no matter how much I run. Oh hell, what's the difference? I'm not walking to get through this foggy stuff out there. I know damn well I could never get through it if I tried. I'm walking because I can't stay still.

I thought I knew all this when I left Tokyo at nine last night, but my nerves have been on edge ever since I started walking. Now my legs are heavy, and these endless rows of pine trees are making me sick. Finally, though, it's not the legs or the pine trees that are bothering me: the ache is in my gut. It's a new kind of pain, one so bad I know I can't go on living a second longer if I don't keep walking, but I have no idea what I'm walking for.

And that's not all. The more I walk, the deeper I tunnel into this out-of-focus world with no escape. Behind me, I can see Tokyo, where the sun shines, but it's already part of a different life. From this world, I can't touch it, no matter how hard I try. They're two separate levels of existence. But Tokyo is still there, warm and bright, I can *see* it—so clearly that I want to call out to it from the shadows. Meanwhile where my feet are going is a formless, endless blur, and all I can do for the rest of my life is wander into this enormous nothing.

I hate to think that this world of clouds is going to be out there, blocking the path ahead, for the rest of my allotted span. Because what that means is that every time anxiety makes me take a step, I walk one step deeper into anxiety. Pursued by anxiety from behind, drawn on by anxiety ahead, I have to keep moving, but I can walk and walk and walk, and nothing is going to be solved. I'll go on walking through an anxiety that will stay unsettled as long as I live.

I'd be better off if the clouds would grow darker every step of the way. Then I could keep going from darkness to deeper darkness. Before long the world would be pitch black and I wouldn't be able to see myself. Then everything would be fine.

The road I'm traveling refuses to be of any help. It won't turn bright, but then, it won't turn dark either. Always somewhere halfway between light and shadow, it remains enveloped in a fog of unsettled anxiety. A life like this is not worth living, I know, but still I cling to it. I want to go somewhere without people and live by myself, and if I can't do that, I might as well . . .

Strange, the thought of the ultimate "might as well" didn't frighten me. In Tokyo I had often been on the verge of committing something rash, but never without a throb of fear. Afterward there would always be a rush of horror at what I'd almost done and I'd be glad I hadn't done it. But this time there was no throb, no rush, no nothing, probably because I was so full of anxiety that the throbs and rushes could have gone to hell for all I cared. And probably, too, I knew in the back of my mind that the "might as well" was not about to happen at any moment. Maybe I figured there was nothing much to worry about. It could have been tomorrow, the next day, a week later. And, if need be, I could have put it off indefinitely. No doubt I was half-conscious of the fact that, whether I was going to throw myself over Kegon Falls or into the crater of Mt. Asama, I still had a long way to go. Who's going to start throbbing before he actually comes to the place where he plans to end it all? That's why I could let myself think about doing it. This out-of-focus world was agony, but as long as there was hope of escaping from it before that throb happened, there was still some point in dragging my heavy legs along. I had decided at least this much for myself, apparently. But I know this now only from having dissected my psychological state after the fact. At the time, I was walking with only one thought in mind: Go into the dark, you've got to go into the dark. Now it seems ridiculous, but there are times in life when we come to feel that the only comfort left us is to move ahead toward death. Of course, the death we're aiming for probably has to be pretty far away for us to feel this. I, at least, believe it would have to be. When it's too close, it can never be a comfort. Such is the fate we know as death.

So here I was, walking along, my head filled with fog—into the dark, got to go into the dark—when someone called me from behind. It's strange: your soul can be ready to drift off into space, but another person calls you and you find it's still anchored down somewhere. I turned around, not quite knowing why. One thing is certain, though: I was not even conscious that this was in response to something. Only when I had turned did I realize that I hadn't gone forty yards from the tea stand. And there in the road in front of it was that cross between a hanten and a dotera, calling me and flashing his huge, tobacco-stained grin.

I hadn't talked to anyone since leaving Tokyo the night before, never dreamed that a person would try speaking to me. I felt absolutely certain that I was unfit to be spoken to. Then it happened so suddenly—he was waving to me frantically and showing me this big, snaggletoothed grin—that the foggy feeling I turned around with cleared itself out, and my feet started moving in his direction almost before I was aware of it.

Now, let me tell you, I didn't like anything about this man—his face, his clothes, his movements. Especially when he gave me the once-over with those white eyes of his, I could almost feel myself beginning to hate him. Less than forty yards later the feeling had disappeared and I turned back to him with a sense of warmth instead, but don't ask me why. My only thought had been to go into the dark. Which means that when I started walking back toward the tea stand, I was moving away from my destination, away from the dark. Still, I was almost glad. I've had plenty of experiences since then, and I've run across contradictions like this everywhere. It's not just me. These days, I don't believe any more in the existence of "character." Novelists congratulate themselves on their creation of this kind of character or that kind of character, and readers pretend to talk knowingly about character, but all it amounts to is that the writers are enjoying themselves writing lies and the readers are enjoying themselves reading lies. In fact, there is no such thing as character, something fixed and final. The real thing is something that novelists don't know how to write about. Or, if they tried, the end result would never be a novel. Real people are strangely difficult to make sense out of. Even a god would have his hands full trying. But maybe I'm jumping to conclusions, presuming that other people are a mess just because I'm put together in such a disorderly way. If so, I should apologize.

Well, anyhow, I walked up to this dark blue dotera and he said to me, "Hello there, youngster," as if he'd known me for years. He had his chin pulled in a little behind his collar, and he was staring at me, somewhere up around my forehead.

Facing in his general direction, I planted my two brown legs and asked politely, "Yes, sir?"

Ordinarily, I was not the sort who would favor someone like this dotera with a cordial reply, especially if I'd been called "youngster." A grunt or a "What?" was about as far as I would go. But at that moment I had the feeling that I and this dotera, with his horrid physiognomy, were human beings on an entirely equal footing. Nor, certainly, was I lowering myself to him in hopes of gaining some advantage. In return, he spoke to me as if he also saw us as equals.

"Hey, kid. Want a job?"

Until that moment, I had been resigning myself to having no other business in life than to go into the dark, so when asked out of nowhere if I wanted a job, I didn't know what to say. I just stood there with my bare shanks planted in the earth, staring at this fellow with my mouth hanging open.

"Hey, kid, want a job? How about it? Everybody's got to work."

By the time he repeated his question, I had grasped enough of the situation to be able to reply.

"I don't mind."

This was my answer. But the fact that my head had managed—in a makeshift fashion, perhaps—to clear itself out enough for these three words to work their way up to my mouth, meant that, in its own simple sort of way, it had passed through a certain process, one that went something like this:

I didn't know where I was going, but I was sure I wanted to go where there were no people. In spite of that, I had turned and started walking toward the dotera. So, while I was walking, I couldn't help feeling a little disappointed in myself. Even the dotera was a human being, after all. Here, someone supposedly heading away from human beings had been drawn back in the direction of a human being, which not only proved how great was the gravitational pull of human beings, it also proved that I myself was so weak that I had to abandon my own resolution. In short, I wanted to go into the dark, but I was actually doing it against my will, and if some entanglement came up to hold me back, I was probably ready to jump at the chance to stay in the real world. Fortunately, the dotera had provided me with the entanglement I needed, and so my feet simply turned around and went toward him. Let's say I Shamefully Betrayed My Ultimate Goal—a little. If the first words out of the dotera's mouth had not been "Want a job?" but instead, "Where you going to do it, kid, the mountains or the fields?" that goal I had been forgetting about would have come back to me with a start, and the thought of the dark place, the place without people, would have filled me with horror. Which only goes to show how my ties with the world had begun to reassert themselves the instant I began to retrace my steps. And the more he called to me, and the more I moved in his direction, step by step, the more these ties seem to have grown in strength, the moment I planted my bare shanks in the earth in front of him being the point at which they reached their highest intensity. It was at that moment he asked, "Want a job?"— an invitation by means of which this scruffy dotera exploited my psychological state with great finesse. My initial response to this unexpected question seems to have been a blank stare, but by the time I snapped out of it, I had become a human being in the real world. *As* a human being in the real world, I had to eat. And to eat, I would have to work.

"I don't mind."

The answer slipped from my mouth without the slightest difficulty. "No, of course you don't! How could you?" the expression on his face seemed to say. Strangely enough, I found this expression perfectly natural.

"I don't mind, but what kind of job?" I added.

"You'll make plenty of money. I guarantee it. What do you say?"

He watched me expectantly, a gleeful grin on his face. A smile from the dotera was not about to charm any hearts, though. His was not a face made for smiling. The more he tried, the worse it looked. Still, I found that smile strangely moving.

"OK," I said, "I'll give it a try."

"You will? Great! There's plenty of money in it for you."

"I don't care about the money."

"Huh?" His voice sounded strange when he said this.

"What kind of job is it?"

"I'll tell you if you promise me you'll take it. You'll take it, kid, right? I don't want you backing down, now, after I tell you what it is. You'll take it for sure, right?"

"I'm planning to."

My reply did not come easily. I more or less had to force it out. Apparently, I was willing to do anything within reason but still wanted to leave myself an escape, which is probably why I said I was *planning* to take it. (I know it's a little strange for me to be writing about myself in this tentative way, as though I were someone not myself, but humans are such inconsistent beings that we can't say anything for certain about them—even when they're us. And when it comes to past events, it's even worse: there's no distinguishing between ourselves and other people. The best we can say is "probably" or "apparently." I may be accused of irresponsibility for this, but there's no getting around it, because it's true. Which is why I intend to continue with this approach whenever anything doubtful comes up.)

The dotera understood my answer to mean that I had accepted his offer.

"Come in," he said. "Relax. We'll have some tea and I'll tell you all about it."

That seemed fine with me. I stepped in and sat down on the bench next to the dotera. A woman in her forties with a twisted mouth set a cup of odd-smelling tea in front of me. The first sip made me hungry. Or maybe I just suddenly realized I was hungry. I was thinking about using the thirty-two sen in my wallet to buy something to eat, when the dotera said, "Have a smoke?" and shoved a pack of Asahis sideways in my direction. Quite the gentleman. I didn't mind that he was offering me such cheap smokes, and I could live with the fact that the corner of the pack was torn. But it was grimy, too, and squashed so badly that the cigarettes inside must have been squeezed together into a single lump. The dotera had no sleeves on his dotera, and probably had to stuff his smokes into the pocket of his *haragake*.*

"No, thanks," I said.

---

*The broad sleeves of traditional Japanese clothing normally served as pockets. A *haragake* is a vest held on by straps that cross in back. Usually made of dark blue cotton, the haragake has a pocket at the lower front and is worn by a workman under a *happi* coat.

With no show of disappointment, the dotera extricated a cigarette from the lump using his dirt-blackened fingernails. Just as I had thought, the cigarette was wrinkled and bent. Still, it didn't look torn, and when he puffed away at it, smoke came from his nostrils. Strange that a cigarette so far gone could perform as it was meant to.

"How old are you, kid?" he asked. I had begun to feel that his tone became a touch more respectful when he was making promises about money, while at other times I was just "kid." He obviously had money on the brain.

"Nineteen," I answered, which was true at the time.

"Still young," said the woman with the twisted mouth. She was wiping a tray and had her back turned to us, so I couldn't see her expression at that moment. I had no idea whether she was talking to herself or to the dotera or to me, but her words seemed to spark something in the dotera.

"Sure!" he exclaimed. "Nineteen is *young*. It's the best time of life for work." He sounded as though he was determined to have me working. Without saying anything, I left the bench.

There was a table for sweets out front. On it, a large platter stood beside a pastry box from which the edge had been broken off. A blue cloth lay atop the platter, not quite covering some round, deep-fried *manjū*.* I had approached the table with the thought of eating some of these, but on close inspection I found that the manjū plate was swarming with flies. The sound of my footstep as I came to a stop by the plate sent them scattering in all directions, but no sooner had I begun to recover from my initial shock and try examining the manjū than the flies, as if signaling to each other that the storm had passed and it was safe now, zipped back down to the manjū. The greasy, yellow crusts received a scattering of black spots. I was on the verge of reaching for a pastry when the spots suddenly arranged themselves into a network of lines, like the constellations on a starry night, and I held back, staring down at the plate.

"Would you like a manjū?" the woman asked. "They're fresh. Fried 'em myself the day before yesterday."

She had apparently finished wiping the tray and was standing now on the other side of the table. I looked up at her in surprise,

---

*A *manjū* is a bun filled with sweet bean paste.

11

and she, for some reason that was unclear to me, suddenly held out a thick hand over the plate.

"Will you look at these flies!" she cried, moving her outstretched hand up and down once, then two or three times from side to side. "Here, I'll get you some manjū if you want."

Before I could say anything, she took a wooden dish down from a shelf and, using long bamboo chopsticks, plopped seven manjū onto it. "I'd better put them over here," she said, carrying the dish to the bench I had been sharing with the dotera and setting it down there.

All I could do was return to my place and sit down beside the wooden dish. The flies had already found it. Staring at the flies and the manjū and the wooden dish, I said to the dotera, "Have one."

This was not entirely in return for his earlier offer of a cigarette. I probably wanted to see, too, whether the dotera would eat these fly-covered manjū that had been fried the day before yesterday.

"Thanks," he said, and popped the topmost one into his mouth without the slightest hesitation. He seemed to find it pretty tasty, judging from the way his fat lips were working, so I decided to take a chance. I picked out one of the cleaner-looking manjū from the bottom of my side of the pile and sank my teeth into it. Immediately the flavor of the oil spread over my tongue, and the rancid filling assaulted my taste buds. I took it calmly, though, given the situation. And when the filling and the crust and the oil had slipped smoothly into my stomach, oddly enough, my hand moved out toward the wooden dish again. By this time, the dotera had polished off a second one and was reaching for a third. His movements were much faster than mine, and he didn't talk when he ate. He seemed to have forgotten about the work and the big money. As a result, all seven manjū disappeared in the space of two or three breaths—and I had eaten only two of them. The dotera had finished off the other five in the wink of an eye.

A thing may be so dirty as to make us flinch, but once we take that first bite, we can go on eating it without too much strain on our sensibilities. This "truth" was something I would come to experience firsthand at the mine, and now it sounds absurdly obvious, but at the time, while I was chewing on those manjū, I was a little shocked to find myself wanting more. I was *hungry*. And besides, my companion was the dotera. Watching him gobble down these sand-flecked manjū, I began to feel a certain competitive urge and an awareness that "sensibilities" were not only useless, they could put you at a tremendous disadvantage. I ordered another serving from the woman.

This time, as soon as the dish hit the bench, I popped one into my mouth, no "Have one" or anything else for the dotera. And he did the same, without a word, least of all "Thanks." Next I took one, then he took one, and the game went on like this until the sixth manjū was gone, leaving only one. Fortunately, it was my turn now, and I grabbed it before he could put his hand out. Then I ordered another serving.

"You really pack it away," said the dotera. I hadn't thought of myself as "packing it away," but now that he said so, I had to admit he was right. Of course, the dotera himself probably had a lot to do with it, the way he stimulated my appetite by tearing into food that I myself wanted to eat. To hear him say it, though, I was "packing it away" entirely on my own. I felt a little like defending myself to him, but the appropriate words didn't come to mind. I just had this foggy notion that the dotera bore some of the responsibility, without any very clear idea of where the responsibility lay. So I kept quiet.

"You're big on fried manjū, huh?" he added.

Sure, I liked fried manjū, *some* fried manjū, but there was no way I could like sandy, fly-covered manjū that had been fried the day before yesterday. On the other hand, I couldn't exactly claim to hate something that I had just eaten three plates of. So I kept quiet this time, too. Suddenly, the tea stand woman piped up—

"Our manjū are famous. Everybody likes them."

I could hardly believe my ears—unless she was trying to make a fool of me. So I kept quieter than ever.

"Unsurpassed flavor," offered the dotera. I couldn't tell if he meant it or was just soft-soaping her. Anyway, to hell with the manjū. I wanted to hear more about this job he had for me.

"Excuse me," I began, "but that business we were discussing earlier . . . It so happens that, due to certain circumstances, it has become necessary for me to work in order to eat. I wonder if you could tell me what this job is that you were mentioning?"

The dotera stared for a while at the table with the sweets, then suddenly turned his face to me and started in again. "You'll make

13

lots of money. I'm telling you the truth. Lots of money. You've got to take this job." He was apparently still determined to make me rich. I took a moment to study this face, now turned full in my direction, as its owner proceeded to tempt me. Beneath prominent cheekbones, the flesh of the face seemed to melt away before it jutted out again at the jaw. The way the sunlight was shining in from the front of the shop, it brought out a deep wrinkle that ran beneath his nose and arched downward on either side of his mouth. The sight of this face made the prospect of making money seem frightening, somehow.

"I don't care about the money. But I *will* take the job. I'll do anything, as long as it's sacred labor."

Somewhere up around the cheekbones, a look of amazement flitted across the dotera's face, but when it was gone, he stretched that arching wrinkle to either side again, revealing his tobacco-stained teeth in all their glory. Then he laughed in his own special way. Looking back on it now, I would guess that the dotera simply didn't understand the phrase "sacred labor." He was laughing out of pity for this poor soul who liked to say fancy things but who lacked the minimum qualification (in his eyes) of a human being: the desire for money. Until only moments before, I had been determined to die—or at least to go where there were no people—or, failing that, to work in order to stay alive. Money was simply not a factor at that point, not a factor at any point for me from the time I was living off my parents in Tokyo. The whole idea of profit was one I found despicable. And I believed that anywhere in Japan I would find only people who thought pretty much as I did. Which is why my only reaction, whenever the dotera opened his mouth about making money, was to find it all very strange. He wasn't making me angry, of course. I was in no position to *be* angry. But it had never occurred to me that the promise of money could be the sweetest words of enticement one could offer a human being. And so the dotera laughed at me, but still the message didn't make it through. What a fool I was!

When his special laugh began to subside, the dotera said, a touch more earnestly, "Tell me something, kid, have you ever had a job?"

A job?! I had run away from home just yesterday. The most "work" I had ever done was fencing and baseball. Not for one day of my life had I eaten food that I myself had paid for with money I had earned.

"No, I've never worked. But I'll have to from now on."

14

"That's what I thought. Say . . . if you never had a job . . . I guess you never made any money."

Here was an observation that required no reply, and I offered none. From behind the table, the woman piped up, "If you're going to work, you might as well make money." As she spoke, she left her seat.

"That's right!" cried the dotera. "But where's the good jobs nowadays? You don't just go out and find them on the ground."

He was beginning to hint at what an exceptional favor he was doing me.

"Sure," the woman muttered, as though not entirely convinced, and she went out the back. I think I expected her to add something to this strangely unnerving remark, and I half-consciously let my eyes follow her into the woods, where, still standing, she proceeded to urinate toward the base of a black pine tree. I quickly shifted my gaze toward the dotera, who went right on with the favors he was doing me.

"You're lucky you met me, kid. Look what a tip I'm giving you—and I don't know you from a hole in the wall. Nobody else would let you in on such a terrific job for nothing."

This was hardly worth replying to. I gave him an extremely formal "Thank you," and left it at that.

"Let me tell you about this job," he went on. I had nothing to say.

"Let me tell you about this job. It's up at the copper mine. If *I* bring you there, you can get work right away. You can be a miner the same day. Pretty good, huh? What do you say? A miner!"

I felt I was being pressed for a reply, but I was not exactly ready to be swept up in his enthusiasm. What was a miner, after all? A laborer who works in the tunnels of a mine. There are many different kinds of laborers in this world, but it seemed to me that the lowliest and most cruelly used was the miner. Far from finding it "pretty good" that I could become a miner so easily, I viewed the prospect with a good deal of alarm. If someone had told me that there are species still lower than the miner, I would have found the concept unimaginable, as if I had been told that there are many days left to the year after December 31. I suspected that the dotera was saying this to me only because he assumed he could put anything over on one so young. He remained surprisingly serious, however.

"So, as soon as you get there, you're a miner. And what an easy

15

life! Before you know it, the money starts piling up, and you can do what you like. They've got a bank up there, too. If you want to save, you can save." He turned to the woman. "What do you say? Isn't that something? He can be a miner right off."

Still wearing the expression she had on while doing her business standing up out back, the woman replied, "You said it. If he starts working in the mines now, he'll have so much money in four or five years he won't know what to do with it . . . He's nineteen . . . best working years . . . have to make your bundle now or never." She spoke in little snatches, as if to herself.

All but insisting that I become a miner, she seemed to be of the same opinion as the dotera. I had no objection, of course. Nor did the prospect of *not* becoming a miner pose any problem for me. I had never in my life been in such an oddly docile mood. I suspect I would have gone along with anything anyone said to me at the time, no matter how outlandish. But why? I had just spent a year so full of duty and desire and agony and my own wrongdoing that everything had suddenly burst and brought about an enormous collision, as a result of which I had come running blindly this far. Nothing in my life before that day should have rendered me so docile, and yet, undeniably, I could not have found in myself the least spark of resistance to anybody. Nor did I consider this either strange or contradictory—if I considered it at all. The only consistent thing about people is their bodies. And because our bodies stay the same, most of us are content to assume that our minds do, too—that we go on being the selves we were, even when we do today the exact opposite of what we did yesterday. When the question of responsibility comes up and we are accused of breaking faith, why is it that none of us even thinks to reply, "Well, that's because my personality is nothing but a bunch of memories. I'm just a mess inside"? I myself have experienced this contradiction any number of times and ought to know better, but still I seem to feel a tinge of responsibility. Which leads me to the conclusion that people are put together in a tremendously convenient way so as to become victims of society.

At the same time, having witnessed the reeling, irregular activity of my fragmented soul, I must conclude from a thoroughly impartial view of the real me that there is nothing so unreliable as man. For anyone aware of his own soul, promises and solemn vows are an impossibility. Only the most uncivilized boor would try to hold another person to a promise. Take a close look at anyone fulfilling a promise, and you'll see he's just doing it under pressure and trying not to let the pressure show. It's not his free will. If I had realized this earlier, I might not have had to go through all the agony—hating people, running away from home to escape the pain. Or, even supposing I had run away and come as far as this tea stand, if I had had the presence of mind to see that my behavior toward the dotera and the woman was totally different from anything I had ever done until the day before, and to compare the two calmly and objectively, I'm sure I would have been able to handle the situation a little more intelligently.

But unfortunately, back then I lacked any capacity for self-analysis. I knew only that I was sad, I was angry, I was in pain, I was disgusted with myself, I was sorry for what I'd done and sick of everything, but I couldn't cut myself off from humanity and I couldn't sit still, so I had started walking and been snagged by the dotera and eaten a bunch of manjū. Yesterday was yesterday and today was today, an hour ago was an hour ago, and half an hour from now was half an hour from now. I had no mind for anything but what was in my mind at the moment. And my soul, disconnected at the best of times, was floating looser than ever, till I could no longer be sure if it existed or not, in addition to which my recollection of the past eventful year had turned into a mass of phantom vapors that were filling the infinite spaces like the dream of a tragic play.

As a result, where ordinarily I would have felt the need to assert myself to the limit, raising question after question—What's so great about becoming a miner? Who says there's anything lower than a miner? Do you think all I care about is money? Is money the only thing that matters?—I remained as docile as could be. Nor was this just a show of docility. There was nothing inside me that wanted to resist.

My only thought at the time, it seems, was that I'd be all right if I had a job to do. As long as I had work, as long as this floating soul of mine could go on bouncing around inside my body, however aimlessly, as long, in other words, as I was not going to force the death of something that could not die on its own, these questions—What was above a miner or below a miner? Was there money to be made or wasn't there?—were of no concern to me, it appears. All I needed was the job. As long as I had that, it probably didn't matter to me that I was being fed a lot of hot air about its status or nature or results, or that these opinions ran counter to my own, or that the hot air was calculated to lure me into something, or that for me to swallow it could only raise serious doubts regarding my qualifications as an intelligent human being. At times like this, the most complex individual is reduced to utter simplicity.

And besides, when I heard that I was to become a miner, I felt strangely elated. First, I had run away from home, set for the possibility of dying. That had changed in the second stage to a desire to go where there were no people. Then along had come the third stage: a determination to work. But if I *was* going to work, something close to stage two would be better than an ordinary job, and better yet would be something connected with stage one. I had seemed to go from stage one through two to three almost before I knew it, but in fact my changing mental state had been pushed along reluctantly from one stage to the next, looking back fondly at each stage it had been forced to abandon. My third-stage determination to work had not been so reckless as to shake off stage two, nor had it moved so far from stage one as to sever all contact with it. If I could work in a place where there were no people and in a state close to death, then I could carry out my final resolution while still, to some extent, satisfying my original goals. What was a miner, after all, but a man in a mine—someone who worked where the sun never shone; who, while in the real world, yet burrowed beneath it; whose only companions in the dark were lumps of ore and earth; and who never had to listen to the voices of the world of men? It was a gloomy life, no doubt, and that's what made it exactly right for me. There were lots of people in the world, but no one as perfectly suited to being a miner as I was. It would be my calling. Of course I didn't have it worked out as clearly as this, but when I heard the word "miner," the gloominess of it struck me, and that very gloominess made me glad. Recalling all this now, from my present vantage point, I can only believe they were the thoughts of someone else.

So I said to the dotera, "I intend to work as hard as I can. I hope that you will help me to become a miner."

With a magnanimous air, the dotera replied, "They're pretty tough about letting anybody be a miner right off, but if *I* put in a good word for you, it's a sure thing."

18

I was keeping my doubts about this to myself when the tea woman piped up again, "All you need is a word from Chōzō here. They'll make you a miner for sure."

I now learned for the first time that the dotera's name was Chōzō. I had a few occasions after that, when we were getting on and off trains, to call him by his name, but even now I am not certain how "Chōzō" ought to be spelled. This was the man who grabbed me by the nose the moment I ran away from home and turned me in a totally unexpected direction; the man, as it were, who contributed a great turning point to my life. How very odd that I should have learned his name by word of mouth but not know how to write it.

So anyhow, since Chōzō and the tea woman both promised me I could become a miner, I figured it was true, and replied, "Well, then, I'll leave it up to you."

Meanwhile, I had absolutely no idea where someone sitting in this tea stand would have to go or what steps he would have to take to become a miner. But I didn't see any need to ask, since Chōzō had pressed so hard and I had said I was leaving it up to him. I was sure he would take care of it.

"All right, then," Chōzō said, vigorously lifting the tail of his dotera from the bench, "let's get going. Are you ready, kid? Don't forget your stuff."

I had left home with nothing more than the clothes on my back. The only "stuff" I could conceivably forget was my body.

"I'm not forgetting anything," I said, standing, but then the tea lady and I looked at each other. Ah yes, the manjū. I had forgotten to pay. Chōzō was already halfway out through the reed blind, looking at the road with an unconcerned expression on his face. I pulled my wallet out and paid for three plates of manjū from my thirty-two sen. While I was at it, I left a five-sen tip.

I can't recall how much I paid for the manjū, but I remember the woman saying, "After you make all that money at the mine, stop by on your way back." I did eventually quit the mine, but I never had occasion to stop by the tea stand.

I followed Chōzō out to the old pine grove I was so sick of, trudging down its single path in ankle-deep dust, and though it had seemed endless before, I was surprised how quickly we got through it this time. The pines gave way at some point, and we found our-

19

selves at the edge of what seemed to be one of the shabby, old post towns on the Itabashi Highway.* It seemed all the more like the Itabashi Highway when a rickety horse-drawn omnibus passed by.†

Walking a step ahead of me, Chōzō turned and asked, "Want to take the omnibus, kid?"

"I don't mind," I said.

"Want to forget the omnibus?" he asked.

"I don't mind," I said.

"What do you want to do?" he asked.

"I don't care," I said.

By that time the omnibus was gone.

"All right," said Chōzō, "let's walk." And he started walking. So I started walking. Ahead, the dust raised by the omnibus filtered into the morning sun, giving the road a cloudy, yellow look. Soon the number of passersby began to increase, and the town itself became a little more presentable. Finally, we came to a spot almost as lively as Kagurazaka in the Ushigome district. In fact, the shops and the people and their clothing looked exactly the same as the ones in Tokyo. There was hardly anybody like Chōzō here.

I asked Chōzō, "What's the name of this place?"

"What? You don't know?" he said with a surprised look, but he told me readily enough, without laughing at me. In this way I learned the name of the town, though I am not going to mention it here. Apparently quite puzzled that I didn't know the name of this bustling place, Chōzō asked, "Where are you from, kid? Where were you born?"

Now that I came to think of it, for someone who was supposed to be introducing me to an employer, it was a little too negligent of

---

*Itabashi was one of the many little post towns along the old Nakasendō Highway, which was one of the five great highways of the Edo period (1603–1868). Like the more famous Tōkaidō, the Nakasendō connected Edo (now Tokyo) with Kyoto, but it passed through the central mountains instead of running along the coast. The first post station, some seven miles northwest of central Edo (but long since absorbed by the spreading Tokyo metropolis), was Itabashi, and the ten-mile section of the Nakasendō from there to Ōmiya was called the Itabashi Highway (*kaidō*). Built to lodge and service travelers, these towns began as long, narrow assemblages of inns and restaurants stretched along each side of the road.

†First used in 1869 between Tokyo and Yokohama, horse-drawn omnibuses had been replaced in the cities by horse trolleys after 1882 and electric streetcars after 1897. By the time of the novel, the run to Itabashi was one of the few routes still served by the omnibus; hence its association with the Itabashi Highway.

Chōzō never to have asked me about my past or my background. Later, I came to realize that he had absolutely no interest in such things. When he asked me where I was born, it was strictly out of a momentary curiosity aroused in him by my ignorance. As evidence of this, when I answered "Tokyo," his only response was "Oh," and he turned into a side street, practically dragging me in after him.

The fact is, I come from a rather prominent family. While it may appear that I had run away from home because things had become too complicated for me, I had not taken this rash step merely to spite my parents. I had come to hate being at home because of a sort of disgust I was feeling for people in general, and once I started feeling that way, I couldn't stand the sight of my relatives, my parents, anybody. At one point I realized what I was doing and tried to fight it, but by then it was too late. The more I struggled, the worse it became, until finally the cork popped and all the reserves of patience I had tried so hard to build were lost. I left home that very night.

If we look into the origins of the matter, the first thing we find is a girl. Next to her is another girl. Around the girls are their parents. Then relatives. And surrounding them all are the people of society. But girl number one looks at me and starts changing: now she's round, now she's square. And when *she* changes, *I* have to change: now I'm round, now I'm square. But vows I was born to with girl number two mean I shouldn't be doing this with girl number one. As young as I am, I know what is happening. But the guiltier I feel, the more I go on turning round and then square. Finally, the change ceases to be one of form and becomes one of internal structure, and girl number two is watching this with eyes full of bitterness. The parents are watching, and the relatives, too. And all those people out there in society can see what is going on. My heart is stretching and shrinking, bending and twisting, and I try my best to cover it up, but girl number one won't leave me alone. She keeps stretching and shrinking and letting me see, and there's no way I can hide what I'm doing. The parents find out, and the relatives find out. They say I'm the villain. Of course, I've never considered myself a hero in all this, but the more I sound them out, the more I realize that what they mean by villain and what I mean by villain are two different things. I try to explain myself, but they won't listen. I'm beginning to feel especially put out that my own parents won't believe me when it occurs to me that if I stay by girl number one, there's no telling what could happen. I may well become the villain they say I am and never be able to explain. But still I can't tear myself away from her. Every day I feel increasingly guilty toward girl number two. Every day these conflicting emotions come rushing at me from all directions, and I'm the maypole in the middle. If I pull on this ribbon, it tangles that one; if I loosen that one, this one tightens up. There's no way I can straighten out all the lines jumbled together in my head. I try twisting and twiddling with them so much I can't stand my own cleverness, but the result is always the same. And then it hits me: since *I'm* the one who's suffering, *I'm* the only one who can put a stop to it. Until now, I've been counting on somebody else to come up with a solution that will work for me. It's as though I've met someone on the road and I'm trying to figure out a way to have him walk around me in the mud while I stand my ground. I've been presenting him with impossible reasons why I should stay where I am and he should be the one to move. There's no point letting your reflection bother you as long as you're standing in front of a mirror. If there's no way you can move the "mirror" called the code of society, then the most sensible thing to do is step away from it.

And so I decided to blow myself out of these convoluted relationships like a puff of smoke. The only way to turn myself into smoke, however, was to commit suicide. I tried it once or twice. But every time I was on the verge of killing myself, I'd be too frightened to go through with it. Finally I realized that suicide is not something you become better at with practice. If I couldn't kill myself all at once, then I could let myself die. But, living the comfortable life of one who, as I said earlier, comes from a fairly prosperous background, there was not much hope of my dying if I simply stayed at home. I would have to run away.

Sometimes it seemed to me that I could never forget these relationships even if I ran away. Sometimes it seemed to me that I could forget them. Finally, I concluded that I would never know unless I tried. Even if the agony came running with me, that was something that concerned me alone. Those I left behind could only be helped by my disappearance. Another thing to keep in mind was that I could not go on running forever. I would run because I couldn't simply die right away, but running would be a step in the right direction. The thing to do was to give it a try and if it looked as though I was going to be pursued and tortured by the past, then it was still not too late to begin making plans to let myself die. And if, after that, it became clear that nothing was going to work, then at last the time would have come for me to perform my act of suicide.

When I write it out like this, I look ridiculous, but these are the bare facts and nothing can be done about them. And it's precisely because I *am* writing it out like this that I look ridiculous. I'm sure that if I were to set down my foggy-brained determination in all its fogginess, then even I would be fully qualified to become the protagonist of a novel.

Or even if not, if I did a splashy job of writing up everything that actually happened then—the two girls, the situation that changed daily, my worries, my agony, my parents' opinions, my relatives' advice—I'm sure I could make a very entertaining newspaper novel. But I have neither the pen nor the time for such things, so I'll forget about that and just tell about the most important thing: my experience as a miner.

Well, anyhow, I had run away with all of this business behind me, and I was ready to be buried alive or to bury myself alive, but when it came to something like my parents' names or my own past history, as desperate as I was, I still didn't want to talk about these to Chōzō. And it wasn't only Chōzō. I didn't want to talk about them to any human being—including myself, if possible. That's how miserable and beaten down I was feeling. And so, although I found it strange that, as a job referee, Chōzō didn't quiz me on my background, I was inwardly very pleased. I might also point out that, at that time of my life, I had not had much practice in the art of lying, and I still thought it a great evil to conceal the truth. Which means that if he *had* quizzed me, I'm not sure what I would have done.

I followed Chōzō down the side street, but before we had passed a block or two of houses, the buildings suddenly became less densely packed, and I caught glimpses of rice paddies between them. I was thinking that all the bustle was stretched thinly along the main street, when Chōzō whipped me around another corner and I was led to yet another lively spot. The street dead-ended at a railroad station. The procedure for becoming a miner required me to take a train, I saw now. I had been imagining that the mine had a branch office or some such thing in this town and that after being taken there I would be escorted to the mine by an official.

A few yards from the station, I called out to Chōzō, who was still ahead of me, "Chōzō, do I take a train?"

This was the first time I had called him by name. He turned somewhat in my direction but gave no sign that he found it unusual to have a complete stranger calling him by his first name. "Right," he said, and entered the station.

I stood in the station entrance, thinking. Did this fellow plan to board the train with me and bring me to the place? If so, he was being a little too kind. There was something fishy about the way he was taking such good care of me. He'd never seen me before in his life. Maybe he was some kind of con man. It had taken long enough for these suspicions to hit me, but once they did I started to have second thoughts about boarding the train. It occurred to me that I probably ought to get out of there fast, and I turned my feet, which until then had been pointing toward the platform, back out toward the street. For a while I just stood there, staring at the red curtain of the station's tea stand, seemingly unable to work up the resolve to start walking, when suddenly a great bellow came from a distance to put a stop to any such plans. When I heard this voice, I realized that it belonged to Chōzō; it was the voice I had been hearing since the pine grove. I turned to find Chōzō's head poking up at an angle in the distance and bobbing up and down, his eyes looking hard at me. The rest of him seemed to be hidden behind the wall of the public urinal. I walked toward that face, thinking I might as well respond to his call.

"You ought to take care of business before we get on the train, kid," Chōzō said.

I really didn't have to, but he kept insisting, so I stood next to him and (if I may broach an unwholesome subject) urinated. At that moment, my thoughts changed again: I don't own anything but my body. With neither property nor honor to be robbed or cheated of, I'm obviously an unpromising commodity. To be frightened of Chōzō means I'm confusing what I am today with what I was till yesterday, which is like worrying about having your pay attached after you've lost your job. Chōzō surely has no education, but you don't need an education to look at someone like me and know right off there's nothing here to be swindled. Maybe he really is planning to take me to the mine and collect some kind of commission. That's OK, too. I'll just have to give him a certain percentage of my pay—and so forth. That's what I was thinking as I stood at the urinal. While the time involved was brief enough, it took me all that weighing and cogitating to reach this puny conclusion. That I was still unable, in spite of these efforts, to grasp the simple fact that Chōzō was, in the purest sense of the word, a procurer—a procurer of laborers for the mine—was due entirely to my being nineteen years old.

Being young is a real disadvantage. One way or another, I had managed, by myself, to grope my way as far as the spot where I had encountered this procurer, and still I was treating him with the reserve I thought I owed him for the kindness he was showing me purely out of the goodness of his heart. What a laugh.

But in fact, when we had wandered from the urinal to the entrance of the third-class waiting room, I turned to Chōzō with some degree of formality and said, in all seriousness, "It was very kind of you to bring me this far, but I really can't ask you to do any more."

Instead of replying, Chōzō looked at me with an odd expression, which made me wonder if I had chosen my words poorly in thanking him, so I tried again.

"You've been tremendously helpful and I want to thank you," I said, nodding repeatedly, "but I can take care of myself from here on out. Please don't bother about me."

"Take care of yourself?" Chōzō said. "You're kidding."

"No, really," I said.

"What makes you think so?"

I didn't know how to respond to this, but I said, with some hesitation, "Well, you can give me the directions, and I can go there, and, if I mention your name, they'll take care of me . . ."

"Look, kid, you don't know what you're talking about. They're not going to make you a miner just 'cause you know my name. It's not that easy."

"But I really hate to bother you . . ."

"Oh, don't worry about me," Chōzō said with a laugh. "I don't mind taking you there. You know what they say. If you even rub sleeves with somebody, karma did it. Ha ha ha ha."

Finally, I said, "I can't thank you enough," and left it at that.

We were sitting together on a bench in the waiting room, and the station gradually began to fill with people. Most of them were country types. One man not only was wearing the kind of hanten-cum-dotera that Chōzō had on, he was even carrying a shoulder pole. On the other hand, there was a very Tokyo-looking merchant wearing a glossy apron and an oddly dented felt hat. After a while, the bench was surrounded by the noise of footsteps and voices, and suddenly the ticket window clattered open. The more impatient people jumped to their feet and crowded in front of the iron mesh, but Chōzō was as cool as ever. With one of his bent Asahis dangling from his thick lips, he turned about two-thirds of the way toward me and asked, "Hey, kid. Do you have the ticket money?"

Again, this will sound as if I am advertising my own immaturity, but until that moment, the thought of the fare had never crossed my mind. It was the height of stupidity for me to be thinking, on the one hand, "Well, I guess I'll be getting on the train," and never to have wondered, on the other, "How much will it cost?" or even "Do I have to pay anything?" I freely admit to the stupidity, but the fact is that, until I heard Chōzō's question, I had been feeling as unconcerned as if I thought I could ride for free. I'm not sure why this was so, but I suppose that, deep down, I had begun to feel strangely dependent on Chōzō, as though, if I stuck with him, he would take care of everything. Of course, I myself was unaware of any such thoughts. Even now, I'm not anxious to admit this about myself. But unless I *was* feeling some such sense of security, I could never, for all my youth and stupidity, have come to a railroad station and failed to have the slightest inkling that there was a fare to be paid. On top of which I had said to Chōzō that I no longer needed his help and that I could go on from here alone. What could I have been thinking? Having encountered situations like this on several occasions since then, I have formulated a theory. Just as illnesses have an incubation period, there is an incubation period for our thoughts and feelings. Although we possess these thoughts and are controlled by these feelings during the incubation period, we remain unaware of them. And if nothing happens in the outer world to bring them to the surface of consciousness, we go on being controlled by these thoughts and feelings for the rest of our lives, insisting all the while that we have never been influenced by them. We try to prove our point through actions and words that negate the thoughts and feelings, but an outsider's view of our actions reveals the contradiction. Sometimes we are amazed to see the contradiction ourselves. Sometimes, without seeing it, we experience tremendous pain. My own suffering at the hands of the girl I mentioned earlier was caused, ultimately, by my inability to perceive what was incubating inside of me. If only we could inject some powerful medicine that would kill off these unknowable creatures before they could violate our hearts—then what contradictions, what misfortunes mankind would be spared! But things do not work out as we would wish them to, and that's too bad for all of us.

And so, when Chōzō asked me if I had the ticket money, I was shocked and flustered. After the manjū and the tip, there was nothing left of my thirty-two sen. I didn't even have train fare, and yet I had promised to become a miner as if I knew what I was doing. When I realized what a phony that made me, I felt my cheeks flush. Looking back, I'm touched by my own innocence. These days, somebody could press me to repay my debts in a crowded streetcar, and while I might be annoyed, I certainly wouldn't blush. To think I could have wasted the sacred scarlet of shame on a lowly procurer like Chōzō! Today, it would be out of the question.

For some reason, I wanted to tell Chōzō that I did have the fare. Of course, I didn't actually have it, so I couldn't lie and say I did. If I could have lied and gotten away with it, I suppose I would have, but if I had lied at that point, only moments before buying the ticket, the truth would have emerged almost immediately. Still, the thought of saying I didn't have it was too painful. I was a child, or, if not exactly a child, I was a slightly grown-up child with adult passions and agonies, and perhaps the tiniest smattering of common sense, which made things all the more complicated. I found myself unable to reply either that I had it or that I didn't have it.

"I've got a little," I said.

It wouldn't have been so bad if my answer had bounced back at him like an echo without delay, but my cheeks had just reddened for this undeserving recipient, and I spoke with extreme hesitancy. What a fool.

"What do you mean, 'a little'? How much have you got, kid?"

Chōzō was moved by neither my red cheeks nor my hesitancy. He obviously just wanted to know how much I had. Unfortunately, not even I knew the answer to that. But one thing was sure: after having paid for three plates of manjū and leaving a five-sen tip from a total of thirty-two sen, there was not a whole lot left. Or if there was something, it was the same as nothing.

"*Very* little. I doubt if I have enough," I answered honestly.

He took this more calmly than I had expected. "That's OK. I'll make up the difference. Just show me what you've got."

I would have been embarrassed to be seen counting coppers, and I didn't want to be suspected of trying to hide what I had. I took my wallet out and handed it to Chōzō, money and all. Now, this was an extremely fine alligator wallet, the high price of which had become the subject of a serious lecture by my father when he had made such an extravagant purchase for me. Chōzō looked at it a moment after it had passed from my hand to his, said only, "Hmm, this wasn't cheap," and stuck it into the pocket of his haragake without checking the contents. I was relieved that he didn't count the money, but then he left the bench and hurried over to the ticket window after pointedly cautioning me, "Now, I want you to stay right here while I buy the tickets. Don't get lost or you won't be able to become a miner." As I watched, he plunged into the crowd, waiting for his turn to come without giving me a second glance. From the time we left the pine grove until now, Chōzō had been close by my side, or, the one time he did leave me for a moment, he had actually stuck his head out of the public toilet and called me over. Once he had my wallet and was buying tickets, though, it seemed as if he had forgotten all about me. Probably he had no chance to look my way because there were so many people about. I, meanwhile, never took my eyes off his back, and I could feel a strange sort of nervousness mount as, from my distant vantage point, I watched him moving closer and closer to the ticket window each time a person ahead of him in line bought tickets. The wallet was impressive enough on the outside, but inside there was only copper. Chōzō was going to be shocked when he opened it and found how little I had. I felt bad about that and I was still worrying needlessly about how much he was going to have to add to my money, when Chōzō came back wearing his usual expression.

"Here, this is yours," he said, handing me a red third-class ticket but offering not a word as to what he had had to pay for it out of his own pocket.

Feeling awkward about all this, I said only "Thank you" and did not bother to mention the money—or the wallet. Chōzō never said anything about the wallet, either. In effect, I had given it to him.

Finally, the two of us boarded the train. Nothing much happened on the train, except that I felt sick and changed my seat once when a pus-eyed man covered with boils and pockmarks sat next to me. In retrospect, this seems pretty ridiculous. You wouldn't expect someone who had run away from home and resolved to descend to the rank of the miners to be put off by most things, but still I didn't want to sit close to anything so repulsive. At that rate, I suppose I would have fled from a man with pus in his eyes right down to the day before I committed suicide. But did I handle everything so fastidiously? No, of course not, which is what bothers me. When I met Chōzō and the tea lady, for example, I took in everything they said without a peep—not a hint of my usual argumentative, self-assertive behavior. Of course, it would be reasonable to try to account for this by reference to the fact that I was starving at the time, but hunger was surely not the whole explanation. Any way you look at it, it's a contradiction. Here I go with the contradictions again. Never mind.

I have a habit of recalling the adventures I experienced back then whenever I have a few spare moments. It was the most colorful period of my life. Each time I bring back those images to savor, I wield my scalpel mercilessly (you can do this with old memories) in an attempt to chop up my own mental processes and examine every little piece. The results, however, are always the same: I don't understand them. Now, don't tell me I've just forgotten because it happened so long ago. I'll never have such an intense experience again in my lifetime. And especially don't tell me that the lines are tangled because those were the frantic acts of a confused adolescent. The acts themselves were confused and misguided, but the only way to understand the processes leading to those misguided acts is to examine them calmly with the brain I have today. It's precisely because I can now look at my trip to the mine as an old dream that I am able to describe it for other people with even this degree of clarity. I'm not just saying that I have the courage to write down everything that happened because the passions have faded; I could never have managed to put down even this much on paper if I didn't have the detachment to drag the old me out to where the present me can see it and study every wart and pimple. Most people imagine that the most accurate account of an experience would be the one written at the time and place, but this is a mistake. Driven by the passions of the moment, a description of the immediate situation tends to convey preposterous misconceptions. Take, for example, my trip to the mine. If I had kept a diary, say, of my feelings just as they were at the moment, I'm sure the result would have been an infantile, affected thing full of lies—certainly nothing that I could have presented to people like this and asked them to read.

When I fled across the aisle from the peril of the pus-eyed man, Chōzō glanced at me and at the man, but he stayed in his seat. I was enormously impressed at how much more robust were Chōzō's sensibilities than my own. My admiration for him faded somewhat when he actually began talking with the man as if it were the most natural thing in the world to do.

"Back to the mine?" the pus-eyed man asked.

"Yup. Got another one."

"That him?" asked the pus-eyed man, glancing in my direction.

Chōzō looked as if he were about to say something, but his eyes met mine and he closed his thick lips, turning away. The pus-eyed man turned away with him and said, "Gonna make another bundle, huh?"

As soon as I heard this, I stuck my head out the window. I let go with a gob of spit, but it flew back and hit me in the face. I was feeling pretty rotten.

There were two men in the seat opposite me. They had a conversation going.

"Suppose a robber comes in."

"Sneaks in?"

"No no, he breaks down the door. And he starts threatening them with a sword or something."

"All right. Then what?"

"Now suppose the owner gives him counterfeit money to get rid of him."

"All right. And then?"

"Then afterwards the robber notices it's counterfeit and starts telling everybody the owner passes counterfeit money. Tell me, Tsune, what do you think—which one is more to blame?"

"Which what?"

"Which man—the owner or the robber?"

"Hmmmm. That's a tough one . . ."

The second man was struggling with this conundrum when I found myself growing sleepy. I lay my head on the windowsill and drifted off.

The minute you go to sleep, time ceases to exist. Sleep is the best medicine for anyone to whom the passage of time is a source of pain. Death is probably just as good. But dying is a lot more difficult than it seems. The ordinary person uses sleep as a handy substitute for death. People who practice judo often have their companions choke them. They spend five minutes or more of some lazy summer day lying dead in the dojo until their friends breathe life back into them and they wake up feeling so good it's as if they've been re-born—or so they tell me. I was always too worried that I might ac-tually die to risk this heroic cure. Sleep may not be as effective, but it avoids the danger that you might not return to life. For anyone with worries, for anyone deep in anguish or unbearable pain, for anyone about to become a miner as a step on the road to self-destruction, sleep is the greatest gift of nature. By sheer chance, this gift of nature now settled itself on my head. Before I could express my thanks, I drifted off, utterly obliterating time, whose passage one has no choice but to be aware of as long as one lives. But then I woke up. I suppose what happened was that, since I had fallen asleep while the train was moving, the sleep lost its rhythm and flew off somewhere when the train came to a stop. Apparently, while sleeping I'm able to forget the passage of time, but I go on reacting to movement through space. Which means that if I really want to forget my anguish, I'm really going to have to die. No doubt, though, the minute the anguish disappears, I'll want to come to life again. The ideal thing for me, to be quite honest, would be to live and die over and over.

This looks like some kind of stupid joke when I set it down on paper, but I'm not trying to be facetious. I mean it in all seriousness. This "ideal" of mine is not something I stuck on just now for fun, as an afterthought while recalling the past. It actually came to me like this when the train stopped and I woke up. It may seem comical because the feeling itself was ridiculous, but all I can do is set down what I honestly felt. The closer this feeling comes to comedy, the sorrier I feel for myself back then, because I realize all the more vividly what a sad state I was in if I could seriously cherish a hope so divorced from common sense.

When I woke up, I found the train had stopped. Before I thought to myself, "The train's stopped," the thought occurred to me, "I'm on a train." No sooner had that first thought crossed my mind than I said to myself, "I'm with Chōzō," "I'm going to become a miner," "I didn't have the fare," "I ran away from home," and so on and so forth, maybe twelve or thirteen such thoughts clumping together and popping out of the depths of my mind all at once. How can I describe the speed with which this happened? Should I say that it was beyond description? Like a flash of lightning? In any case, it happened with terrifying swiftness. I later heard that some drowning people have seen their whole lives flash before their eyes, complete in every detail, and judging from my own experience at that moment, I would have to conclude that such stories are true. This is how swiftly I became conscious of my position and condition in the real world. Simultaneous with the return of consciousness came a feeling of disgust. Actually, "disgust" can't fully describe what I was feeling, but I'll settle for it since there's no other word that will do the job. Those who have experienced the feeling will know immediately what I'm talking about, and those who haven't should count themselves lucky. It's nothing you'd ever want to learn.

Before long, two or three people in the compartment stood up. Two or three other people entered the compartment from the outside. What with those who were casting about for a seat and those who were searching for articles they might be leaving behind, plus the others with no particular business who were shifting in their seats, sticking their heads out of windows or yawning, the entire world seemed to be crumbling into a state of unrest, and I became aware that everything in my immediate vicinity had begun to move. With that awareness came the realization that I was different from ordinary people. I was an outsider who did not become swept up in the mood of movement even when everyone around me was moving. I felt like some ghost who had strayed in from the world beyond. My sleeves might brush theirs or my knees touch those of the person opposite me, but our souls remained utterly separate. Until this moment, I had managed one way or another to keep in tune with the normal run of men, but the second the train stopped, the world became bright and ascending, while I became dark and descending, and all hope was lost for contact between the two. At the thought, I felt myself shriveling like a pricked balloon, my chest and back pressing my innards together until they were as thin as a piece of paper. Alone, my soul suddenly plunged down through the surface of the earth. I was defeated, overwhelmed with a dizzying feeling of shame and remorse.

At that point, Chōzō stood and approached me. "Hey, kid," he said, "still asleep? We get off here."

"Oh," I thought, "so that's what's happening," and I stood up. Funny, your soul can be halfway through the earth, and as long as the blood is still coursing through your veins, when you call it, it comes back. If things go a little too far, though, the soul won't return to the body as ordered. When I was in a shipwreck off Taiwan some years later, for example, my soul pretty nearly gave up on me, which was quite an ordeal. No matter how bad the situation, there's always worse. You should never relax because you think you've come to the end of the line. This was a brand new feeling for me at the time, though—and a bitter experience.

Sniffing after the tail of Chōzō's dotera, I passed through the wicket and out to the main street of a large town. It was the usual long, straight road you find in the old post towns, but it was surprisingly broad, and it was *so* straight that it seemed to clear the mind. Standing in the middle of this wide street, I saw all the way down to the far edge where the town came to an end. As I did so, I was struck with an odd kind of feeling. Since this was another of those feelings that I was experiencing for the first time in my life, I will take a moment to set it down here. I had just come out to the street, restored to a more or less human view of the world after having barely succeeded in calling back my soul, which had nearly escaped when the bottoms of my lungs fell out. The soul had finally found its way back into my lungs with my most recent inhalation, but it was still noticeably wobbly, and far from settled in. So while *I* was here, in the world (I was the one who had just left the train, come out of the station, and was standing in the middle of the street), my soul possessed only the most bleary sort of consciousness, as if it were reluctantly performing at minimum capacity and could not fully grasp the fact that these functions were its professional responsibilities, accepted in all solemnity. Thus, when, dizzy and half-conscious, I opened my sunken, staring eyes, bereft as they were now of interest in anything, my field of vision, which until that moment had been restricted to the cramped cube of the train compartment, suddenly leaped a thousand yards ahead down the length of the far-stretching road. And although my eyes came to rest at its end on a mountain fairly dripping with lush greenery, the mountain was too far away to feel like an obstruction; instead, it absorbed my leaden gaze into its green depths. Which is how I came to have this odd feeling I mentioned.

First of all, the flat, perfectly straight road has a bracing simplicity about it, as though it's been built to fit the phrase from the Book of Songs, "The Great Road was like a whetstone."* Or, more simply stated, it doesn't confuse the eye. "Here, come with me, don't worry," it seems to beckon; "there's no need for hesitation or reserve." And because it does say "Come with me," if you stick with it, you can go forever. The eyes don't even want to turn down side streets, for some strange reason. The farther the road continues on straight ahead, the more the eyes have to move straight ahead if they are to avoid constraint and discomfort. I firmly believe that the great ribbon of highway has taken its form parallel to the free movement of the eyes. And in looking at the row of houses on either side (some of which are tile-roofed, others thatched, but I make no distinction between the two), the farther off I look, the lower and lower the roofs drop, and the hundreds of houses stretch on forever, moving away at an angle and all in perfect alignment, as though a wire has been passed through them from the far end to the near in order to regularize the slope. The farther away they stretch, the nearer they come to the ground. The two-story buildings to either side of where I stand—I recall them as inns—are tall enough so that I have to look up at them, but peering through to the end of the town, the eaves there look low enough to fit between two fingers. The houses are not entirely uniform, to be sure—a few have shop curtains fluttering in the breeze, one a large clam drawn on the front shoji door—but when you follow the line of the eaves into the

* "The way to Chow was like a whetstone, / And straight as an arrow." James Legge, *The Chinese Classics*, 5 vols. (Hong Kong: Hong Kong University Press, 1960), 4: 353.

distance, a couple of miles come leaping into the eye in half a second, so brilliantly clear is the scene.

As I've already said, my soul was completely hung over. And in that state, with no warning, the second I came out of the station it ran smack up against this brilliantly clear scene, one that would have been clear to a blind man. Of course there was no way it could avoid a shock, and that's just what it got. But a little time had to go by before it could overcome the inertia of its shaky, wobbling, hang-back condition. Now, this odd sort of feeling I've described was something that occurred in the critical interval between the moment I sensed the brilliant clarity of the scene and, shortly afterward, the moment my soul flopped over in its sleep. This clear, expansive scene so totally unsuited to my emotional state was a wonderfully lively thing, but no amount of brightness or expansiveness could prevent it from becoming a mere fact of reality once my startled soul began to involve itself seriously with the outer world. Even the holiest of lights must lose some of its glory when it is reduced to a function of the real world. Because my soul had been in an unusual state—because it had been able to perceive the bright outer world in all its brightness but had not been functioning acutely enough to attain the self-awareness that this was actually happening—I had had the good fortune to see this straight road and these straight eaves as a brilliant dream with the impact of reality. As a result, I felt exactly as I would have in encountering a phantasm from the world beyond with a degree of clarity visible only in this world and with an accompanying sense of exhilaration. True, I was standing in the road; the road was tremendously long and straight; if I wanted to, I could walk its entire length and pass through the town; if I wanted to touch the houses on either side, I could reach out and touch them; if I wanted to climb to a second story, I could climb to a second story. I knew full well that all these things were possible, but I had lost track of the *concept* of their being possible as I stood there simply receiving an acute sense impression through the eyes.

I'm no scholar and have no idea what you call this kind of feeling. Not knowing what to name it, I have ended up describing it at such lamentable length. I suppose I'll be laughed at by people with an academic background who see this and think, "Is *that* all?" but it can't be helped. Since then, I have experienced feelings similar to this on several occasions, but never again with such intensity. I have gone to the trouble of writing this down in the hope that the information might possibly be of use to someone. As soon as it came to me, though, the feeling was gone.

I noticed that the sun was on its way down. Judging from the angle of the light (it was early summer, when the days are longer), it was probably some time after four o'clock, probably not yet five. The weather was not as good as I had thought, possibly because this place was near the mountains, but I couldn't exactly have called it bad, since the sun was shining. Noting the sun, which was striking the long street at an angle, I concluded that *that* must be the west. I knew that I had kept myself running straight north from Tokyo, but I had lost all sense of direction by the time I left the train. If we follow the road north through the town, we'll come to the mountain, I thought, and if I'm right about the directions here, the mountain, too, is north, so Chōzō and I are still going to be headed north.

The mountain seemed to be pretty far away, and it was by no means small. Its color was blue, but the brightness of the side where the sun was shining gave the shaded side a blackish hue within the blue. Of course this might have been owing to an abundance of cedars or cypress rather than to the angle of the sun. In any case, it was obviously dense and deep. When I shifted my gaze from the setting sun to this blue mountain, I wondered whether it was standing there alone or was part of a chain of mountains lying beyond. As Chōzō and I began moving gradually northward, walking side by side, I could not escape the feeling that the mountains stretched out and out endlessly beyond this one mountain I could see before me, and that all these mountains continued on to the north in an unbroken chain. I suppose you could say that this was because the mountain appeared to be retreating before us step by step, since walking toward the mountain resulted only in our walking toward the mountain and didn't bring our feet any closer to its base. You could also explain it this way: As the sun sank lower and lower, the upper edge of the shaded side of the blue mountain and the lower edge of the blue sky forgot their proper places and began to invade each other's territory; soon I could no longer distinguish between the two, and when I shifted my eyes from the mountain to the sky, I lost any conscious sense of their having left the mountain and saw the sky as a continuation of the mountain. And the sky was huge.

And it stretched northward without limit. And Chōzō and I were walking north.

Ever since I had tucked up the skirts of my kimono at the Senju Bridge on the edge of the city the night before, after leaving Tokyo, I had forged onward with bare shanks, whether plunging into the pine grove, sitting at the tea stand, or taking the train, and still I had been fairly hot. Since entering this town, however, I had begun to feel sort of cold with my legs bare. More than cold, I had probably begun to feel lonely. Silent, and moving nothing but our legs, it seemed as if Chōzō and I were making our way through autumn. Then I got hungry again. I know it doesn't look good for me to keep writing about my empty stomach, and it's particularly unpoetic in this context, but that can't be helped. I really got hungry. All I had been doing since leaving the house was walk, never eating any normal human food, as a result of which my stomach would empty all of a sudden. However bad you may feel, however great your anguish, however convinced you may be that your soul is trying to escape, your stomach empties itself out just fine. Or rather, it might be more appropriate to say that, in order to keep your soul in place, you *have* to eat. You have to provide it with food. Undignified as it may sound, I traversed the length of that long, narrow town, walking in the middle of the street with Chōzō, swinging my head back and forth, back and forth, looking into all the eating places on either side. And there were lots of them. Forget about the high-class inns and restaurants. Everywhere, I could see these plain old eateries that would be fine for Chōzō and me. But he didn't look ready to go into any of them. He didn't ask me, "Want to eat?" the way he had asked me if I wanted to take the omnibus before. Still, he was obviously looking back and forth from side to side just like me, as if he were trying to find something. Firm in my belief that at any moment Chōzō was going to find a good place and take me inside for supper, I patiently endured my hunger, walking ever northward through the long, long town.

Now, it's true that I was hungry, but not so hungry that I was about to collapse. I could tell there was a little manjū left in my stomach from before. I could walk if I wanted to. It was just that my sinking spirit had been shocked awake when it was hurled into the middle of the street upon leaving the train, and it reacted by instantaneously translating the sudden chill of the mountain evening air into a desire for something to eat. I could get by without eating if I had to. It wasn't so bad that I was willing to ask Chōzō to feed me. Probably my mouth needed something to chew on, which made it hard for me to ignore the restaurant signs. And when I saw that Chōzō was looking into the shops on both sides as if he had the same thing in mind, my hunger grew worse. In passing through this long, narrow town, I counted nine eateries that looked right for Chōzō and me. When I reached the ninth, I realized that, for all its length, the town was about to come to an end. Another hundred yards and we'd be through it. I was beginning to feel a tremendous letdown when I spotted one more sign on the right: "DRINKS/ EATS." "This is it," I thought. "My last chance." Perhaps the thought was responsible for the intensity with which the thick letters on the shoji beneath the sooty eaves burned themselves into my mind: "DRINKS/EATS," "SNACKS." And I can still see each word now, indelibly etched on my brain: "DRINKS." "EATS." "SNACKS." Whatever senility may lie in store for me, I know that I shall never lose the ability to write these three words exactly as I saw them then.

Incredibly, my own lingering glances at my last chance for drinks, eats, and snacks were matched by Chōzō's concentrated gaze at the shoji. "At last," I thought, "even the unyielding Chōzō will go in for a bite to eat." But he did not go in. On the other hand, he did come to a sudden stop. Beyond the shoji, I saw something red moving. Judging from the expression on Chōzō's face, he seemed to be staring at this red thing. Yes, the red thing was a human being. I had no idea why Chōzō had stopped to stare at this red human being. It was undoubtedly human, but its features were entirely obscure. It was just this gloomy, red THING. I, too, stopped to marvel at this phenomenon when a red blanket came flying out through the shoji door.* There may be some readers who feel that a blanket should not have been necessary in May, however deep in the mountains this town might have been, but in fact this fellow had himself wrapped tightly in a red blanket. On the other hand, the only thing he had on underneath was a handwoven summer kimono, which meant that he wasn't wearing much more clothing than I was. Of course I dis-

---

*The wearing of a red blanket as a kind of winter poncho was formerly common enough in rural areas for the term "red blanket" (*akagetto*) to be a synonym for "country person."

covered only later that he was making do with a single, unlined kimono. At the time he came flying out through the shoji, he was just red.

Chōzō walked right up to this red fellow and said, "Hey, kid, want a job?"

Since "Want a job?" was the first question Chōzō had asked me, I thought, "There he goes again, putting somebody to work," and I observed the two of them with considerable interest. This was when I realized clearly for the first time that Chōzō was a man who would approach anyone he judged to be a suitable young fellow and ask, "Hey, want a job?" It was simply his business to find work for others. He was not recommending me to become a miner because he found me uniquely qualified for the position. He was probably capable of tirelessly repeating "Hey, want a job?" in the same mechanical tone of voice to anyone anywhere. Come to think of it, it was amazing he could continue in this line of work year after year. Not even Chōzō could have been born with a natural gift for asking people, "Hey, want a job?" Like anyone else, he must have been repeating himself by force of circumstances. Viewed thus, he was a perfectly innocent individual. He pursued this work because he didn't know how to do anything else, but he gave no sign of anguish at his lack of ability. Indeed, he performed his chosen task with the confident air of a man convinced that there was no one else in the whole, wide world who would be capable of asking, "Hey, want a job?"

It would have been fun if I had been able to formulate such a replete Theory of Chōzō back then, but having nearly been deserted by my soul, I could not have attained the necessary degree of detachment. No, my Theory of Chōzō has just begun taking shape now for the first time, while I look back at myself as a stranger and set down these recollections of my youth here on paper. It exists only on paper, and I suspect it's very different from any Theory of Chōzō I could have arrived at back then.

As I stood there listening to Chōzō and the red blanket, I realized that Chōzō took absolutely no cognizance of my individuality. (Yes, I know it's a little funny for me to bring up the question of individuality at this point, and that a ridiculous contradiction is involved when someone who's just run away from Tokyo and sunk to the depths of becoming a miner starts insisting on his individuality. I almost burst out laughing when I wrote the word here. I'm in a far better position now than I was then if I can feel like laughing when I look back on my past. Back then, laughing was the last thing I wanted to do.) Clearly, Chōzō did not recognize my individuality. By which I mean that he had buttonholed this young fellow who had come flying out of the eatery and was urging him to become a miner as if the red blanket were simply another me, using exactly the same tone, the same attitude, the same words, and, I think I may presume to say, the same degree of enthusiasm. Somehow, I found this a little insulting. An explanation for this would go roughly as follows:

Not even I, who at the time had placed my common sense in hock, could go along with Chōzō's claim that being a miner was a wonderful profession. I knew full well that the miner ranked only above the ox and the horse among beasts of burden and that it was no honor for me to become one. I may have been thinking that I was the only candidate for a miner, but I had enough sense to know that it was nothing for me to get worked up about when another one suddenly materialized from the door of a tavern in the form of a red blanket. But when I saw that he and I were being treated in exactly the same manner, I felt not so much annoyed that the manner was the same as that he and I were the same person. I had arrived at the odd conclusion that if the manner of treatment were the same, those receiving that manner of treatment must be the same. (I seem to have stumbled onto that one.) Chōzō was now offering a job to the red blanket, and the red blanket was me. I couldn't believe that some other person was standing there with a red blanket on. My soul had abandoned me, flown into the red blanket, and was being urged by Chōzō to become a miner. This started me feeling sorry for myself. As long as I was dealing directly with Chōzō, I could forget about my "individuality," but how pitiful to stand aside and watch myself, as the red blanket, being promised by Chōzō that I would make "lots of money"! I looked hard at the red blanket and, with some disappointment, thought, "So this is the real me."

But what really struck me as odd was that the red blanket gave Chōzō the same kind of answer that I had. This young man was the same human being as myself, not just in the red blanket he had on, but down to the very bottom of his heart. I didn't like this one bit. Another thing that bothered me was Chōzō's disgustingly impartial manner. He gave no hint whatever that I was more suited to being a miner than was the red blanket. He was absolutely mechanical in his approach, to the point where I began to feel that I deserved at least a little special treatment as the one who had come first. (This just goes to show what a stubborn thing human vanity is. Here I was, in such desperate circumstances that I was on the verge of becoming a miner, and still I was vain enough to be bothered by something so trivial. This was probably the same sort of phenomenon as "honor among thieves" or "courtesy among beggars.") I was a lot less bothered by this affront to my vanity, though, than by my realization that the red blanket and I were one and the same.

The two quickly wound up their business as I stood there blankly, watching in annoyance. Not that Chōzō was so clever: the red blanket was a fool. I don't mean to dismiss him as a fool by way of contrasting him to myself. In my readiness to go along with Chōzō, in the ease with which I agreed to become a miner, and in all sorts of other ways, I was just as much of a fool as this young man. If I had to come up with a difference, about the only one I could name would be that he wore a red blanket and I had on my blue-and-white lined kimono. When I call him a fool, I mean it only in the sense that he was just as pitiful a creature as I, and implying the sympathy of one fool for another.

And so it came about that Chōzō headed for the copper mine with two fools in tow. The moment I started walking next to the red blanket, though, I noticed that my feeling of annoyance had disappeared. Human thoughts are the most changeable thing in the world. The minute you're happy to have one, it's gone. The second you're pleased to be free of one, it's back. Maybe a thought is there, maybe it isn't; you can't put your finger on it for sure. Once, I was staying at a hot spring, bored, so I borrowed a book from the inn and found it to contain a bunch of nonsense from the Buddhist scriptures. One phrase struck me, though: "The mind is unknowable in all three worlds."* The "three worlds" business is a lot of hot air, but I think the part about the mind being unknowable is the kind of thing I'm talking about. True, one person I told this to said I was talking about ideas, not the mind. I didn't contradict him, since

*A reference to the *Diamond (Kongō, Vajra) Sūtra*. The three "worlds" are past, present, and future.

41

you can call it anything you like. Disputes of this sort are absolutely pointless; they arise because there are lots of people around who are very clever but who don't know the first thing about the human heart. It frustrates me the way they think that, just because it's a solid object, the heart stays the same (as long as the worms don't eat it) year in and year out. And the shocking thing is they openly manipulate other people any way they see fit, educate them, and make them behave according to their own wishes, all based on this cheerful misconception. They don't realize that water never comes back once it's flowed away; while you're dillydallying, it evaporates.

In any case, you only need to remember here that my earlier annoyance had evaporated by the time I started walking with the red blanket. I was shocked to find myself actually pleased to be walking next to him. On the other hand, this fellow was a real bumpkin from Ibaraki or thereabouts. His pronunciation was funny, as though the words were escaping from his nose. He pronounced "potato" "p'tater," but that belongs to a later anecdote. When we first started walking together, I wasn't too thrilled with the noises he made. And his face was not fully formed. By comparison, Chōzō, with his square jaw and thick lips, was a man of regal presence. In addition, he had been running around all his life in the fields of Ibaraki, had never set foot in Tokyo. And his red blanket had a funny stink about it. Still, I was happy to have found a companion in this mountain village who would go with me to the mine. I was aiming to bury myself, but I preferred to be buried with company rather than alone. Going to ruin by yourself is far lonelier than going to ruin with someone else. Rude though it is of me to say this, I didn't like one thing about the fellow, but I was tremendously pleased and grateful that he would be going to ruin with me. All it took was a few words between us when we started walking to draw us close together—which leads me to suspect that, if I were drowning in a river, I'd probably want to drag a boatman or two down with me. And if it turned out that I had to go to some kind of hell when I died, I'd probably choose a hell with demons over one where there was nobody besides me.

In this way, I suddenly found myself liking the red blanket, and after walking a couple hundred yards, I noticed I was hungry again. It may sound as if I was constantly getting hungry, but this was just a continuation of the earlier hunger, not a new one. To review the order of events: First, my spirit had dimmed and I had left the train when my sense of reality was at its weakest; then, I had looked straight down the straight road to the mountain at the far end of town and finally returned to normal. This had led to my feeling of hunger, then my awareness that my individuality was being ignored and a strong accompanying feeling of annoyance, which had been followed immediately by the advent of a companion in mining and a partial recovery of my declining energies. This explanation should help you to grasp the sequence resulting in my return to hunger.

In any case, I was hungry again, but we had already passed the last eatery and were coming to the end of the town. Ahead lay only the dark mountain road. My need was obviously not going to be fulfilled. And the red blanket from Ibaraki, having just eaten, bounded ahead energetically. I gave up. As a last, desperate measure, I spoke to Chōzō.

"Could you tell me, Chōzō, are we going to cross that mountain?"

"That one right there? Hell, no! We go left soon," he said, hurrying along. There was only one thing for me to do.

"Are we going far? I'm kind of hungry," I said, confessing my need for food at last.

"Oh, yeah? You need a sweet potato." Before the words were out of his mouth he went flying into a potato shop on the left. Amazing: it just happened to be there. Call it (with some exaggeration) a Gift from Heaven. Even now, when I recall how perfectly that moment worked out, I'm not only tickled but downright happy. Of course, the place was not as nice as a potato shop in Tokyo. It was the blackest potato shop I've ever seen—almost indescribably so. And it wasn't just a potato shop, though I couldn't exactly tell you what they sold besides roasted sweet potatoes. Probably I was too busy eating to remember.

A moment later, Chōzō emerged from this black potato shop balancing potatoes on both hands. Having no container, he simply held his hands out to me and said, "Here. Eat."

I said only, "Thanks," and went on looking at these sweet potatoes that had been thrust before my eyes. Not that I was trying to decide which potato to choose. These were not the sort of potatoes that permitted one to indulge in such nice distinctions. They were red and black and emaciated and dampish, the skins were ripped in a few spots, and the exposed sections looked like nothing so much as verdigris. It wouldn't make any difference which one I happened to grab. On the other hand, you shouldn't get the idea that I was hanging back out of some queasiness induced by this gruesome potato spectacle. Judging from the condition of my stomach, I had more than enough appetite to appreciate even these pariahs among sweet potatoes. It's just that, when I had them thrust before me with the command, "Here. Eat," I felt somehow intimidated and couldn't simply put my hand out for one. Probably there was something wrong with the way Chōzō had said, "Here. Eat."

Meanwhile, Chōzō looked a little frustrated watching me watch the potatoes, and again he said, "Here," gesturing with that chin of his toward the potatoes and flexing his outstretched wrists as a signal to eat. Come to think of it, he had his hands full of potatoes, and until I did something to change the situation, Chōzō would not be able to bring one to his mouth, however badly he might want to eat it. His impatience was only natural. Finally, I realized what was happening and stretched my right hand toward the potatoes, arching my arm up and over in a strange sort of way. But as my hand was moving toward its destination, a potato rolled from Chōzō's hand and fell to the street. Immediately the red blanket picked it up and announced, "This is a good p'tater. I'll take it." Which is how I learned that he pronounced "potato" "p'tater."

I recall that I took sweet potatoes from Chōzō twice: three the first time, two later, for a total of five. As I ate them with the pleasure of meeting an old friend, we finally reached the end of the long town, where another event occurred.

At the end of the town was a bridge. Beneath the bridge was a stream, its blue waters flowing. While it had crossed my mind that the town was coming to an end, I was so taken up with eating the sweet potatoes that I didn't notice the stream until I was actually on top of the bridge. Suddenly there was the sound of water, and with a start I found myself on the bridge. There was the stream. The water was flowing. (There's something ridiculous about all this, but if I'm going to narrate things as much in accord with the actual facts as possible, this is probably the best way to write it out. I'll leave it as is. These are not figures of speech, the kind novelists use that are seven-tenths hot air. And if they're not figures of speech, then it becomes all the more obvious how much I was enjoying those potatoes.) When I was startled by the sound of water and looked over the railing, I saw why the stream made so much noise: it was full of big rocks. They were irregularly shaped and, lying down or thrusting upward, they seemed to be there for the express purpose of blocking the flow. The water was crashing against them, and it was running at an incline. It came dancing down as if it were being pursued, spreading out the force of its fall from the mountains in easy payments. So while it might be called a stream, in fact it was more like a broad waterfall paid out in monthly installments. Thus, for a stream with so little water, it was surprisingly turbulent. The water came rushing down with the reckless abandon of a pushy Tokyoite and flowed past, spouting white foam and twisting and turning like blue, sticky strands of candy. It was awfully noisy. Meanwhile, the sun was going down bit by bit. I looked up but couldn't find anyplace it was shining. There was just a soft glow over where it had sunk down, and the mountains shouldering that portion of the sky stood out greenish-black. The time of year was May, but it was cold. The sound of the water alone made it seem like anything but summer. And the color of that mountain, with the setting sun on its back and its face in shadow—what could you possibly call that color? You could get away with purple or black or green if you simply wanted to give it a name, but how do you set down the way that color felt? The mountain looked as if at any moment it was going to lift up, float over my head, and crunch down on top of me. That was probably what was making me feel so cold. Vaguely aware that, in another hour or so, every last thing all around me was going to turn the same eerie color as that mountain over there, and that Chōzō and Ibaraki and I were going to be wrapped in that single, world-enveloping hue, I must have realized that the color that everything would be in an hour or so was the color of that one special place where the sun was going down, and sensed that at any moment the color of the mountain was going to spread from the one special place to take in everything, and this was what had made me feel as if the mountain was going to lift up and crunch down on top of me—which is the analysis of the situation that I came up with just now, sitting at my desk. I'll have to stop this. Free time inspires a lot of pointless activity. I was just cold, that's all—so cold that I began to envy Ibaraki his red blanket.

Just then, from beyond the bridge—but I should point out that beyond the bridge there were no houses of any kind, just the moun-

tain straight ahead and the forest on either side. (Actually, it had
never occurred to me until my feet hit the bridge that all signs of
human habitation would disappear so suddenly.) From the direction
of the empty mountain, a solitary boy appeared. He was thirteen or
possibly fourteen and he wore shabby straw sandals. At first, I could
barely make out his face. He came down the slightly brighter swath
cut through the gloomy forest by the rock-strewn road, moving toward us with quick, small steps. I had no idea where he had come
from or how he had gotten there. Perhaps, because the single path
beneath the dark trees took a sharp curve some hundred yards
ahead, disappearing from view, the road functioned as a device for
making unexpected entrances and exits, but the time and place
being what they were, I was somewhat startled by him. Holding my
fourth potato to my lips, I forgot to move my jaw as I watched him
for a while. By "for a while" here, I mean something like twenty
seconds, that's all. I'm sure I started chewing again right away.

Whether or not the sight of us had startled the boy, I couldn't tell
for certain; he approached us without hesitation. When he had
come within some thirty feet or so, I saw that he had a round head,
a round face, a round nose. Everything about him was put together
round—and with a quality of workmanship far superior to that of
the red blanket. He made as if to pass us by, apparently unperturbed
that the three of us were blocking the way from the bridge to the
path. He was absolutely calm.

Chōzō called out to the boy, "Hey, young fella."

"What?" the boy answered without the least show of fear, coming
to a sudden halt. I was amazed at his confident manner, but perhaps
it was to be expected from a young boy who comes down from the
mountains alone at sundown. When I was his age, I was a little
frightened to cut through Aoyama Cemetery at night—and that's in
the middle of Tokyo.

I was thinking to myself what an admirable little fellow this boy
was, when Chōzō said, "How would you like some sweet potatoes?" and generously dangled two of the uneaten ones in front of
the boy's face. The boy immediately yanked them from Chōzō's
hand and, without a word of thanks, started eating one of the potatoes. Taking in the remarkable swiftness of his every move, I
sensed, with renewed admiration, that a boy who would come

down alone from the mountain like this had to be more than a little different from myself. Unaware of my feelings, the boy went on eating with total abandon. And because he swallowed each mouthful with barely a wetting of saliva, his throat seemed to make little gulping sounds. I thought he would have an easier time of it if he'd eat a bit more calmly, but my concern was wasted on him. He went on gulping down mouthfuls as if to say that it was not as painful as it might look. True, he was eating sweet potatoes, nothing hard. They wouldn't injure his throat, no matter how he wolfed them down. But his throat was crammed full of potatoes, and until they passed down the food pipe, there was some fear that he could suffocate. The boy himself had no such fear. His throat twitched with one gulp after another, as if each swallow of potato were chasing the previous one down to his stomach. His two potatoes were especially big ones, but they quickly disappeared, and the boy himself evidenced no ill effects. The three of us stood around him, watching him eat, but until he was through, no one said a word. I felt there was something a little odd about him, but I also found him rather sad. This was not merely out of sympathy. It had only been a few minutes earlier that I had felt hungry enough to ask Chōzō for sweet potatoes, which meant that my memories of hunger were still pitifully fresh, but to watch this boy eat, he was two or three times hungrier than I had ever been.

"Good?" Chōzō finally asked him. Having myself gone so far as to thank Chōzō for the potatoes before I even put my hand out for them, I assumed that the boy would say *something* once he was through eating, but he offered not a word. He just stood there in silence. Then he turned and looked toward the darkening mountain. Only later did I realize that the boy was entirely a creature of the wild; he did not know how to express thanks. Once I learned that, it didn't bother me too much, but at the time I thought him an unfriendly little brute, in contrast to his appearance. When he tilted that round face of his, though, and gave an odd, long look toward the peak of the gradually blackening mountain, I again found him touchingly sad. I also found him a little disturbing, though I'm not sure why. Perhaps some deep, fatal bond linked the small boy, the tall mountain, the dusk, and the mountain town. I haven't read much poetry or other literary stuff, but I suspect it's written by

47

making a big deal out of this kind of bond between things. That way, you can come up with a poem or a story in the most unlikely places. Wandering all over the country for years now, I've sometimes encountered such links and found myself reacting to them with a sense of something uncanny. Usually, though, if I think about it calmly, the mystery is solved. Probably this boy was, for me, almost the embodiment of the ghostly "little boy who flew down from the mountain" in the song I knew from childhood. Enough on that subject. I won't bother thinking about it any more deeply than this. All that matters is that the boy was staring at the black mountain peak with a strange look on his face.

Chōzō asked him, "Hey, where you going?"

The boy quickly turned his gaze from the black mountain and replied, "Ain't goin' nowhere." His unfriendly tone did not match his face.

Chōzō took it calmly. "Heading home, then?" he asked.

The boy was equally calm. "Ain't goin' home," he said.

The more I heard of this dialogue, the more disturbed I felt. This young boy was a drifter. I had never in my life imagined the existence of such a small, lonely drifter—and one so self-possessed. Thus, while I realized that he was a drifter, I found that the feelings of pity that normally go along with an ordinary drifter naturally tended to give way to a sense of dread. Chōzō seemed to have no such reaction to him. Probably all he cared to know was whether the boy had a home or not. Having heard that the boy was bound nowhere in particular, Chōzō said to him, "Well, then, come along with us. I'll show you how you can make some money."

And the boy, without a moment's reflection, said, "OK."

I was amazed at the speed with which Chōzō's "negotiations" could be concluded, whether with the red blanket or with the boy. If human beings were put together this simply, life would be a lot easier for everybody. But even as I say this, I have to recall that I was no more difficult to win over than the red blanket or the boy. Strange. I was shocked to witness the boy's casual acceptance of Chōzō's offer, but at the same time I came to see that there were a considerable number of people on this earth who, like me, would follow wherever led, satisfied to drift along with the flow. In Tokyo, people are dizzyingly mobile, but even as they move, their roots are firmly planted. About the only one in the whole place whose roots happened to work loose was me, I figured, when I took off from Senju with my skirts tucked up, which is why I was feeling twice as hopeless as anyone else. Then, in this town, I had unexpectedly latched onto the red blanket. Before another twenty minutes had passed, I had latched onto the boy. And both their roots were far looser than mine. With traveling companions coming to me like this, one after another, it didn't much matter where I was headed. For better or worse, I had been born into a family of more than middling means, and until nine o'clock the night before, I had lived as the classic pampered son. My anguish had been the pampered son's anguish, and the flight I attempted when that anguish reached its peak was the flight of a pampered son. Thus, whether or not I was attaching some exaggerated significance to this flight of mine, I did consider it one of the great turning points in my life. I thought of it as the parting of the ways between life and death. Which is to say that, in a world seen through the eyes of a pampered son, there has never been such a flight—or, at least, nowhere but in the newspapers. But flights in the newspapers are two-dimensional, ink on paper, nothing you can sink your teeth into. They're like phone calls from another world. You listen and say "Yes, yes," and that's the end of them. Your own flight, then, comes to seem like the only true, authentic one, and you feel pleased with yourself. Meanwhile, mine was a simple case of anguish and flight. Having read little poetry or other prettified writing, I was free of the pretensions it takes to view your own situation as a novel, to go dashing back and forth across the novelistic landscape making a great show of your pain and sorrow, all the while observing your own pitiful state from a place apart and gushing over how terribly poetic it is. When I say that I was attaching disproportionate value to my particular flight, I am merely pointing to the fact that, as a result of my inexperience, I was overly impressed with and bewildered by things that really didn't deserve such exaggerated attention. And it was the boon of experience, finally, that was responsible for the sudden dilution of my bewilderment when I met the red blanket and the boy and saw how confidently they handled themselves. I must confess that both of them now seem far more admirable to me than I do myself when I look back and see what we were like at the time.

It was nothing at all for Chōzō to win over the red blanket and then the boy. Not that I put up much of a struggle, either. Come to think of it, Chōzō's job wasn't exactly killing him. I had been assuming that the only one stupid enough to go along with him so easily was somebody like me who had run off at night with his skirts tucked up. It would follow from this that, in such an undemanding line of work as Chōzō's, the whole of Japan could be covered by one man, and if he was going to make a living, that one man would have to have been born with the good fortune to bump into me. By rights, then, Chōzō should have been attacking his work in full recognition of the fact that it was going to take a lot more patience than catching a three-foot carp from the river bank, but he wore an expression that all but said such determination was unnecessary, and he blithely went on collaring men on the street as if it were the most ordinary work in the world, something that carried the official sanction of society. Miraculously, the collared men themselves went along with him, no questions asked. His success could almost make you wonder if, in fact, this *was* the most ordinary work in the world. Any business this successful needed more than one practitioner for the whole country. There should be lots of them. Chōzō himself probably thought so. I know *I* did.

And so the four of us—the happy-go-lucky Chōzō, the happy-go-luckier boy and red blanket, and I, who, by following their example, was learning to be enormously happy-go-lucky—crossed the bridge and took the path to the left. Chōzō cautioned us to walk with care now that we would be climbing along the stream. Having just eaten the sweet potatoes, I was no longer hungry. My legs were exhausted from walking since the night before, but they could still carry me if they had to. I followed Chōzō and the red blanket with all the care I could muster, as Chōzō had suggested. Since the path was not very wide, we could not walk four abreast, which is why I fell behind. As the smallest in the party, the boy followed along one step behind me, sticking close.

What with my heavy belly and heavy legs, I didn't feel much like talking. Chōzō, too, fell silent once we had crossed the bridge. The red blanket had not had much to say from the time Chōzō caught him in front of the eatery, and now, for some reason, he spoke even less. The most uncommunicative of all was the boy, whose only sound was the slapping of his straw sandals against his heels.

Now that we had stopped talking, a stillness hung over the mountain path. The darkness of night gave the place an especially desolate air. Of course, the "night" had barely begun, the sun having just set. I could at least make out the path. Maybe it was my imagination, but the water rushing down to our left seemed to shine a little now and then. Not a brilliant glow, no. It was just that something dark and moving out there looked as though it had a shine to it. The water crashing against the rocks was fairly clearly white, and it made a continuous rushing sound. It was pretty noisy, and that made it pretty desolate.

Before long, the narrow path seemed to be climbing gradually upward. The slight incline by itself was no great trouble, but the ground was all pits and bumps. Probably the same scattering of rocks that littered the bottom of the stream continued on up into the path and raised sudden obstructions or left hollows in the surface of the ground. My geta caught on these pits and bumps. The worst trip-ups made my innards bounce. It became a major ordeal. Chōzō and the red blanket seemed to be used to climbing mountain paths. They walked along through the darkness under the trees without the slightest hesitation. This was only to be expected, but the boy—the boy was downright spooky. He hopped easily over the dark pits and bumps, his straw sandals flapping all the while. And he never said a word. It wouldn't have bothered me so much during the day, but in this gloomy place the slapping of the sandals against his heels was preying on my nerves. I felt as though I was walking with a bat.

Soon the path became steeper and steeper. Before I knew it, the stream was far away. I was out of breath. The pits and bumps were growing worse by the minute. Suddenly my ears started ringing. If this had been some hike in the woods, I would have made a fuss long before, but I was running away, after all, and this was supposed to be the first step toward death for someone who had failed at suicide. I could hardly start bringing my complaints to someone just because it hurt a little. And whom would I have complained *to*? There was only me. All right, maybe there *was* somebody else besides me, but I didn't have the guts to open my mouth. And if I had, they wouldn't have listened to me anyhow. *They* weren't having any trouble. They just went zipping along. They didn't even talk. There was no way for me to approach them. All I could do was follow them docilely, in silence, though my ears were ringing and I was out of breath. I had known the word "docile" since I was a kid, but I

51

had never understood its meaning until now. I suppose you could laugh this off as the beginning and end of my enlightenment, but once it began, this insight continued for some time, reaching its ultimate form in the mine. When docility attains its highest state, tears flow less easily. People often say that so-and-so brought tears to their eyes, but if you can cry, you've got nothing to worry about. As long as you have tears to shed, you can still laugh.

Strange that anyone who was so under the spell of docility should have changed so completely. There's nothing docile about me now. In fact, I'm considered to be rather difficult. If Chōzō could see me now, after the way I put myself so totally in his hands back then, he'd say I've gotten too big for my britches. Meanwhile, if my present friends could see what I was like back then, they might say I was pitiful. But so what? It's only natural for the docile creature of yesteryear to become difficult today. That's just the way people are. You can try forcing someone to remember how he felt in winter and keep shivering after summer comes, but it won't work. A person might not be able to eat beef while he's sick, but nobody can order him to give it up for the rest of his life. You hear about people warning others not to forget what they've done for them in their hour of need, but of course they're going to forget. Swearing otherwise is just a lie. This may sound like some kind of rationalization, but it's not at all. I'm telling the honest truth. The trouble with people is they think they're solid as a rock. They don't look at another person's surroundings but try to force him into some predetermined slot. They assume it's perfectly reasonable to treat others this way, but I don't think I've ever heard of anyone who was happy to squeeze himself in where he doesn't fit. If you go at everything like this, you're going to have to run away from the three-dimensional world to one that's perfectly flat. People who loudly accuse others of bad faith or dishonesty or a change of heart are duly registered citizens of Flatland, raising their battle flags at the sight of printed hearts. There are lots of this type among the ranks of the pampered sons and daughters, scholars, innocents, and great lords, most of whom have no idea how things really work. If I hadn't run away back then, if I had calmly entered adulthood as my family's sweet, little sonny boy, if I had grown up unaware that my heart is constantly on the move, convinced that it doesn't move, doesn't change—mustn't move, would be a sin to change—if I had been satisfied to go to school, collect a salary, have a tranquil home life and ordinary friends, never feeling the need for introspection—never knowing the lively mental metamorphoses that make introspection possible—if pain and poverty and homelessness and wandering and weariness and agony and winning and losing and possession and deprivation had not bestowed on me this experience of mine and given me, finally, the ability to dissect my experience with an open mind and to evaluate each little piece of it (and, thank goodness, I *do* have this great gift)—then I would never make such drastic pronouncements. Not that drastic pronouncements are anything to boast about. I'm just describing things as they are. And, things being what they are, there's no telling when the docile one who became difficult might change from difficult to docile.

My legs felt as if they were going to fall off. I stopped and planted them like poles in the earth, listening, and from the distance to my ringing ears came the sound of rushing water. I grew increasingly docile.

In this state, I covered a lot of ground—too much for me to guess how many miles it was. Walking at night, it would have seemed long under the best of conditions, but in negotiating the pits and bumps my calves began to swell, my knees were scraping against each other, and my thighs felt ready to fall to the ground. I was beyond worrying about distance. Yet as evidence that I was still alive, I managed to keep walking, never more than thirty feet or so behind Chōzō. This was not merely a result of my having docilely resigned myself to submerging my individuality. As soon as the distance between us grew to much more than thirty feet, Chōzō would turn around and wait for me to catch up, then start walking again before I had actually reached him, urging me on little by little this way. It was amazing how Chōzō could see behind him—and at night! The path was so dark that only upon looking up did I sense how the black trees thrusting straight up into the sky on either side of us left a narrow, open band above our heads. People talk of "starlight," but it doesn't amount to much. And of course no one there happened to be carrying a lantern. For my own part, I kept my eye on the red blanket ahead. He wasn't red at night, but somehow or other he seemed very much like the red blanket anyway. This was probably because I had fixed on him while it was still light and followed after him, concentrating on "that blanket, that blanket," like repeated invocations to the Buddha. Eyes encountering him for the first time after dark would not know what they were seeing, but to me he looked exactly like the red blanket. No doubt this kind of thing is the source of what they call the power of faith. I had managed, thus, one way or another, to find myself a guide in the darkness, but there was simply no way that Chōzō could tell how far behind him I was. And yet he did it all the same. As soon as I dropped back more than thirty feet, he would stop and wait for me. At least I *think* he was stopping for me. He might have been stopping because he felt like it. In any case, he was stopping. This was a feat beyond the powers of an amateur. In my misery, I still could not help admiring Chōzō. It was a skill he needed for his work, I felt, which he had brought to this level of perfection after long years of practice. Walking beside Chōzō, the red blanket stopped whenever Chōzō did. And as soon as Chōzō started up again, the red blanket did, too. Here was a man who functioned like a puppet. He was probably far easier to manipulate than I, who tended to fall behind. And the boy—the boy had disappeared. At first, I had assumed that he was falling behind because he was a youngster, and I even figured I'd give him a little encouragement if he tired, but after I'd seen the way he went skipping along the pitted road with his sandals flapping, I had abandoned any hope of keeping up with him. But that had been quite some time ago. For a while, I had climbed with the flapping right next to me. Now there was nothing left of him—not even a shadow. While he was next to me, he walked with almost too much vigor for such a little boy. This in itself wouldn't have bothered me, but in addition, his silence was extreme, which gave me a very creepy feeling. Before you start laughing at me, imagine for yourself an extremely small, tremendously lively, and completely silent animal, and you'll see what I mean. This was no ordinary creature. Anyone crossing a mountain at night with an animal like that would be scared. I feel strange just thinking about him even now. Earlier, I said he was like a bat, and that's exactly what he was: a bat. I suppose I was OK because Chōzō and the red blanket were there. But honestly, if I had been alone with the bat, I wouldn't have made it.

Suddenly, out of the darkness, Chōzō shouted, "Halloo!"

I don't know if any of you have heard the sound of a human voice without warning on a lonely road at night, but let me tell you, it can make you feel very weird. An ordinary speaking voice might be all right, but a loud "Halloo!" is not going to do wonders for your nerves. There I was, on a mountain path, in the dark, where not a soul was passing by, and to make matters worse, I was walking with some kind of bat. Chōzō picked just the moment of mounting terror to raise his voice as if there were something happening. "Halloo!" he cried, when nothing should have been happening in a place where anything could happen, bringing together the unexpected and the all-too-expected in a way that sent weird reverberations into my head. Had it been a cry directed at me, I would have made do with a simple start: "Uh-oh, something's wrong." But his shout was so loud that it could not possibly have been meant for me, walking thirty-some-odd feet behind him. Besides, it was moving in the wrong direction. It wasn't aimed toward me. It sped off to the right and left, but, blocked there by the trees, it fled far ahead down the narrow path until it sent back an echo from a long way off. There was definitely an echo but apparently no answer. Then Chōzō shouted, even more loudly than before, "Hey, you! Boy!"

Now that I think of it, Chōzō seems a little ridiculous yelling "Boy!" to this boy whose name he didn't know, but at the time he didn't strike me as ridiculous at all. The moment I heard Chōzō's cry, I thought to myself, "The bat's gone into hiding." The normal thing in a situation like this would have been to think, "He's gone ahead," or, at worst, to conclude that the boy had run off, but if the first thing that crossed my mind was that he had gone into hiding, there's not much doubt that I was under the spell of the bat. The spell broke when the sun came up the next morning, and I kicked myself for being such an idiot, but in fact, when I heard that shout of "Hey, you! Boy!" it really shook me up.

As before, the reverberations trailed off into the distance, meeting up with nothing. They faded away, like the tail of a shooting star, and, as if in response, the trees and hills and valleys fell silent. There was no answer. Nothing. In that interval while the reverberations, though still barely hanging on, were gradually fading away, and from the moment they disappeared completely until the entire world fell silent, the three of us, Chōzō and the red blanket and I, stood in silence, nose to nose in the dark. This was not a very pleasant sensation.

Finally, Chōzō said, "If we go a little faster, maybe we can catch up with him." To me, he added, "OK, kid?"

No, of course, it was not OK, but there was nothing much I could do about it. I agreed and hurried after him. Now, I knew damn well I couldn't "go a little faster" at this point if my life depended on it. I didn't have it in me—I didn't have it in my legs—to go faster, but, strangely enough, I said I'd do it. I probably had a funny look on my face at the time, but once I'd said I'd hurry, I hurried, whether I thought I could do it or not. How I managed the next part of the trip, and what kind of places we passed through, well, I suppose the best thing would be for me to say flat out that I don't know. At some point, Chōzō stopped short, and that brought me around. We were standing in front of a house. There was a lamp lit inside. The light of the lamp spilled out onto the road. I was overjoyed. I could see the red blanket clearly. And the boy was there. His shadow cut across the road and fell into the valley on the other side. It was a long shadow for such a little fellow.

Finding a human habitation in a place like this was the last thing I had expected to do. My head was swimming, my ears were ringing, I had been rushing along blindly with no idea of where I was headed and no hope of getting there, when all of a sudden we had come to a stop in the glare of lamplight. It was a shock, but at the same time it was tremendously moving to realize what a human thing the light of a lamp could be. To this day, I've never been so grateful for a lamp as I was at that moment. I learned afterward that the boy had beaten us to the lamplight and waited for us to catch up. He had heard both of Chōzō's shouts, but he hadn't bothered to answer. What an amazing little fellow!

So now our group was back together again. Docile as ever, I stood there wondering what would happen next, when Chōzō, leaving us by the side of the road, entered the house alone. I keep calling the place a "house," but really the word was more than the place deserved. If it had had cows, it would have been a barn; for horses, it could have been a stable. They sold straw sandals there, I guess; I didn't see anything but walls, straw sandals, and a lamp. The whole facade was six feet wide, and the door's storm shutter was half closed. Probably they left the thing half open all night. Or maybe the shutter had eaten its way into the groove and couldn't be budged. The roof was thatched, of course, and the straw was old and crumbling, probably from having soaked up rain, which gave it a vague sort of look. It was so mushy you couldn't tell where the roof and the night met. This, then, was the "house" that Chōzō entered. You had the feeling more that he had crawled into a hole or something. He stayed there, talking. The three of us stood outside. I don't know what my own face looked like, but I could see the faces of the red blanket and the boy clearly in the light of the lamp that came streaming out of the shed at an angle. The red blanket's face was as blank as ever. I was sure he would wear that same expression in any situation—in the midst of a massive earthquake with roof beams falling all around him or by the bed of a parent on the verge of death. The boy was looking at the sky. He was still frightening.

Then Chōzō appeared. He didn't come out to the road, though. Stepping up to the threshold, he stood facing our way, allowing only a narrow beam of lamplight to escape between his legs. It seemed as though the lamp had been moved to a lower position in the meantime. Of course, I couldn't see Chōzō's face very well.

To me he said, "You'd never make it over the mountain if we tried crossing now, kid. We'll stay here tonight. Everybody come inside."

The moment I heard this, my docility blew apart, and the flesh sagged on my bones. Not even with this barn staring me in the face had the thought crossed my mind that spending a night here could give me such relief. We had found a place to rest, but I was probably still too docile even to think of resting. This goes to show that human beings are the easiest things in the world to control. They'll take the most outlandish orders with profound respect and, far from putting up a fuss, they'll thank you for them. Whenever I recall those days, along with the memory comes the conviction that I was the most obedient, dutiful person imaginable. It has even crossed my mind that the way I was then is the way a soldier always has to be. And this has brought with it the realization that if one is able to ignore the use of an object, he is also able to forget the use of an object.

This is how my thought came out on paper, but I don't understand it myself now that I read it over. It's actually much simpler than this, but it ended up looking difficult because I crammed it into too short a space. Here's an example. Say you know that you have no right to drink sake. As long as you are able to convince yourself that sake, by nature, is something the presence of which is of no concern to you, then a whole row of sake bottles can be standing in front of you and it won't even occur to you that sake is for drinking.

Probably what saves us all from becoming thieves, finally, is the manner in which we are artificially acclimated to such a state of mind from childhood. On the other hand, a state of mind like this comes about as the result of anesthetizing a part of our humanity, so while they're forging ahead feeling very pleased with themselves, people end up as idiots. Now, granted, you don't want anybody turning into a thief, but it is my humble opinion that the most virtuous deed one can perform for another is to make it possible for him to exercise all his other psychological propensities in a suitable manner. If the old me had survived unchanged to the present day, I would be plenty obedient and hardworking, but I would also be an idiot—probably worse than an idiot—and it would be obvious to anyone who bothered to notice. Human beings are *supposed* to get angry now and then, they're *supposed* to rebel. That's how they're *made*. Forcing yourself to become a creature that doesn't get angry and never rebels is tantamount to happily educating yourself to be an idiot. It'll ruin your health, first of all. If you don't like what I'm saying, then you'd better arrange your life so that nothing ever makes you angry or rebellious.

Back then, I was following Chōzō's instructions to the letter in every situation, and as far as I'm concerned that was the most natural thing for me to do. Given my present position in life, though, a hundred Chōzōs could yank at me for seven days and seven nights, and I wouldn't budge an inch because that would be the most natural thing for me as I am now. And I believe that for me to change like this is the very thing that makes me human. I mention Chōzō merely as an example to help you understand what I'm saying, but if you look at the matter closely, you'll see that human character changes by the hour. The process of change is entirely normal, and it is just as normal for contradictions to arise as the process goes on. There are, in other words, many contradictions in human character—so many, in fact, that it makes no difference whether we conclude that character exists or doesn't exist. If you think I'm lying, try an experiment. It would be wrong of you to experiment on other people, so try it first on yourself. You won't have to stoop to becoming a miner for this to work. And you won't obtain any better results if you try asking a god for the answer. The god that understands this kind of reasoning lives inside you—down in your gut.

Sorry for these pseudo-academic noises I'm making without any academic background. I really wasn't planning to go on huffing and puffing like this, but here's what got me started. People often used to complain to me that I was full of contradictions. And every time they did it, I would put on a sour face and apologize. I found myself just as upsetting as they did. It worried me that I couldn't pass for an ordinary human being. If I didn't do something to reform myself, I might lose my credibility and end up on the streets. But then I started experimenting on myself, observing myself in different situations, and I realized there was no need whatever for me to reform. This was the real me, and it was all that made me human. I then tried my experiment on other people, only to find that they were made just like me. It was hilarious. The complaints they brought to me could just as well have been brought to them. When they got hungry, they'd eat; when they were full, they'd get sleepy; hard up, they'd turn bad; with their pockets full, they'd keep to the straight and narrow; falling in love, they would marry, and falling out of love, they'd divorce. It was as simple as that. They were playing it by ear, and this was all it took to be human.

There. I was so impressed with my own ideas I just wanted to say them. I really shouldn't be carrying on as if I know what I'm talking about. There are plenty of scholars, priests, and educators in the world, and each of these demanding fraternities examines such matters with its own professional expertise.

That's enough hot air for now. Back to the docile attitude and the story of what happened in the mountains.

When, standing on the threshold and facing the road, Chōzō brought up the idea of spending the night in this place, I was so totally unprepared for the concept of spending the night anywhere that it only dawned on me at that moment, not so much that it was possible to spend the night in a hovel like this, as that the original purpose of all human habitation was precisely for spending the night. Meanwhile, I was so tired my body was as limp as a wet noodle. Ordinarily, every organ in my body should have been bursting with the need to stop and rest, but this fatigue of mine had occurred *after* I had resigned myself to the ego-submerging business of becoming a miner—that is, to this final degeneration as a kind of warm-up for letting myself die, which is why, in spite of its need for rest, my body did not put in a request to my soul for lodging. Then, suddenly, the order came from nowhere—first to my soul, which, in a somewhat confused form, sent the message on to my arms and legs, and when they reacted with extraordinary joy, my soul finally noticed that it was time to be grateful for Chōzō's kindness. I know this sounds as though I'm trying to be comical, but I'll never be able to describe my mental state at the time without adopting some such figure of speech.

As soon as I heard what Chōzō had to say, my nerves went slack and I headed for the doorway, dragging along my legs, which were no longer usable for standing. The red blanket plodded in after me, and the boy flew in. No, I suppose he didn't *fly* in, but it seemed that way to me, what with the energetic flapping of his straw sandals against his heels.

Inside, the place stank, though I had no idea what from. I saw the boy's nose twitching, so I knew he was aware of the smell, but Chōzō and the red blanket paid it no mind. After a day on the road in geta without socks, I felt I ought at least to wipe my feet with a rag before stepping up from the dirt-floored entranceway to the tatami mats, but the boy slipped out of his sandals and hopped right up. This was particularly unforgivable in his case, I thought, since the tail ends of his sandals had been worn away and he had been as good as walking barefoot on the ground. I stood there, looking at his feet, when Chōzō urged me to "Step right up. You've been wearing geta."

I did as I was told, though I didn't feel very good about it. When my foot came down on the tatami, it sank into the wavy straw. The boy was already sprawling on the rotten old mats. I carefully lowered just my bottom onto them and sat cross-legged inside, next to the shoji, of which there were two in the doorway, one having been slid open atop the other. I turned to see Chōzō and the red blanket stepping out of their straw sandals. Both took handkerchiefs from their sashes and swatted the dust from their feet, then immediately stepped up to the tatami. Apparently, washing their feet would have been too much trouble. At that point, the proprietor appeared from the next room, carrying tea and a tobacco tray.

All of this sounds very ordinary—"proprietor," "the next room," "tea," "tobacco tray." But if I were to go into detail about what each of these items was really like, you'd be amazed at how mistaken your impression had been. Still, it's a fact that the proprietor brought tea and a tobacco tray from the next room. And he struck up a conversation with Chōzō. I don't remember what they talked about, but it was obvious from the way they were talking that they knew each other from before and that there were some kind of debts outstanding between them. Something about a horse kept coming up. The man asked not a thing about me or the red blanket or the boy—not that he considered us beneath his notice, surely. Chōzō had probably told him everything about us there was to tell when he went in alone earlier to arrange for our lodgings. Either that or the proprietor was unconcerned about us because Chōzō was always bringing such carefree fellows through here on the way to the copper mine.

Listening to the conversation, I began to doze at some point. Right about the time someone was saying he had failed to sell the horse and something-or-other, things were becoming fuzzy, and Chōzō simply melted away. The red blanket melted away. The boy melted away. The proprietor and the tea and the tobacco tray melted, and when the shack itself melted away, I snapped awake. My chin had fallen to my chest. Startled, I raised my head, finding it extremely heavy. The proprietor was still talking about the horse, but even as that thought came to me, I started to drift off again, and I just let it happen, drifting farther and farther until my eyes suddenly opened wide. Shadow-like amid the gloom, Chōzō and the master of the house were sitting on the matted floor, knee to knee. At that moment, the master was saying something about his loan and laughing jovially. This man had a very long forehead that drew back toward the crown of his head at an angle. Viewed in profile, it was reminiscent of the Kiridōshi Slope in Tokyo. The higher up the slope, the more hair he had. It grew in shaggy patches, some an inch long, some an eighth. When I bolted awake from my dozing and my eyes snapped open, the first thing to flash into them was this head. In the feeble light of the soot-smeared lamp, the head, too, appeared soot-smeared to me. And yet it was quite close by. Which meant that the image reflected in my eyes was a clear one. In other words, the very second I came back to myself from the non-perception of sleep, I saw this clear and at the same time hazy head of the proprietor. It was not a pleasant sensation. The queasy feeling convinced me to put off sleeping for a while, and I began to examine the room. In the far corner sprawled the boy. Stretched out next to me was Ibaraki, his big feet sticking out from under his blanket. Straight ahead was the wall, and in the corner of the wall was a hole, the depths of which were pitch black. Above was the underside of the roof, the chillingly blackened thatch appearing to tremble when struck by the mixture of light and smoke rising from the lamp. I became sleepy again. My head dropped again. I tried to raise it because it was so heavy, and again it dropped. At first it worked like this: My head, once raised, would begin sinking as I grew drowsier and drowsier until, at the extreme point of drowsiness, it would fall to my chest and I would leap back to consciousness. After three or four times, though, I might open my eyes, but my mind would not clear. Foggily, I would return to the world, and immediately sink once again into unconsciousness. Then, as usual, my head would drop. I would feel as if I were only marginally alive. And then I would enter the Great Emptiness. Finally, it ceased mattering to me that my head had fallen forward. Probably what happened was that the weight of my head hanging down pulled me over sideways. In any case, I slept soundly until dawn and when I awoke, I found that I was no longer dozing in a sitting position but was stretched out full length on the tatami in the ordinary sleeping position. And I was drooling. I had started dozing listening to the conversation about the horse, opened my eyes to hear the conversation about the loan, picked up on the dozing where I had left off, repeated that a few times, and, finally giving up dozing for the real thing, stretched out, and that was the last I heard from my soul, so when I opened my eyes and the sun was up and I saw that the world had switched a hundred and eighty degrees from Yin to Yang,* I just lay there with my eyes open, drooling. If you could be conscious and dead at the same time, it would be like this. I was alive, but the urge to move was not forthcoming. I remembered the night before in minute detail, but I couldn't bring myself to believe that last night's minute details had carried over into today. Everything about my experience was new and intense, but the new, intense things were somewhere far away. Or, rather, I felt as though a thick partition had formed between last night and today, marking a sharp distinction between the two. If the mere appearance and disappearance of the sun is going to disrupt the continuity of my heart this way, then I become strangely unsure of who I am myself. Life is like a dream. Or so I began to think as I lay there steeping in my own thoughts without

*Yin = dark, Yang = light.

wiping the drool, when Chōzō, still on his side, went into a long stretch, bringing his clenched fists up above ear level. His fists shot straight out along the tatami. When his arms had reached their full length, the tension left him and he went limp. For a moment, I thought he was going back to sleep, but then he brought his right hand down again and began scratching vigorously at his sunken cheek. Maybe he was awake? But soon he started mumbling to himself, and I decided he must be asleep. That was when the boy flew up. Literally. In the air. With a huge, resounding thump that threatened to cave the floor in. Perceptive as ever, Chōzō stopped his mumbling and raised himself on an elbow. He was blinking..

Since I couldn't go on endlessly steeping in my own thoughts, I got up. Chōzō also raised himself the rest of the way. The boy stood up. Only the red blanket was still asleep. He lay there, snoring contentedly, his big feet sticking out from under the blanket. Chōzō tried to wake him.

"Hey, kid! Hey! Better get up! We want to get to the mine by noon."

After three or four *Hey, kid*'s, the red blanket was still sound asleep. Chōzō had no choice but to try shaking him. "Hey, hey," he yelled, his hand on the red blanket's shoulder.

"Hey," the red blanket responded in kind, standing up, more or less. Now all of us were sort of up, and I was wondering what to do, having neither washed my face nor eaten, when Chōzō took me by surprise.

"Well, let's get going!" he said, stepping down into the entryway. The boy followed him, and the red blanket let his big feet dangle down uncertainly to the dirt floor. Now it was my turn to make a move. The last of the group, I stepped into my geta and moped around waiting for Chōzō and the red blanket to tie on their straw sandals.

Now that I was down in the dirt, the obvious questions—Don't we wash our faces? Aren't we going to eat breakfast?—began to seem like outrageous demands, and making them was more than I could manage. Funny how something we've come, through habit, to view as indispensable, can suddenly turn superfluous. It happens all the time, though, I realized later in thinking about this topsy-turvy event. What's "normal" is what everybody does; what's "dispensable" is what you alone do. The only way to become "normal" is to make a lot of allies and do the abnormal as though it were the most normal thing in the world. I still haven't tried this, but I'm sure it would work. After all, look at the changes that even as unlikely a pair as Chōzō and the red blanket were able to bring about in me.

Having tied his sandals and thus disposed of any business he had with his feet, Chōzō suddenly raised his face. He looked at me. And he said, "You don't need breakfast, do you, kid?"

Of course I needed breakfast, but it wouldn't have done me any good to say so. I just said "No," and let it go at that.

Chōzō, however, would not let it go. "Want to eat?" he asked, grinning.

He did this for one of two reasons: either a desire for food deeply ingrained in my nature was showing just a bit on my face, or the thwarting of nineteen years of expectation by a breakfastless departure on rising brought forth from me a look of dismay. Otherwise, he would never have asked such a thing after having finished tying his sandals. It's obvious. He didn't pose the question either to the boy or the red blanket. Now that I think of it, it does seem as though he should have asked them, too. Only an authentic vagrant or something close to a vagrant would set off on a hike of ten or twenty miles without breakfast. They were wide awake and the sun was up, but these people didn't associate those things with steam on the morning broth or the aroma of pickled vegetables, which meant they were that unfortunate (or fortunate) type for whom it is natural to let things take their course, happy each day just to keep body and soul together, with no thought for tomorrow. It occurred to me that, for the first time in my nineteen years, I had just spent a night with people like this and that we were going to walk out of there together. When neither the red blanket nor the boy showed the slightest facial evidence of expecting breakfast, I sensed that they belonged to a species of humanity unfamiliar with that particular custom, and I saw that my fate had slipped to something well below that of a miner even before I had become one. Not that the realization was particularly sad; I didn't cry, of course. It still rankles me, though, that Chōzō never asked the others, whose experience of breakfast was so limited, "You kids want to eat?" Would they have said, out of sheer force of habit, "No, that's all right," or, aroused by an unforeseen hope that there just might be something for them to eat, would they have answered, "Yes"? It's a minor point, but I still wish I could have heard their answer.

Standing on the dirt floor, Chōzō turned back partway and called, "See you later, Kuma. Thanks for everything." He stamped lightly on the ground a few times.

"Kuma" of course was the name of the proprietor. He was still in back, sleeping. The shaggy head that had given me the queasy feeling the night before on the edge of sleep, I now peeked in to find sticking out from under a quilt—or, rather, a mattress. Apparently, it was his style to put a sleeping mat on top of himself when he slept. When Chōzō spoke to it, the shaggy head jerked up from the floor mats and out came Kuma's face. It didn't look as odd to me as it had at night. But there was no denying, even in the morning light, that the forehead drew back at an angle running straight up to the top of his head.

"Oh, don't mention it," said Kuma from under the covers. And he was right. There was nothing to mention. He was the only one with a quilt. "Weren't you cold?" he added. Here was a man who believed in taking it easy.

"No, not at all," said Chōzō, stepping across the threshold.

"Stop by on your way down," Kuma said, yawning, to his back.

So now Chōzō was out in the road. I followed him, a step behind the boy and the red blanket. They were all in a tremendous hurry—and all thoroughly used to this kind of traveling, it seemed. According to Chōzō, we would be crossing over the mountains now, and we were hurrying because we had to reach the mine by noon. He didn't say *why* we had to reach the mine by noon, and I didn't have it in me to ask. I just followed along silently. Soon the road started to climb, as Chōzō had said it would. Having had my fill of climbing the day before, I found this hard to believe, but in fact I could see nothing but mountains in every direction. Mountains within mountains within mountains. We were going so deep into the mountains it was almost ridiculous. The copper mine was obviously in an isolated place. I climbed along vigorously, panting with the effort, but all the same I felt discouraged. When it crossed my mind what a time I would have trying to find my way back to the city from a place like this, I started blaming myself for having come here on a whim. Of course, I had run away precisely because I didn't want to stay in the city. I was *supposed* to be going someplace hard to leave, where I could rot away without fear of encountering my family. Scaling a high slope, I paused now and then to catch my breath and survey the surrounding mountains. Each was covered with a dark, forbidding growth of trees and all were swathed in clouds, and as I looked at them, they seemed to draw off into the distance. Perhaps it would be more accurate to say they faded away. Fading, they would slowly withdraw into the depths of the mist until all traces were lost of what had been no more than a shadow. No sooner had that happened than the clouds would move past the face of the mountain, its pale shadow emerging from the white, swirling mist. Beginning at its edge, the shadow would grow gradually thicker, and by the time the color of the trees became clearly visible, the cloud had flowed to the neighboring peak. Then another cloud would come and obscure the color of this mountain that had managed to emerge, until, finally, it was impossible to tell where the mountains were or what they looked like. Trees, mountains, valleys would appear at random from the mists as I stood looking. Even the sky above came falling down from its infinite heights to within touching distance.

"It's going to rain," grumbled Chōzō to himself.

No one answered him. The four of us kept climbing through the clouds, which continued streaming at us, swirling around us, burying us. As far as I was concerned, these clouds were a joy. I had wanted to make myself invisible, and thanks to them I was able to do just that. I could walk through them without undue suffering. I could move my limbs freely without any constricting sense of being closed in, even while enjoying the advantage of concealing myself from the eyes of the world. This was what it meant to be buried alive. It was the one and only ideal for me at the time. And so I was tremendously grateful for those clouds. Or perhaps "relieved" would be a better word. When the clouds began to bury me, it was not so much gratitude as relief that I felt. Now that I think of it, I can't imagine why. Call me crazy, I don't know. Given the proper time and circumstances, maybe even tomorrow, I might wish I had those clouds back again. Strange, I feel as though I can't be sure I'm really here, as though I myself am not myself.

But the clouds, at least, those clouds were a joy. I've never forgotten how the four of us moved through them, drawing apart, bunching up, screened from each other, enveloped together. The boy would emerge from the clouds and plunge back in again. The blanket from Ibaraki would turn red, then white. No more than thirty feet ahead, Chōzō's dotera would grow solid, then fade. No one said a word. Speed was everything. I'll never forget how those four shadows, cut off from the world, went forging through the clouds, pulling ahead, falling behind, drawing together, springing apart, never increasing, never decreasing, but always four, we had to be four, as if it could never be any other way.

I was buried in the clouds, and so were the other three. Clouds were the world, and we four the only people in it. All three of the others were homeless vagrants. For them it was natural to wander through the clouds without washing their faces or eating breakfast. When I had climbed more than two miles and descended almost five with these companions through the blowing clouds, and my legs were ready to give out, it started to rain. Since I had no watch, I didn't know what time it was. From the look of the sky, it could have been morning, but it might just as well have been afternoon or evening. The world was as out of focus as my mind, though one thing I couldn't help noticing was the color of the mountains filtering through the rain. It was completely new. Suddenly the trees were gone and the hills were bare, transformed almost before I knew it into patchy bald heads as red as cinnabar. I had staggered this far with nothing more on my mind than to keep my legs moving as quickly as possible, the clouds a huge brushstroke blotting out whatever bound me to the world at large. When these red hills suddenly appeared before me, I snapped out of the spell of the clouds. I had never imagined that color could have such an impact on me. (By nature, I'm so indifferent to color that I wouldn't be surprised if I turned out to be color-blind.) The moment the red mountain made its fairly violent attack on my optic nerves, I thought to myself, "Finally, we're coming close to the copper mine." Perhaps it was just a presentiment of some kind, but I'm sure I associated the color of the mountain with copper. In any case, when I sensed intuitively that we had arrived ("intuitively" having no deeper meaning most of the time than this), Chōzō said something like what I had been thinking:

"We're almost there."

Within fifteen minutes, we came to a town. Having burrowed into mountains within mountains and passed through clouds within clouds, I was so amazed at the unexpected sight of this new town that I wanted to rub my eyes in case they were deceiving me. If the place had been a post town or village that had some ties with the old days of the shōguns, I wouldn't have been so surprised, but here everything was brand new—new banks, new post office, new restaurants, even new women with makeup on their faces. It was like a dream, and before the surprise could register on my face, we had passed through the town and come to a bridge. Chōzō stopped on the bridge and glanced down at the water flowing beneath.

"This is the entrance," he said. "We're here now. Better keep that in mind."

I had no idea what he meant by this last cautionary remark. I just stood on the bridge, looking from the entrance at what lay beyond. There were hills on the left and hills on the right. I could see houses scattered on the slopes. The wood of the houses looked as new as the town. A few were white stucco or painted. They, too, were new. The only thing old and peeling was the mountain itself. I was beginning to feel a little disappointed, as though I were being dragged back into the real world. When he saw me standing there, peering beyond the bridge, Chōzō asked, as he had before, "You doing okay, kid? You all right?"

"I'm fine," I answered clearly, but inwardly I was not the least bit fine. For some reason, Chōzō was concerned about no one else but me. He never asked the boy if *he* was "doing okay" or the red blanket if *he* was "all right." Obviously, he was taking it for granted that both of them were predestined to become miners and to end their allotted span in the copper mine. Which meant that I was the only one he couldn't count on. Maybe he had been suspicious about my qualifications all along. So much for my inflated self-image.

The four of us crossed the bridge. There were some impressive-looking houses off to the right. Chōzō pointed to the most imposing one among them and said it was where the manager lived. Then, looking to the left, he said, "Over here's the hole. OK, kid?"

I had never heard the expression "the hole" before, and I strongly considered asking him about it, but I decided to accept the fact that something over here was probably "the hole" and just keep quiet. Later, when I was in a position where I had no choice but to understand the word clearly, it turned out to be not much different from what I first figured. Soon we went left and walked more in the direction of the hole. Following the rails, we climbed higher and higher. There were lots of shabby little houses all around. Chōzō said that these were where the miners lived, and I assumed that I, too, would be living in a house like this from now on, but I was wrong. There were two small rooms (six mat and three mat) in each of these shacks, and, true, there were miners living here, but only miners with families. Bachelors like me were not allowed in. We continued to climb, weaving our way among the shacks. The next thing that came into view were some long, narrow barracks perched under rock cliffs. At first, I thought there were just a few of these buildings, but the more we climbed, the more we saw. They were all pretty much the same size and shape, and all were built up against cliff walls, but each faced in a different direction. Since they had been squeezed willy-nilly onto what little land could be reclaimed from the mountain slope, such fine distinctions as southern exposure or eastern view had been sacrificed. For one thing, the road itself meandered all over the place. When you thought you were going to pass to the right of a building, you'd end up in front of it. Another you thought was directly overhead and expected to reach it soon, but suddenly the road swerved off and you never came near the place. You never knew where you were. And there were faces sticking out of these long, narrow buildings. Now, there's nothing unusual about faces in the windows of a house, but these were not ordinary faces. Each in its own way was poorly formed, and the color was bad. Even the extent of the badness was out of the ordinary. The blue-gray, blackish, brownish color was something that life in the city could never prepare you for. Hospital patients are nowhere near as bad. When, climbing the mountain road, I first saw these faces, I felt I understood "the hole" even though I still had no idea what it was. Nevertheless, I told myself, "hole" or no, there couldn't be too many faces like this. I was wrong. Every one of these barracks I passed had faces showing, and they were all the same. By the time we reached our destination at one o'clock, I had been presented with so many awful faces and had had my own face stared at so much—all the faces in the barracks windows were looking at us, without exception, and all with a vicious kind of expression in the eyes—that I concluded the hole must be a truly horrible place.

Our "destination" was one of the long barracks. They called these dormitories "boilers," though I'm not sure why. Maybe because that's where they boil the rice they feed the miners. Later, I tried asking one of the miners about the meaning of boiler, but all I got for my pains was a bawling out. "What the hell are you talking about? A boiler is a boiler." The jargon they use in this little society—"the hole," "boiler," "jangle"—consists entirely of words that have come into being and circulate through sheer chance. Anger is the only reply for anyone foolish enough to ask what they mean. There's no time to ask the meaning of things, no time to answer, and anyone who tries to find out is considered a great fool, so language here is extremely simple and absolutely practical.

As a result, I still don't know the original meaning of "boiler." Just keep in mind that a boiler is one of those long barracks at the base of a cliff. So, anyhow, we finally got there. Why we chose that particular boiler is something that only Chōzō can explain. As far as I could tell, Chōzō was not the exclusive supplier for this one place. No sooner had he dumped me at this boiler than he took the red blanket and the boy off to another one. I realized later that this meant they would be taking their meals at some other boiler. Once Chōzō took them off, I never heard from them again. I never once ran into them in the mine. What a strange business. I had fallen in with the red blanket, who had come flying out of the eatery, and with the boy, who had suddenly materialized on the dusky mountainside; we had led and followed each other through the summer night and slept together beneath the dilapidated thatched roof, finally reaching our aimed-for boiler after another half-day in the clouds, only to have the red blanket and the boy suddenly disappear into nothingness. At this rate, my book will never turn into a novel. Life is full of such events that seem as though they ought to fall into place but never do—events, I might add, that are like episodes from a badly written novel. Looking back across the years, it seems to me that the most interesting experiences are precisely the ones with long, floppy tails that disappear somewhere into the vastness of the sky. All past events worth recalling are dreams, and it is in their dream-like quality that the nostalgia lies, which is why there has to be something vague and unfocused in the past facts themselves for them to contribute to the mood of fantasy. Far more interesting than fully developed events that satisfy our expectations of cause and effect are pictures such as a night and a day in the life of the red blanket, only the middle part of which floats before our eyes, the head and hindquarters lost in secrecy. It seems like something that could turn into a novel, yet it never does. There's something pure about that, something free of the stench of everyday life that I find refreshing. And it's true not only of the red blanket. It's the same with the boy. And Chōzō. And the woman in the pine-grove tea stand. On a larger scale, it's true of this whole book. All I'm doing here is recording facts that don't fall together. There's no novelistic fabrication involved, so it's not interesting the way a novel is. But it's a lot more mysterious than a novel. Natural facts, which have been dramatized by fate, are freer of laws than a novel devised by human design. Which is why they're mysterious. Or so I've always thought.

The disappearance of the red blanket and the boy was something that occurred later, of course; they were still part of the group when we arrived at the boiler. It was at this point that Chōzō began his negotiations in support of my application to become a miner. Putting it this way makes it sound as if he went to a great deal of trouble, but in fact his "negotiations" were simplicity itself: "This fellow says he wants to become a miner. How about hiring him?" That was all. He spoke not a word about my name, place of birth, family background, personal history, or anything else. Of course, knowing nothing about such things, he couldn't have discussed them even if he'd wanted to, but I never imagined he planned to settle the matter with such dispatch. The experience of entering middle school had led me to believe that you couldn't be hired— even as a miner—without following the appropriate procedures. I had been assuming that some personal referee or guarantor or somebody would have to place his seal on some kind of document and that, when the time came, I would ask Chōzō to do it for me. But no sooner had Chōzō begun his "negotiations" than, much to my surprise, the boss of the boiler (of course, at the time, I didn't know that this *was* the "boss"; he was just a sturdily built man in his early forties with thick eyebrows and the blue traces of a heavy beard) said, "He wants a job? Sure, leave him here with me."

It was the simplest thing in the world, like the delivery man plopping a bale of charcoal down in the kitchen. There was no appreciation that a human being had trudged long miles across the mountains for the express purpose of becoming a miner, and I found myself resenting him somewhat. This was a mistake on my part, the reasons for which will become clear soon enough.

A boiler boss is a kind of captain among miners. He is in charge of one boiler and he controls everything in the lives of his miners, which means he is very powerful.*

Having completed his minute-long "negotiations" with this particular boss, Chōzō said, "Well, then, I leave him in your care," and he went out with the red blanket and the boy. I figured he'd be back, but I never saw him again, and eventually I realized that I had been dumped. What an awful man! He sounded so concerned for my welfare while he was dragging me out there, but once he was through with me, he couldn't spare a simple goodbye! Still, I must say I have no idea when or where he received his procurer's fee.

Perceived by the boss as a bale of charcoal, tossed in by Chōzō like some kind of parcel, I was not feeling much like a human being, which was getting me down, when suddenly the boss, who had watched the three others leave, looked my way. His face was different now. It could never have been taken as the face of a man who would treat someone as a bale of charcoal. He was someone you might encounter any morning or evening on the streets of Tokyo, a man whose bitter experience of life had taught him much.

"Unless I'm mistaken, son, I'd guess you haven't been a laborer all your life . . ."

Even before he had finished speaking, the boss's words made me want to cry. On the point of resigning myself, thanks to Chōzō, to a life in which I would never again rise above being anything but "kid," I was suddenly "son" again. The joy of having my individuality recognized in a totally unexpected place, the warm familiarity, the memories of the past (I had not become "kid" until the day before yesterday, after all)—a crowd of emotions welled up inside me, in addition to which the man's tone was so polite and kindly! Since that day, I have encountered many different situations in which I wanted to cry, and I can see from my present jaded state that most of them were not worth the tears. But the tears that welled up inside me at that moment—oh, yes, they might just come gushing out even today if I were to find myself in the same situation. Tears of pain, of hardship, of regret, of defeat: these can be overcome with experience. Even tears of gratitude need not always be shed. But the tears

---

*The "boss" or *hanba-gashira* was a semi-feudal figure who ran the dormitory for the mine owner and collected a percentage of the miners' pay. The system, inaugurated in the Meiji period, was known for its brutality.

of joy felt when someone recognizes one's old self in spite of the intervening degeneration, these must stay with one until death, so strong is the human sense of self! Mistaking such tears for tears of gratitude and priding oneself on having shed them may be the same thing as hiring a student houseboy mainly to do chores for you while telling yourself that you're doing it primarily to help him out.

This, then, is how I came to feel like crying when the boss began to speak, but in fact I did not cry. True, I was feeling down, but I was still in control. A desire to stand my ground had materialized out of nowhere. The only problem was that my mouth wouldn't work. I just listened in silence to what he had to say. In tones so kind that they filled me with joy, the boss went on:

"I have a fair idea how a young lad like you might end up in a place like this—especially since that man brought you here. Come, though, think it over one more time. I'm sure he fed you a line about how you could become a miner right away and make lots of money. In fact, you'll never make a tenth of what he promised you. Becoming a miner sounds easy, but it's not the kind of work that just anyone can do. Especially someone educated like yourself. There's no way you can make a go of it here."

Having said this much, the boss looked straight at me. I had to say something. Fortunately, by this time, I had passed through the feeling of wanting to cry, and my mouth was working again. "I . . . I'm not looking for money," I said. "I didn't come here to get rich. I know what you're telling me. I know about that."

I remember quite clearly repeating myself at the time. "I know," I said, "I know," which was a most presumptuous, even defiant way to speak to the man. While I was young, I could go straight from dejection to impudence depending on the other person's attitude. I blush to admit it now. And my claims to know what he was talking about meant only that I was fully aware of the fact that Chōzō, the man who had brought me here, was a kind of agent working on commission, and that he partook of the gift of exaggeration shared by all such agents, which "knowledge" was not worth boasting about. There was nothing to be gained at this point by explaining that I had not been deceived, that I knew precisely what I was doing in asking to be made a miner. When you're young, though, the need to defend your vanity is strong (not that it's exactly weak even now). I still break out in a cold sweat to recall the stupid insistence with which I sought to justify myself. Fortunately, though, I was dealing with a man whose kindness and sincerity far outshone the needs of his profession. Through an excess of pity for my lack of experience, he chose to overlook my impudence, and I escaped without a beating. For this I am truly grateful. After I came to live in the boiler, I saw with a shock what broad powers the boss wields over his men, and I would blush to recall my "I know, I know." I might mention here that the boss's name was Hara Komakichi. I still think it's a nice name.

Mr. Hara gave no sign of displeasure as he quietly listened to me make excuses for myself, but then he shook his head. It was a big, round head bristling with close-cropped hair, which was receding at the forehead much as if it had been rubbed off by a fencer's face mask.

"This's just a whim," he said. "So what if you dragged yourself all the way up here? You didn't leave home with your mind made up to work in the mines. It's just some bright idea you hatched. And I know what's going to happen: you'll get in there, and you'll get fed up with it right away. So don't even start. I've never had a student last ten days in the mine. What's that? Of course they come. Lots of 'em. And they all cut and run when they get a taste of the work. It's not something that just anybody can do. So don't worry, I'm not going to blame you for going home now. It's not hard to make a living if that's all you want. You don't have to be a miner."

At this point, Mr. Hara, who had been sitting cross-legged on the floor, began to unfold his legs and lift himself from the mats. I was obviously going to fail the test. This came as a great blow—as a result of which I stopped thinking about becoming a miner and began examining myself apart from that question. Suddenly I felt cold. My kimono had become soaked in the rain. My legs were bare. In these mountains, May was like February or March in Tokyo. It hadn't bothered me as long as I was hot with the climb, and excitement had kept me going until the moment Mr. Hara rejected me. But when I stopped to rest at the boiler and, in addition, my hopes of becoming a miner were suddenly dashed, I began to shiver with the combined impact of the disappointment and the cold. The look on my face at that moment must have been unbearably ugly. Though he had abandoned me shortly before and had gone off without so much as a goodbye, I began to wish I had

Chōzō with me again. If Chōzō were here, he'd do his best to see they hired me as a miner. Or if he couldn't make me a miner, he'd work *something* out. He paid my fare for me, didn't he? He'd at least lead me to someplace where I could find my own way. He got whatever money I had when he took my wallet. How am I supposed to "go home" if all I can do is die of hunger on the way? Maybe I should go running after Chōzō right now. If I look in every boiler, I might run across him. If I explain the situation to him and throw myself on his mercy, he can't just ignore what we've been through together. He'll come up with something clever to help me out, won't he? On the other hand, a man who would go off like that without a nod in my direction . . . I stood before Mr. Hara with these leisurely thoughts racing through my head. How could that be? How could I carry on such a fevered mental dialogue with Chōzō, who wouldn't give me the time of day and had disappeared from my life, while standing in front of Mr. Hara, whom I liked? Things like this happen all the time. It's important in times of crisis not to fall into the habit of assuming an enemy's an enemy and a friend's a friend but to keep a free and open mind, searching for friends among your enemies and detecting enemies among your friends.

Young and inexperienced, I couldn't grasp such a state of mind. I stood before Mr. Hara, trembling and uncertain. I guess he felt sorry for me and made an offer: "If you want to go home, I'll do what little I can to help."

His words took me off guard and filled me with gratitude. Which would have been the obvious reaction, but there was more. I suddenly realized that, apart from this man who had just rejected my hopes, there was no one I could turn to for help. The moment I experienced this realization, my mouth stopped working again. Once again, I could only stand there, incapable either of pleading to be made a miner or of asking for the fare to return home. This realization, however, led nowhere. I seem to recall that what I did then was ball my right hand into a fist and rub my cold upper lip. I had often been to the variety halls and seen storytellers perform this conventional struggle against tears, but this was the first time I had ever done it myself.

When he saw this, Mr. Hara said, "I don't mean to sound presumptuous, but if you're worried about the fare, you needn't. I'll take care of it."

I didn't have the fare, needless to say. The taint of money was nowhere to be found on my body. Even somebody prepared to die by the roadside feels more secure if he has money—especially someone like me who could be satisfied with a nice, slow wasting away. I wouldn't have sneezed at a single five-sen coin. Had it been decided that I was going to go home, I would have begged Mr. Hara for the fare if it had meant rubbing my face in the dirt. I would have accepted the money in any manner required, however unseemly. Pride and dignity can go to hell when you're actually in a scrape like this. I'm sure most people would do the same. And they should. Not that there's anything admirable in such behavior. I openly set this down merely to write the truth of human nature as it is in actual fact, and not because I think it's anything to boast about. Some people will tell you that man is by nature so-and-so, as if that makes the so-and-so all right, but this is like concluding that because sweet bean paste is made from beans, you might just as well chew the raw beans as eat the paste. Whenever I recall this scene in the boiler, I feel disgusted with my own shabbiness. Anyone who can live his life without ever entering into such a sordid state of mind may be short on experience, but he is nonetheless fortunate. And he is far nobler than anyone like me. He is a lucky person who spends his life enjoying sweet bean paste without ever knowing how bad raw beans can taste.

I was on the verge of clasping my hands together and accepting some small bit of charity from this man I had never seen before in my life. That I was able, finally, to resist was owing to a vague awareness on my part that whatever money he might put together for me out of the goodness of his heart would be gone after I had endured a night or two in a flophouse somewhere, after which I would have to begin wandering aimlessly again. I gallantly declined his offered solatium. This appeared to be an act of great personal integrity—even to me. But close inspection leaves no doubt that it was based on a judgment of where my best advantage lay, as weighed on the scales of desire. The best proof of this is what I said to Mr. Hara as I was declining his offer:

"Instead, let me become a miner. Since I went to all the trouble to come up here, I want to give it a try, no matter what."

"You're crazy, you know," he said, cocking his head and looking at me. Finally, almost sighing, he said, "You really don't want to go home, do you?"

"I can't go home. I don't have a home to go to."

"But—"

"It's true. I'll have to try begging or something if I can't work in the mines."

In the course of this give-and-take, I began to find it tremendously easy to talk. The mood came upon me, probably, as a result of my forcing myself to say these things that I knew I shouldn't say. I suppose you could view the change as a sort of mechanical transformation, but strangely enough, the mechanical transformation had a converse effect on my spirit. As these things I wanted to say began to flow out of me (and the tongue is such a mechanical device that in some situations, some people happily gush things they *don't* want to say), as the device gained accelerating force through usage, I became increasingly bold.

Anyone who wants to criticize me for putting it backward is free to do so: "You *first* started feeling bold, and *that's* why you were able to blurt out what you wanted to say." All right. But that's too trite, and insisting on this order will often misrepresent the truth. Those who cannot be satisfied with lies and clichés will admit the justice of what I am saying.

So I became bold. And the bolder I became, the more determined I was to live there as a miner. The more I chattered on, the more convinced I was that I could become a miner. Through all the complications leading to my flight from home, it had never once occurred to me to go to the mines. Far from it. If becoming a miner had been the fixed purpose of my escape, I would have been, in a way, embarrassed, and might have decided to put off my departure for a week or so until I had had time to think things over more carefully. I *was* going to run away. That much was definite. But I would do it like a gentleman, one who has never known want. Surely, in my mind, there hadn't flickered the slightest shadow of a thought to run away for the purpose of becoming a lowly creature who digs in a hole in the ground, a man indistinguishable from a lump of earth. But, clenching my teeth with the cold and carrying on this inescapable give-and-take with Mr. Hara, I began to feel that it had become my predetermined fate—nay, my very calling—to work as a miner.

Having conquered the mountains and the clouds and the rain to come this far, I could never be forgiven if I did not become a miner. If my candidacy should be rejected, it would be, for me, a complete loss of face. (The reader may find this comical, but I am describing my emotions at the time with utter sincerity. The funnier others find this, the sorrier I feel for my former self.)

It remains unclear to me whether I was driven by a strange kind of determination, or a refusal to admit defeat, or simply a fear of collapsing by the wayside if I should dare to head for home. Whatever it was, I pressed Mr. Hara with all the zeal I could muster:

"I understand your objections, but please hire me anyway. If it turns out I'm really unsuited to the job, I'll have to face that fact, but I've never even tried the work. Give me one or two days, that's all. Think of it as a trial period. Otherwise, what's the point of my having come across the mountains? And if it turns out that I can't handle it, I'll leave. Just like that. I promise. I would never try to force myself on you if I couldn't do my fair share of work. But I'm nineteen. I'm young. These are my best working years . . ."

I let loose with everything I had, including the very words the woman at the tea stand had spoken to me the day before. Now I see that these were words more appropriate for others to say about me than for me to use in order to sell myself. Mr. Hara laughed a little when he answered me.

"All right," he said, "if you want it that badly, there's nothing I can do. Maybe you were meant to come here. Give it a try. But I'm warning you, it's going to be tough." He glanced up toward the red mountain in back of the barracks. Probably checking the weather. I turned my gaze with his. The rain had stopped, but the sky was dark and overcast and almost frightening in its weirdness. Such was the moment my wish came true and I more or less became a man of the mountains. It was then, too, that Mr. Hara's "warning" began to seem strangely disturbing. A reaction often sets in when people attain their present goals, and suddenly they begin to resent the very fact of the attainment. My feelings bore some resemblance to this when I was granted this oral certificate enabling me to settle here in accordance with my wishes.

"All right," said Mr. Hara, speaking somewhat more curtly now, "have a look inside the hole tomorrow morning. I'll send somebody down to show you around. And then . . . let's see . . . oh, yes!

There're a few things I'd better get straight with you before that. People think there's nothing much to being a miner, but it's not as easy as you might hear on the outside. A man doesn't just become a miner right off." He stared at me for a moment. "With *your* build, you might not be able to manage it at all. Think you can be satisfied with some other kind of work?" he asked with a hint of pity. I now began to see that you needed a good deal of training and had to work your way up through several ranks before you became a miner. No wonder Chōzō was always making such a fuss, as if it were some great honor.

"You mean there are other jobs here? Not everybody who works here is a miner?" I asked to confirm my suspicions. Giving no indication that he thought me a fool for asking, Mr. Hara proceeded to explain the organization of the mine.

"You know, we've got ten thousand men in this place. They're divided up into four groups: diggers, setters, shoppers, and miners. A digger is somebody we can't use as a full-fledged miner—a miner's helper, you could say. A setter is a kind of carpenter who works in the hole. And then there are the shoppers. All they do is break up rocks. They're mostly kids—you know, like the one who came with you. We keep them around for a while until they learn to be miners. That's pretty much it. A miner gets paid according to what he produces. On a good day, he can make himself one or two yen. A digger gets paid by the day, though. He goes on, year after year, making do with thirty-five sen a day. Out of that, his foreman takes five percent, and if he gets sick or something, his pay is cut in half to seventeen sen, five rin. Out of that he has to pay quilt rental of three sen (though of course he needs two when the weather is cold, for a total of six sen), plus fourteen sen, five rin a day for rice (that's *just* rice; whatever goes with it is extra). So, what do you think? If you can't make it as a miner, are you willing to work as a digger?"

I didn't have the energy for a resounding "Yes!" but having come this far there was no way I could refuse and still hold my head up. With as much energy as I could muster, I said, "Yes."

I can't say for sure whether Mr. Hara took my answer for a firm resolution or forced enthusiasm born of false pride, but he responded warmly. "Well, then, come right in," he said. "And have a look at the hole tomorrow. I'll send someone to show you around. Anyhow, what with ten thousand men here, and all the gangs they're divided into, just being in charge of one boiler gives me nothing but headaches from morning to night. They beg me to hire them, so I do, and then they run away . . . It's true. Every day, maybe two or three men. Then I get some guy who keeps quiet and minds his own business, and the next thing I know he gets sick and dies. Nothing ever goes right. Hardly a day goes by we don't have half a dozen funerals . . . Well, then, if you're sure you want to work here, give it your best. Come in, come in."

Listening to his detailed account, I began to feel that I owed it to him to work with my whole strength at any job they gave me, be it digger or shopper or whatever. In my heart I resolved never to do anything that would cause Mr. Hara grief. (I was nineteen, after all, a simple age.)

Following his instructions, I sat on the edge of the raised wooden floor, wiping my feet, when an old woman appeared from the back, so suddenly that she gave me a start.

"Come with me," she said.

With a perfunctory bow, I followed after her. She was a little thing, and from the back she looked delicate, even fragile, but there was a lively spring in her step. She wore a narrow, brown sash tied in a simple square knot, and her sparse hair came together in a bun at the nape of her neck, where it was held by a long pin the color of lead. The sleeves of her kimono were fastened with cords. Obviously, she had been hard at work in the kitchen—or, if there was no kitchen, somewhere else in the back—when she was called out to show me the way, which was why she hurried along like this, tail wagging. Or maybe it was because she had spent her life in the mountains. No, probably the boiler did this to everyone. You couldn't take it easy here. And, starting today, the same would apply to me. As long as I was going to be eating the rice of this boiler, I couldn't just sit around with my arms folded. Doing everything with this old woman's energy would be an absolute must. Must. I must. The thought struck me with such force that the "must" charged into my wobbly arms and legs and I felt as though the very cells of my head and chest had changed to some extent. The momentum carried me pounding up the broad stairway after my guide. But no sooner had my head popped up a foot above floor level than my resolution fizzled.

As my head and shoulders rose up to the second floor, the sight was a shock. Where I was expecting an ordinary room of six or eight mats, the size of this place would have to have been measured in the tens of mats, and they stretched off into the distance as far as the eye could see, unobstructed by a single wall or partition of any sort. The place was like a judo gym or a variety theater where the audience crowds together on an unbroken expanse of floor mats, but it was two, maybe three times bigger than that. It felt not so much big as empty. I knew I was seeing floor mats, but I felt as if I were in some vast wilderness. That alone was enough to cause a shock, but into this field had been cut two large sunken hearths, around each of which were huddled some fourteen or fifteen human beings. Cowardly as this may sound, I think the withering of my resolve was owing entirely to these people. It's true I always used to put on a bold front, but young as I was, I had rarely had the experience of appearing before crowds of complete strangers. Ceremonial occasions make me nervous at the best of times. But here I had suddenly been captured alive by a group of miners, and the sight of this black clump of humanity made me falter somewhat. Now, it would have been an entirely different matter if these had been ordinary human beings.

Wait, that doesn't make much sense. If it had been a matter of ordinary human beings having become miners, there wouldn't have been any problem. But the second my head and shoulders came up through the floor, all parts of this clump turned in my direction as if at a signal. Their faces—well, I admit it, they scared me to death. By which I mean these were not ordinary faces. These were not ordinary human faces. They were pure, unadulterated miner faces. There's no other way to describe them. If you insist on more of an explanation, I'll give it a try. Their cheekbones soared up and up, their chins thrust out, their jaws spread sideways, their eye sockets collapsed inward like caverns, sucking their eyeballs still deeper into their heads, and the wings of their noses dropped down. I suppose I could just say that every trace of flesh had gone into full retreat while every piece of bone had charged outward with victorious shouts. They were so craggy I didn't know if I was looking at the bones of faces or faces of bone. One interpretation might be that they had aged prematurely as the result of harsh working conditions, but the sheer natural phenomenon of "aging" could never do *that*. Search all I might, I couldn't find a hint of warmth or softness anywhere in these faces. In a word, they were savage faces. Mysteriously, the savage physiognomy appeared to be a communal possession of this entire body of men. When the blackened things seated around the hearth turned in my direction, a split second produced a perfectly uniform assemblage of fifteen savage faces. The bunch surrounding the hearth at the far end of the room must have had the same sort of faces. Which means the faces of all ten thousand men living in the barracks were probably savage. I was ready to shrivel up and die.

Just then the old woman swung around and said to me impatiently, "Come over here." I screwed up my courage and moved toward the savages. When I neared the edge of the hearth at last, she said, "Have a seat," by which she meant I should find a place to sit, not that there was already someplace designated for me. I avoided the black clump and sat on the open stretch of mats by myself. The savage eyes were glued to me this whole time. None showed the slightest restraint. And no one said a word. Until I could find an opening, there was no way for me to join the group, but sitting out there all alone just made me a target for savage stares. It was not the old woman's place to make introductions. After mechanically ordering me to sit, she disappeared down the steps, wagging her rear end with its square-knotted sash. I felt as if I had been abandoned in the middle of a variety theater to be ridiculed by a gang of ushers. Of course I didn't know what to do with myself, which only served to increase my sense of helplessness. I was also freezing cold with nothing on but my kimono. If the savages had to sit around a hearthful of hot coals in May, you know it was cold! All I could do to hide my confusion was unbutton my undershirt and shove my hands in under my arms, draw up my knees and fiddle with my big toes, rub my thighs, and do whatever else I could think of to keep warm and busy. At times like this, you're at a big disadvantage if you haven't mastered the art of sitting with a relaxed expression on your face—or, better yet, with true, inward equanimity. Since there was no hope of attaining such accomplishments at the age of nineteen, I sat there going through the aforementioned catalogue of ridiculous gestures, when suddenly someone cried out, "Hey!"

At that moment, I happened to be looking down, retying my cotton sash, but when I heard the cry, the cords in the back of my neck yanked my head up like some kind of electrical device. The same faces were assembled there, where they had been before, all eyes turned on me and shining. I didn't know which face had been the source of the "Hey," but that didn't much matter. All were equally savage, and now I saw that all were clearly etched with contempt, derision, and curiosity. I discovered this fact the moment I raised my head, and no sooner had I discovered it than it gave me the most disagreeable feeling. There was nothing for me to do but wait, face raised, until the "Hey" came again. How many seconds this took, I don't know, but I seem to have remained in this pose for some time in a state of anticipation. Then, unexpectedly, someone said, "Too good for us, huh? The bastard."

The voice that said this was a little more husky than the voice that had said "Hey." I figured it was a different person speaking. But since the remark itself was not exactly a question calling for an answer, I continued to remain silent. Inwardly, though, I was pretty shaken up. The only people I had spoken to since coming here had been Mr. Hara and the old woman. Being a woman, she used polite expressions as a matter of course, but Mr. Hara was far more courteous in his speech than I had anticipated—and he was a boss. I had assumed that if even a boss was like this, the ordinary miners couldn't be very rude, so when this crude language came flying at me out of the blue, I was not so much horrified as dumbfounded. The matter might have been settled right off if I had given tit for tat and either been beaten to a pulp or treated as an equal, but I didn't try to come up with anything. As a Tokyo native, I should have had a good crack or two ready, but I responded neither in kind nor with a more ordinary retort. Why was that? Because I figured he was too far beneath me to bother with? Or because I didn't have the guts to open my mouth? I like to think it was the former, but I'm pretty sure it was the latter. Probably it was a little of both. There are plenty of things in this world that you can despise and fear at the same time. There's nothing contradictory about this.

Whatever the reason, I didn't respond to the curse, and the miners, taking this to mean that I intended to let it pass, burst out laughing. And the greater my restraint, the more their laughter echoed through the boiler. They were enjoying the chance to make fun of an ordinary person who had strayed into the mine. This was a way to get even with society for snubbing them when they themselves went out of the mine. I was acting as the lone recipient of these miners' resentment toward society. Until coming to the mine, I had convinced myself that I could not fit into society. Here, in the boiler, the treatment I was receiving all but told me that a person like me would not be allowed to become one of the fellows. I was in a perfect fix, wedged between ordinary society and the society of the miners. When the laughter of these fourteen or fifteen men exploded so close to me, it brought a glow to my face; I felt not so much sad or embarrassed or confused, but more sorry for myself that I had before me such a group of uniformly heartless brutes. Education was obviously not to be found among them, and I had no intention of making demands of a sort the uneducated could not hope to fulfill. But I assumed they at least possessed the human qualities they had brought with them from their mothers' wombs. When I heard their outsized laughter, I thought to myself: animals. To me, they were not human. Nowadays, as a result of experience, the gap between the "human" and the "animal" has narrowed for me a good deal, and my considerably duller sensibilities would probably overlook such a minor affront, but the impact of this derisive laughter on a tender new brain that had only been in use for nineteen years was a painful one. Whenever I recall that moment, I feel enormous pity for that sweet, sad little boy, and I want to wrap his whole nervous system in cotton and put it away where it will be safe.

When the malicious laughter died down, it was followed by a question: "Where you from?"

I knew the exact source of the voice because the one who had asked the question was the one sitting closest to me. He had a pale blue towel sort of thing pulled tightly around his waist for a sash and he kept his back turned, his face twisted around toward me at an angle. The lower lid of his eye looked as if it were permanently pulled down, revealing the conjunctiva, which was gorged with blood.

When I answered, "I'm from Tokyo," the red-eyed one sucked in his fleshless cheek and, with a mocking smile, jerked his chin toward the miner sitting four places away from him. The recipient of this signal, a scruffy fellow looking like a beggar-monk who had stopped shaving his head, now took his turn:

"Listen to the schoolboy! 'I'm from Tokyo,' he says. What happened, schoolboy? Whores take your money? You oughta be ashamed of yourself. Schoolboys got no morals any more. Kids like you can never stick it out here. Go home, boy. Skinny arms like those won't do you any good in this place."

I kept quiet—for so long it maybe took some of the fun out of their jeering, which began to let up a little. Then one of the miners—this fellow had a normal face. His features worked together well enough that they could have passed as ordinary in society. Each time I had looked up at the black clump while they were jeering at me, I had taken in a new impression—the number of men, their clothing, the degree of their savagery—and at first the only things that had struck me about their faces as a whole were that they were made of bones and eyes and that a greasy film of animal lust clung to them all, no single face being distinguished from any other. By the third or fourth glance, however, as I began to tell them apart, this one miner's face stood out from the rest. He was probably under thirty and he was powerfully built. Where his eyebrows and the bridge of his nose met, the flesh was sunken in somewhat, as if by the constant wearing of eyeglasses. The feature suggested a permanent fit of temper, but this perhaps had the converse effect of reducing the apparent degree of savagery in his face. Now this miner spoke for the first time:

"What the hell do you think you're doing here? You'll never make any money in this place. We're here because we can't make a living anywhere else. Get out. Go home. Deliver newspapers. Anything. You wouldn't know it to look at me, but I used to be in school. I'm here because of liquor and women. Once you get like me, you've had it. You can't leave even if you want to. Go back to Tokyo now, before it's too late. Get a paper route. No schoolboy's going to last a month in this place. Get out of here now. I won't blame you for going. You got the idea, right?"

This advice was tendered with some sincerity. Even the savages had to listen to it without butting in. Its impact on all hearers caused a moment of silence after the advice itself had come to an end. I sensed that the cause of the silence might well be that this particular miner wielded a certain degree of influence here and that the others treated him with respect. An indefinable kind of happiness welled up inside me at the thought. There might be some small differences in physiognomy between this miner and the others, but finally they all went down into the same hole to scrape ore out of the mountain. This was not exactly an art in which there could be vast differences in skill. Which meant that the source of this man's influence over the others must lie in his ability to read, his ability to understand and reason—in short, his education. They were making fun of me now. They were heaping insults on me as if I were a semi-human unfit to join the ranks of the lowliest laborers. But once I plunged into this society and became one of the savages myself, after living here a month or two, I might be able to rise to a position of influence on a par with this man. I *should* be able to. I *would* be able to! Yes, I would show them! No matter what anyone said, I would not go home. I would become a full-fledged member of this society—and more!

What stupidity. Though, even now, I can see a certain degree of logic to my thoughts. I respectfully lent an ear to this miner's advice, but I did not, as he would have wished, respond with a farewell. Soon the tongues of derision, which had fallen momentarily silent, began to wag again.

"You can stay if you want," said one man, "but we've got our ways of doing things here, and you'd better damn well learn them."

"What kind of ways?" I asked.

"Stupid, you know what I mean!" he screamed. "We've got bosses and we've got brothers."

"You mean like boiler bosses?" I asked, though at first I thought I might keep quiet. He sounded ready to bite my head off. But I was afraid that if I didn't know their rules, I might get in trouble later by breaking one.

Another miner replied without hesitation, "Don't you know anything? How the hell can you be a miner if you don't know about bosses and brothers? Get the hell outa here, boy, right now."

"Yeah, bosses and brothers. That's why you'll never make any money here. Get out!"

"Make money? Shit! Get outa here!"

"Get out!"

"Get out!"

Obviously, they weren't telling me to get out for my own good. They were saying it because they wouldn't let me be one of them. They wanted me to give up and get out because only they, not I, could make any money doing this work. That's why they kept telling me to get out but said nothing about where I ought to go. As far as they were concerned, it could be the bottom of a river or the back of a cave. I said nothing.

It's easy to imagine the outcome if this state of affairs had continued for any length of time. The enemy was not ranged solely around the nearby sunken hearth. As I mentioned earlier, they were clumped together in another big black circle farther off. Had the far troops come to reinforce the near group when I was already fully occupied with them, there would have been hell to pay. While I was being ridiculed, I kept my future enemy (they held their ground, but, at this rate, anything human was going to look like an enemy to me) under observation, sending sidelong glances their way lest they suddenly rush me. My mind thus moved off simultaneously in all directions, unable to stand alone in its divided pursuit. There's nothing more painful than chasing around trying to catch something that's just ahead of you. What is it they say? Meet the enemy and swallow him. If you can't swallow, be swallowed. If neither side can manage it, cut cleanly and stand alone, keeping watch. The position of greatest disadvantage—and thus of greatest inferiority—is to be unable either to merge with the enemy or to ignore him, making it necessary always to be sniffing at his haunches. Having encountered such situations from time to time, I have closely studied many different routes of escape, but I never take my own hard-won advice. Which means that the three options I have presented here may sound impressive, but they don't mean a thing. The more you dwell on a platitude that's obvious without a big lecture, the more foolish you appear. Without a proper education, you're really at a disadvantage in a situation like this. You can't tell what's worth including and what ought to be left out.

With my attention flying off in all directions at once, I sat there desperately trying to shrink my existence down as much as possible, when the voice of the old woman resounded nearby:

"Enjoy your meal."

My soul at that point had shriveled to about the size of a pigeon's egg. Until the moment her voice reached my ears, I had been totally unaware that the old woman had come upstairs again. Now I saw that she had set a small lacquered table in front of me. The lacquer had been chipped away in spots. The tray-like table held an inverted rice bowl ready for use, the edge of which had been chipped away,

too. There was also a small tub of rice. The lacquered chopsticks
were half red, half yellow, but most of the yellow was gone, leaving
the bare wood exposed. To go with the rice, there was a dish of gela-
tinous noodles. When I lowered my eyes to survey this spectacle, I
felt an enormous urge to eat. Not a drop of water had passed my lips
since I had awakened this morning. My stomach was absolutely
empty. Or, if not empty, it contained nothing more than the fried
manjū and the sweet potatoes from the day before. Nearly two days
and nights had gone by since I had been anywhere near a bowl of
rice. However shriveled my soul might have been at that moment,
the sight of the rice tub brought a huge wave of hunger surging up to
my throat. So much for jeers, and to hell with appearances. I scooped
out the tub and filled my rice bowl to overflowing. Even this simple
procedure seemed to take far longer than I was willing to wait.
I grabbed up my chopsticks, plunged them into the rice—and
couldn't believe what happened next. The rice would not come with
the chopsticks. I plunged the chopsticks in again, with added force
this time, digging down to the bottom of the bowl, but the same
thing happened. The grains of rice slipped from the ends of the chopsticks and refused to leave the bowl. Having lived nineteen years
without the benefit of such an experience, I was simply amazed.
After trying and failing two or three more times, I rested the hand
holding the chopsticks and thought about what was happening to
me. I must have looked absolutely mystified. The miners, watching
me, burst out laughing. As soon as I heard that, I brought the bowl
to my lips and scraped in a mouthful of the dingy-looking rice. The
weird taste I experienced at that moment all but caused my soul to
concentrate itself entirely in my tongue, such that the laughter, the
miners, and even my hunger ceased to exist. I could not believe that
what I had in my mouth was rice. It could only be wall mud. There
is no way I can describe the sensation of having that wall mud melt
in my saliva and spread itself throughout my mouth.

"Good, huh?" said one of them with a sneer.

"You think it's a holiday or somethin'?" said another. "That's the
only time you'll get the good stuff around here. Why do you think
we're tellin' you to get out?"

"Yeah," added a third. "You're makin' a big mistake, fella, if you
wanna be a miner and don't even know what cheap rice tastes like."

All I could do, while they were having fun at my expense, was gulp down the disgusting mouthful. I considered stopping at that point, but I knew they'd start in on me again if I didn't eat what I had piled into the rice bowl. I forced myself to cram at least that much into my stomach, telling myself it was good for me—like taking bear's gall.* Hunger had nothing to do with it. How much tastier yesterday's fried manjū and steamed potatoes had been! Never in my life had I tasted such low-grade rice.

This was how I managed to finish off the first bowl of rice, but I couldn't force myself to take a second. I ate the noodles and set my chopsticks down. That led to another round of jeers, despite my efforts to force down the foul-tasting rice. At the moment I found the ordeal excruciating, but after that it became necessary for me to eat this kind of rice three times a day. Not only did I become accustomed to the taste of wall mud, I came to perceive it as something that human beings could eat—indeed, as a delicacy they should eat, in no way different from the so-called good stuff. Once that change in outlook was accomplished, I felt ashamed of myself for having hesitated to eat what the woman served me that day on the chipped table. No wonder the miners made fun of me. If I were now to witness the spectacle of such an inexperienced, aristocratic miner suffering over a bowl of cheap rice, I myself might find it comical— or at least worth a good-natured laugh, if not a full-fledged jibe. People certainly do change.

Sorry, I really ought to drop this subject of cheap rice. I don't know how long the sarcastic remarks on my bungling would have continued if they had been allowed to run their course, but suddenly they were interrupted by a sound rather like the smashing together of metal wash basins. Not just one smash. The repeated metallic clashing set up a rhythm as it drew closer and closer, and soon it was joined by a lumber hauler's chant. Not a real lumber hauler's chant, of course. That was the closest thing I knew to what I was hearing. All at once the jeering stopped. As the clanging echoed through the hushed mountain air, something drew slowly nearer, raising a bizarre plaint.

"It's a jangle!" shouted one of the miners, all but slapping his knee in surprise.

"It's a jangle!" The others took up the cry. "It's a jangle!"

*A bitter-tasting traditional health tonic made from a bear's gall bladder dried complete with the bile.

The black clump scattered, heading for the windows. I had no idea what a jangle was, but as soon as the others' attention was diverted from me, the feeling of relief made me want to see the jangle, and with that came renewed vigor. The human heart, it seems to me after careful consideration, is like water. Push it and it gives way; pull back, and it comes flowing in. You might say our life is like a continual shoving match without hands. So, after everyone else stood up, I stood up. And when they went to the window, I went over to the window. I stretched to see over the black heads that filled the bottom of the frame. Around the corner of the stone wall where the road curved away at an angle, two men in blue, narrow-sleeved kimono appeared. After them came two others. These were holding a round metal thing in each hand, something like a wash basin squashed and hammered thin. The moment it occurred to me that those were the things I was hearing, the two men brought them smashing together. The discordant sound struck the sheer stone wall, echoed against the rock-strewn mountain behind, and before it had died away, another pair of men appeared after the others, smashing the metal things together. And another pair, though these were not carrying the flattened wash basins. Instead, they were singing the lumber hauler's chant—which is what I called their song before, but now their voices sounded more like the weird battle cries the chanter makes in Naniwa-bushi.*

"Hey, where's old Kin?" yelled one of the black heads in front of me. Since everyone was looking out the window, I couldn't see the man's face.

"Yeah," answered another miner without hesitation, "He oughta see this."

Almost before he had finished speaking, five or six of the black heads whirled around toward me. I stood there, resigned to hearing more comments of the kind I had endured earlier, but, amazingly enough, the eyes that had turned this way were not aimed at me. Their line of vision seemed to run toward something in the far corner of the large room. I twisted my head around, allowing my gaze to follow theirs, and found the "something" lying down. A thin quilt lay atop him.

---

*A popular narrative form originating in the late eighteenth century, performed by a single chanter. The chanter was accompanied by a shamisen and recited tales often dealing with military exploits.

"Hey, Kin!" yelled one of the men, but there was no answer.

"Hey, Kin, get up!" another one yelled, but still there was no reply. Three men left the window, headed for the far corner. They stripped away the quilt, revealing a man in a sleeping robe.

"Get up, I said! I've got somethin' for you to see."

Finally the man stood, leaning heavily on the shoulders of two who had gone to rouse him. He looked this way. The single glance I had of his face at that moment sent a shudder of horror through me. This was not a man who had been lying down merely for the sake of rest. He was very, very sick—too sick even to stand up by himself. He was close to fifty. His face had shaggy stubble that suggested he had not shaved for several days. Even a savage looks pitiful when he has wasted away to this extent. He was so pathetic, in fact, that he was frightening. At its height, the pity I felt the moment I saw him turned to fear.

Held up by the men flanking him, the sick man approached the window, dragging his useless legs. The crowd at the window greeted this spectacle with gleeful shouts.

"C'mon over, Kin. It's a jangle! Hurry up and look!"

"I don't want to see any damned jangle," the sick man replied feebly as he was being dragged along against his will. It made no difference what he wanted to see or not see. They rushed him to the window, where the sliding shoji had been pushed aside.

The jangle continued indifferently to appear around the corner of the stone wall. Was it never going to end, I wondered, stretching to look down at the road, which brought me another rush of horror. Between the bearers of the wash basins, dangling in space as it made its way down the mountain road, was a square coffin. The top had been covered in a white sheet, a bare cedar pole passed through the wooden loops at either end, and there was a man shouldering each end of the pole with all the matter-of-factness he might have evidenced if entrusted with a load of water. From here it looked as if they, too, were cheerfully singing the chant. It was then that I realized the meaning of "jangle." The moment of understanding came with a piercing clarity I shall never forget for the rest of my life, whatever else is left in store for me. A "jangle" was a funeral, a kind of funeral that can only be performed—indeed, *must* be performed—for miners of the four classes—miner, digger, setter, and shopper. It was a funeral in which phrases from the sutras are sung in the emotional Naniwa-bushi style, the music of shattering wash basins is played, the coffin is carried past the barracks, dangling like a barrel of water on a pole, and, finally, a half-dead miner is dragged from his bed and, despite his protests, forced to look on. It was the height of innocence, the height of cruelty.

"How about it, Kin? Get a good look? Pretty good, huh?"

"Yeah, yeah, I saw it. Now, take me back and let me lie down, for heaven's sake," Kin pleaded.

The two who had brought him over now took Kin between them and, with small, quick steps, led him to where the quilt lay on the floor.

Then, as if the entire overcast sky had suddenly turned to powder and come filtering down, it began to rain. Smashing its way through this rain, the jangle continued on down toward town.

"More rain," the men grumbled, shutting the window, each then finding his way back to the hearth. At some point in the commotion, almost before I knew it, I had been admitted to the ranks of the savages and was now able to approach the fire. This occurred through both chance and design. By which I mean that, without fire, I would be very cold up there in the mountains—too cold to survive wearing my one thin kimono. And, in addition, it had begun to rain. This was the kind of fine-grained rain that might just as well be called mist. It hid the surrounding rocky peaks and blotted out the sky, drenching everything below. Even sitting indoors, you felt as if the microscopic drops were infiltrating through your pores and deep down into your guts. This was something you needed fire to endure.

Taking a seat at random, I felt what little warmth there was to be had at the sunken hearth bathing over my face. Much to my surprise, the others were ignoring me now and I escaped without further ridicule. Perhaps because I had taken the initiative to enter their ranks, the others had decided to tolerate me as just another savage. Possibly the sudden appearance of the jangle had distracted them enough to make them forget about me for a while. Or maybe they had simply run out of jibes or had their fill of cursing. Whatever the reason, once I found this new seat I felt somewhat more relaxed. Of course, the many voices around the hearth now concentrated on the jangle.

"I wonder where it came from?"

"What's the difference? A jangle's a jangle."

"Maybe from Kuroichi's. Somewhere up there."

"I wonder where you go after a jangle."

"To the temple, stupid. Everybody knows that."

"Who you callin' stupid? I'm talkin' about after the temple."

"He's right. It sure as hell doesn't end at the temple. You gotta go somewhere."

"That's what I mean. The last place. I wonder what it's like there. Think it's the same as here?"

"Sure. Human souls go there. It must be pretty much the same."

"I think so, too. If you go somewhere, it's gotta be there."

"They talk about 'heaven' and 'hell,' but ya hafta eat there, too, I guess."

"I wonder if they've got women."

"Of course they've got women. There's no place in the world without women."

This more or less sums up the kind of nonsensical talk that followed the jangle. At first, I thought I must be hearing a joke. Figuring it was probably all right to laugh, I took a quick survey, the corner of my mouth twitching, but obviously I was the only one who wanted to laugh. The other faces around the hearth were as hard as if carved in stone. These men were discussing the question of the afterlife in deadly earnest. There was an intensity to be seen on each furrowed brow that could only be described as unbelievable. One glance was enough to expunge my initial urge to laugh. It took me completely by surprise that such bold, reckless men—men who knew when they went down into the mine with their oil lamps that they might never again see the light of day, savages who were more machine than human, more animal than machine—should be so deeply concerned about what lay in store for them. No wonder men needed religion to guarantee an afterlife. I was not actually aware, of course, when I raised my eyes and surveyed the men sitting crosslegged around the hearth, that a combination of restraint and awe had wiped the nearly formed smile from my face. I merely felt a need to observe decorum, as if I had opened my eyes expecting to see a comedy, and found there instead a throng of fierce guardian deities in full armor. In other words, what happened, surely, was that I witnessed for the first time in my life the germ of all true religious feeling and, in the presence of these half-animal–half-humans, felt a genuine sense of awe. (Nonetheless, I myself still possess no religious feeling.)

Just then, the sick man in his corner began to moan. This had no special significance, of course. It was simply the usual moaning of a sick person. But, to these men now sunk in their worries about the life to come, it must have had an uncanny ring to it. They looked at one another anxiously.

"Somethin' hurtin' you, Kin?" shouted one man loudly.

The moan that came back in response might have been an answer or just a moan.

"Forget about your old lady," shouted another man from his place by the hearth. "He took her. She's gone. No use groanin' about it now. You're the one who pawned her. When you don't pay up, somebody else gets her. That's the way it works."

I couldn't tell if this was meant to comfort the sick man or torment him. From the miners' point of view, the two were probably one and the same. All the sick man did was groan back—or, rather, just groan. The men gave up their attempts to comfort him, and the embryonic dialogue reverted to chatter around the fire. The focus of discussion, though, remained on Kin.

"You know why he lost her, don't you? 'Cause he got sick. It's his own damn fault," said one, as if Kin himself had done something wrong by falling ill.

"You said it!" chimed in another. "He gets sick, so he borrows money. He can't pay it back, so they take his old lady for collateral. He can't crab about that."

"How much did he pledge her for?"

"Five big ones," shot back someone on the far side.

"So old Ichi came down and took Kin's place? Ha ha ha!"

It was painful for me to go on sitting by the fire. My back was shivering with the cold, but my armpits were streaming.

"Kin better get well fast and take his old lady out of hock."

"And take Ichi's place? No problem!"

"Yeah! Or the smart thing would be for him to make a bundle and get himself a piece of collateral that's worth more."

"That's the ticket!"

This remark set off a burst of laughter. Enveloped in the mirthful sound, I was yet unable to laugh. I lowered my gaze. Then I realized that I was kneeling formally with my knees together. Stupid. I lowered my buttocks to the mat and crossed my legs. The way I felt inside, though, was nothing like this relaxed posture.

Not long afterward, the sun began to set. This wasn't simply a function of the passage of time. The darkness came early here because of the weather and the surrounding mountains. I listened for the sound of rain falling, but I couldn't hear any. Maybe it had let up. But that seemed unlikely, considering how dark it had become. The window was, of course, shut tight. There was no way I could tell what it was like outside. The dank night air filtered through the shoji paper, assaulting the broad open spaces around the hearths. The faces of the fourteen or fifteen men around the fire began to go out of focus. At the same time, the red glow of the coals piled high in the middle seemed to rise gradually to the surface of the mound, sending its warmth in all directions. I was beginning to feel somewhat as if I were sinking to the bottom of the mine while the fire was gradually rising up out of it. Suddenly the room grew bright. Someone had switched on the electric lights.

"Let's eat," said one of the men. The others responded as if recalling something left behind.

"Eat and then it's our shift again, huh?"

"It's kinda cold today."

"Still rainin'?"

"I dunno. Go outside 'n' look."

Each man contributing his crude bit to the noise, they stood and climbed down the stairway. I was left alone in the huge room. The only one there besides me was the sick man, Kin. He still seemed to be moaning faintly. Sitting cross-legged by the hearth, holding my hands out over the fire, I turned my gaze in his direction. His head was under the covers. His feet, too, were pulled up. He lay there, small and flat, beneath his single quilt. Pitifully small and flat. Before long, his moaning seemed to stop. Again I turned my head, now to stare into the fire. I couldn't get Kin off my mind, though, and once again I looked to the side. He lay there just as small and flat as before. Only, now he was silent. Was he alive or dead? It had been bad enough while he was moaning, but his silence had me even more worried. The worry rose in pitch to fear and I raised myself slightly from the floor, dropping my buttocks to the mat again after more or less convincing myself that he must be all right: people don't just pop off so suddenly.

At that point, I heard some men coming noisily up the stairs. Could they have finished eating already? It was much too soon for that, I told myself, shifting my gaze slightly in the direction of the stairway, where there appeared two men entirely different from the ones I had expected to see. They wore jackets of some indefinable dark color—black or navy blue—and tight-fitting pants of the sort workmen usually wear, also that blue-black color. They carried oil lanterns, and both men were wet and muddy. Neither said a word. They stood stock still, glaring at me. Men like this could only be robbers. Eventually, they threw down their lanterns, loosened their buttons and took off their jackets. Then their pants. Taking down wide-sleeved robes from the wall, they put these on over their underwear, wrapped towel-like sashes around their waists, and, still without a word, clumped down the stairs. As soon as they were gone, more came. They, too, were wet. And muddy. They threw down their lanterns. Changed. Clumped downstairs. More came. They continued coming like this by turns—a good number. Each, without fail, darted a glance at me, eyes flashing from within. One said to me, "You new?"

I answered, "Yup," and let it go at that. Fortunately, these newcomers left me pretty much alone. Each new arrival was in such a hurry to go back downstairs, I suppose, that he had no time for the kind of jeering the others had given me. On the other hand, not one of them failed to dart me a piercing glance. Eventually they stopped coming and I was finally able to relax, staring at the red-glowing coals and thinking. My "thoughts" were completely disconnected, of course, and each new one was more ridiculous than the last, but this was unavoidable, the way these crazy snatches came flaring up from the burning coals. In the end, I had the strange feeling that my soul had slipped out of me and into the red coals, where it was dancing like mad. Then suddenly someone said, "Go to bed. You must be exhausted."

I looked up to find the old woman standing over me. She still had the cords holding her kimono sleeves up for work. I had been totally unaware of her coming upstairs. My soul had been galloping around in the fire, turning into girl number two, Tsuyako, then girl number one, Sumie; my father, old Kin; pretty jackets, pompadours, the red blanket, moans, fried manjū, Kegon Falls—countless images were whirling madly in the fire, and just as tumbling clouds of them flared up within the rising flames, like dust in a shaft of sunlight, I saw her there with a start. She looked incredibly strange to me at that moment, but her words, "Go to bed," must have registered clearly in my mind.

"All right," I answered simply.

Pointing to the closet behind me, she said, "The quilts are in there. You have to take your own. Three sen each. It's cold, so you'll need two."

"All right," I said again.

The old woman left without another word. Now that I had been given permission to sleep, I could stretch out properly without fear of being taken to task. Following her instructions, I opened the closet, and there they were. Piles of quilts. And every one grimy. They were nothing like the quilts we had at home. I slipped out the top two and looked at them beneath the light. They were made of pale blue cloth with a white pattern. A layer of filth coated the surface of each, discoloring it—especially the white places—to a degree that I would normally have found unbearable. And they were the hardest quilts I had ever seen. The cotton stuffing was squashed together into a leathery consistency and had nothing whatever to do with the cloth covers, as if someone had wrapped a freshly pounded rice cake in a piece of sheet.

I spread one of these flat quilts on the matted floor and lay the other atop it. Stripping down to my undershirt, I crawled in between the two. When I stretched out my legs in the damp space into which I had fit my body, my heels ended up on the floor. I pulled them in just a bit. Neither in the stretching nor in the bending did my legs move with their accustomed smoothness. The knees were so stiff they practically creaked when I flexed them. Stretched out on the floor like this between the covers, my legs were not merely heavy, they weighed a ton. I felt as if everything below the knees had been cut off and replaced with artificial legs of wood and metal. They were two poles that just happened to possess the sense of touch. Out of concern for these cold, heavy legs of mine, I pulled my head in between the covers. This was a desperate move borne of the frail hope that if my head, at least, could be warmed up, my legs would compromise to some extent.

But the worst thing was the tiredness—worse than the cold, the legs, the stink of the quilts, my anguish, my world-weariness. It almost seemed I'd be better off dead than to be that tired. Which is why as soon as I lay down—or, at least, as soon as I had managed to pull in my feet and head—I fell asleep. Fast asleep. Out cold. What happened to me after that, not even I can write . . .

Suddenly a needle stabbed me in the back. Whether this had happened to me in a dream or waking, the sensation was too indistinct to tell. Nor would I have cared if the matter had ended there, be the offending object a needle, a thorn, or anything else. All I had to do was drag the waking needle into my dream or bury the thorn of my dreams beneath the bed of unconsciousness. But things didn't work out that way. By which I mean that I was beginning to drift off and forget about the needle, even as the awareness of having been stabbed was still in my mind, when I got stuck again.

This time I opened my eyes wide. Stuck again. And again, while the shock of the last one was still fresh. It finally began to dawn on me that something awful was happening when another one got me in the thigh so painfully I wanted to jump. Now, for the first time, I reverted to being a normal human being. And I discovered that the pinpricks were happening all over my body. I slid my hand in beneath my undershirt and rubbed. My whole back felt gritty. When I first touched myself, I was convinced I had contracted some terrible skin disease. But when I pulled my fingers a few inches along the skin, the gritty stuff fell off. Something serious was going on here. I jumped out of bed and went to the hearth, though dressed in nothing more presentable than an undershirt. Between my thumb and forefinger I was squeezing something the size of a rice grain, which, upon inspection, turned out to be a strange little bug. Never having seen a bedbug before, I would not have been able to declare that that's what it was, but I sensed intuitively that it must be a bedbug. I know I shouldn't be using such highfalutin language to describe a situation so vulgar, but there's no other word for it. I "sensed intuitively" that it was a bedbug. In the course of my inspection, I came to hate the thing. I put it down on the rim of the hearth and crushed it with my thumbnail. The bug gave off a sharp, grassy, indescribable sort of smell that, in a way, made me feel good.

Look at me, writing down such unpleasant stuff in perfect seriousness. That's how crazy I was. In fact, it was not until I smelled the grassy odor that I felt I had gotten back at the little devils. I kept catching them and crushing them, one after another, and each time

I crushed one I'd bring my thumbnail to my nose and sniff it. My nose became clogged with the smell. I was on the verge of tears, feeling very sorry for myself. But each whiff of my thumbnail cheered me up. Just then a roar of laughter echoed from downstairs. I immediately gave up crushing bugs. Surveying the huge room, I found no one else there—just old Kin, lying flat and quiet. Neither his head nor his feet were visible. And there was one more person. Of course, I didn't think at first that he *was* a person. All I saw was this strange white thing, maybe made of canvas, stretched between a pillar and the window sill, with something wrapped inside it. More careful inspection revealed a black thing sticking out of the white thing at an angle: the fuzzy, round head of a human being. In the whole large room, there was no one besides me and these other two. And yet the electric lights were burning brightly. I was thinking to myself how very quiet it was when there was another burst of laughter downstairs. Probably the bunch I had been with before, or men who had returned from their shift, were together down there having fun. Head still in a fog, I returned to where my quilts lay on the floor. Stripping off my undershirt, I shook it out and put on the kimono and sash I had left by my pillow. Then I folded my two quilts very nicely and put them back in the closet. Then I didn't know what to do. I wondered what time it was. The night showed no sign of ending. I stood there, thinking, with my arms folded. My insteps started itching again until I couldn't stand still.

"Damn!" I muttered, doing a few little dance steps. I rubbed my right instep with my left foot and my left instep with my right foot, grinding my teeth in anger. Were they going to keep coming at me after all this? I couldn't run outside, I didn't have the courage to go back to bed, and I certainly didn't have the energy to wedge myself into the circle downstairs. Recalling the abuse I had suffered earlier, the thought of joining those men was even worse than the bedbugs. Wishing that the morning would come, I walked to the window that faced the road. A pillar stood near the window. I stayed on my feet, leaning my back and buttocks against it. Soon the soles of my feet began to slide along the woven straw surface of the floor mats, moving farther and farther away from the pillar. I straightened myself up again. Again my feet began to slide. Again I stood. This kind of thing went on for a while, but at least I had no bedbugs. Every now and then, a burst of laughter would resound from downstairs.

Unable either to lie, stand, or sit, I remained in motion, though I cannot say for how long. Exhausted to begin with, I managed to tire my legs and arms even more, only falling asleep, probably, when I was so tired that not even bedbugs could bother me. When morning came, I had slid to the bottom of the pillar, back curled against it, legs stretched out on the floor.

It's odd that after so much suffering, it took only two or three nights for the bedbug bites gradually to stop hurting. In fact, after a month, the bedbugs could be crawling all over me but were of no more concern than so many grains of rice, and I slept soundly every single night. Of course, as the others told me, the bugs for their part become more restrained as time goes by. They go crazy over newcomers and swarms of them torture you all night at first, but if you stand it for a while, they lose interest and leave you alone. One fellow told me it was because they get sick of eating the same human flesh day after day, but someone else said it's because the flesh itself improves in quality; it takes on the smell of the mine, which the bugs find rather daunting. Viewed in this light, bedbugs and miners have a lot in common. And not just miners. Bedbugs and the greater part of humanity in general seem to be controlled by the same psychology. In its equal applicability to both insects and humans, this is an attractive theory, the beauty of which would surely be pleasing to philosophers, but I myself don't subscribe to it. I would say that it's not a matter of the bugs' acting out of restraint or surfeit, but rather a loss of sensitivity on the part of the human beings who are eaten by them, entirely as a result of habit. The bugs go on eating as before but the humans no longer mind. Of course, there is a significant difference between not feeling it when you are eaten and not feeling it when you are not eaten, but since, in effect, the two are indistinguishable, there can be little practical purpose served in debating this point. So I'll stop.

I opened my eyes to find that the night had ended. Downstairs there was a babble of voices. Good. I stuck my head out the window and saw that it was raining again. Though not exactly. The thick clouds couldn't quite manage to turn themselves into raindrops, sending only those few drops that did form down to earth in slim streaks. Which is why the air was not thick with fog. The clouds were turning themselves into rain very very gradually, and as this happened the threads from the clouds descended through transparent air. Not that there was anything to see through that air but mountains—mountains almost bare of trees and grass, and wholly devoid of moisture. All around me were hills so red and barren you knew that even their inner depths must become hot under the summer sun. Without exception, they were wet with rain. Since the mountains themselves contained no moisture, this was rather like spraying a fine mist on an unglazed vase to make it look cool for summer guests: it would absorb so much that you could never wet it enough. Meanwhile, I was feeling cold. I was about to draw my head in when something caught my eye. Below the far stone wall appeared a few men in jackets. With towels draped over their heads and some straw things on their buttocks, they were walking up the road down which the jangle had passed the day before. They looked pathetic from a distance—frail and unsteady. It suddenly occurred to me that, starting this morning, I would be one of them, and as their shadowy, towel-draped forms moved off in the distance, I could not help feeling a twinge of pity, as much for myself as for those rain-soaked forms. Then an old hat came out of the rain. After it appeared another jacketed form. I guessed it was time for the men of the morning shift to head for the mine. Finally, I drew my head in. At that point, a half dozen men came barging up the stairs. "Here they come," I thought to myself, but there was not much I could do about it besides lean against the pillar with my hands shoved up my sleeves. They quickly changed into the same outfit and went downstairs again. More men came. They, too, put on jackets and went down. Soon it appeared that all the men of the boiler had gone out to work on the morning shift.

If the whole boiler was going to be active like this, I couldn't simply hang around. But no one came to tell me to wash my face or eat breakfast. Even for a pampered youth, there was such a thing as having too much time on one's hands. I forged boldly downstairs. I was by no means calm, but I behaved like a big tipper at an inn. However intimidated I might feel, it was the only way my parents' son knew how to behave. At the bottom of the stairs I ran into the old woman, who had come galloping out of the back with her sleeve cords on and holding a pair of straw sandals.

"Where do I wash my face?" I asked.

"Over there," she said, barely glancing at me and continuing on to the front door. I had no idea where "over there" was, but figured it must be where she had just come from. Walking in that direction, I came to a large kitchen, in the middle of which sat a huge rice tub that looked like a barrel cut in half. When it occurred to me that this thing must be crammed full of that awful rice I had eaten last night—more in this one tub than I could possibly consume in a month of eating it for three meals a day—my appetite died on the spot.

I found the place for washing. Stepping down from the kitchen, I approached a long sink and patted a little water on my cheeks. In my situation, there was no point in doing a proper face wash. (Keep this attitude up, and next I'd be saying to hell with washing my face at all. The others the day before—the red blanket, the boy—had probably passed through this evolutionary stage.)

At last, with no assistance, I washed my face. Eating was another matter. I wandered back to the kitchen, wondering how that was to be accomplished. Luckily, the old woman came back in just then and put together a meal for me. I was pleased to see that this one included miso soup, which I proceeded to dump over the rice before shoveling it down, thus concealing the taste of wall mud.

"Don't take too long," the old woman said to me. "Hatsu is waiting outside to take you into the mine when you're finished."

She started rushing me like this before I had a chance to rest my chopsticks. In fact, I had just been thinking that I'd better have another bowl of rice, at least, if I was going to make it through the day, but now there was no point in asking for seconds.

"Oh, really?" I replied, standing. Out front I found a man sitting with his feet down in the entryway.

"You the one that's goin' down?" he demanded with all the force of someone smashing chips from a rock.

"That's right," I replied simply.

"Let's go."

"Excuse me, but will these clothes do?" I asked politely.

"Hell, no! You gotta wear this stuff," he said, flinging down one of those jackets I had seen. "I borrowed 'em from the boss for you. Here's the pants," he added, throwing a pair of those tight-fitting pants at my feet.

Picking them up, I found that both pieces were damp and had bits of mud clinging to them. They seemed to be made out of plain duck cloth. So now my turn had come, I thought, to wear the miner's uniform. I took off my kimono with its blue-and-white splashed pattern, replacing it, top and bottom, with solid navy blue. At a glance, I might have looked like a cabinet member's porter, but I felt even worse than that. Assuming my preparations were now complete, I stepped down into the dirt-floored entryway.

"Hold it, hold it," cautioned Hatsu forcefully. "This goes on your ass."

He held out an odd-looking object: a kind of straw quilt, round, like the cap of a charcoal bale, with a couple of strings attached to it. Following his instructions, I tied it over my buttocks.

"That's your seat-pad," he said. "Got it? Next, your chisel. You stick it in your sash like this . . ."

The thing he called a chisel was a sharp-pointed steel rod a good foot-and-a-half long. I slipped it under my belt like a sword.

"You wear this the same way," said Hatsu, holding out a hammer. "Watch it, it's kinda heavy. Get a good grip on it or you'll hurt yourself."

He was right. The hammer was heavy. How did they manage to walk through the mine with such things hanging from their belts?

"Heavy, ain't it?"

"Yes, it is."

"And that's a light one. The really heavy ones go six, seven pounds . . . Got it now? OK, shake your hips. OK? Now, this."

He started to hand me a lantern, but then said, "Hold on. Get your sandals on before you take the lantern."

There was a new pair of straw sandals on the threshold by the entryway. These were probably the ones I had seen the old lady carrying. I fit my bare feet into them, but when I strung the cord behind my heel and gave a tug, Hatsu yelled at me.

"Not so tight, stupid! Loosen it up between your toes."

Despite the yelling, I managed to fasten them on my feet.

"OK," he said, handing me a coolie hat and the lantern. "That does it."

The hat was the kind worn by prison laborers, round on top, like a manjū cut in half, but I put it on docilely and took the lantern, letting it dangle by my side. The lantern was made expressly for hanging down like that. The body was a kind of oil can holding maybe a cup and a half, with a filler spout and a hole for the wick. Over the hole was a long, narrow tube, the top of which bent somewhat to the side and then spread out into a cup. You stuck your thumb into the cup and let the lantern dangle from your thumb— an extremely practical design that allowed one digit to do the work of five.

"You put it on like this," explained Hatsu, shoving his thumb—as hard and brown as a dried chestnut—into the hole. It fit perfectly. "Now, watch."

He swung his arm a few times like the pendulum of a clock, and the lantern showed no sign of falling from his thumb. I gave it a try, with the same results.

"That's it. Pretty good," he said. "OK, ready to go?"

"I believe I am."

I followed him out front. It was raining. The first thing the rain struck was my hat. When I looked up at the sky, the drops hit my chin, my mouth, my nose. Then I felt them on my shoulders. My legs. As I walked along, my whole body became damp, and the moisture that soaked through my clothing was turned to steam by the energy of my skin. The rain was cold, though, and it seemed to be gradually reducing the warmth of my body, but Hatsu went so quickly up the slope that by the time we reached the mine entrance, the rain that had soaked through all but boiled out of my pores.

The entrance was big—maybe as big as a train tunnel. Arched at the top like a cake of fish paste, the opening must have been a good twelve feet high. The rails emerging from it also gave it the appearance of a train tunnel. Hatsu said this was where the electric trains ran. Standing outside, I tried peering into the depths of the tunnel. It was dark inside.

"This's the door to hell," said Hatsu. "Got the guts to go in?"

He spoke with a touch of derision. Abuse had been showering down on me all along the road from the boiler to the mine as heads poked out of windows growling, "That guy from yesterday is still here," or "It's the new one." The way they looked at me, I couldn't believe their attitude came from sheer curiosity as a result of being closed off in the mountains. Down deep, their words were meant to mock me. In one sense, they were saying, "So now you're in this hole with the rest of us. Good! Serves you right!" And in another sense, their words meant, "It won't do you a damn bit of good to come here. A weakling like you won't last a minute." Thus, their curses reflected their pleasure at the fact that I had fallen so low as to taste the suffering that they themselves must taste, plus their contempt for me as one who would never be able to endure the pain. Not only did they exult at having dragged someone down to their own level, but they seemed to enjoy kicking him once again after they had him down by hinting at their superior ability to endure the fall. Each time I had heard their curses on the road to the mine, I had lowered the brim of my coolie hat and passed by with my face half hidden. Which is why, when Hatsu added his own contemptuous remark, I answered him a little testily.

"Of course I can go in. Look, they've even got streetcars running here."

"Think you're tough, huh? We'll see about that."

Of course, if I had said I was afraid to go into the mine, he would have heaped curses on me for being a coward. I had to lose either way, so I wasn't sorry for my answer. Hatsu charged into the mine and I followed. It became dark more quickly than I had expected it to. The most frightening thing was the suddenly uncertain footing. Even with the rain falling, the outside now came to seem bright and cheery. To make matters worse, the tunnel on either side of the roadbed was a mass of mud. Apparently still smoldering from my remark, Hatsu forged ahead. I forged on after him, determined to keep up.

"You gotta behave yourself in the hole," he said, suddenly coming to a stop in the dark, "or they throw you down the pit."

At his waist I could see Hatsu's chisel and his seven-pound hammer. Shriveling up in the dark, I said, "All right. I'll be careful."

"OK, got it straight? If you're plannin' to come out alive, you're better off not goin' into the hole in the first place."

Hatsu spoke these words—as much to himself as to me—after he had turned away and begun walking again. I was more than a little taken aback. Because of the strong echo in the tunnel, his voice bounced off the rock walls, ringing in my ears. If what he said was true, I had gotten myself into a terrible place. I had decided to become a miner precisely because of the work's similarity to death, but if I was now actually going to die—if it was such a frightening job—if I was going to be killed—if I was going to be thrown into the pit . . . the pit. What was the pit?

"Pardon me, but what's the pit?"

"How's that?" asked Hatsu, swinging around toward me again.

105

"I said, 'Pardon me, but what's the pit?'"

"It's a hole."

"What?"

"A hole! A hole! We throw the ore in and take it down together. You get thrown in with the ore and . . ."

Cutting himself short, he hurried on again.

I came to a stop and stood there for a moment. Glancing back, I saw that the tunnel opening now looked like a tiny moon. Upon entering, I had thought to myself, "Well, if *this* is all there is to the hole, it's not as bad as they say." But after Hatsu's frightening comments, this otherwise very ordinary tunnel had begun to take on an entirely new air for me. I longed for the tapping of cold raindrops on my prisoner's hat. Then I glanced back toward the tunnel entrance and realized I had come so far inside that the entrance looked like a tiny moon. Cloudy as it might be outside, that was where I longed to be. I found it disturbing the way the pitch-black tunnel ceiling pressed down on me. And it seemed to be coming lower and lower. No sooner had these thoughts struck me than we cut across the tracks and turned right. The road began to slope gently downward. I couldn't see the entrance anymore. There was nothing behind me but solid darkness. The tiny moon, the window to the world of men, had been slammed shut, and Hatsu and I moved steadily downward. As we walked, I stretched out my hand and touched the wall. It felt as wet as if it had been rained on.

"Still with me?" Hatsu asked.

"Yes," I replied meekly.

"Wait. Pretty soon we get to the Main Street of Hell."

With that, our brief exchange ended. Just then a point of light appeared somewhere up ahead. It shone like one eye of a black cat in the darkness. If it was a lantern, it should have been flickering, but it moved not at all. Neither could I judge its distance or direction, which was not in a straight line from here. The only sure thing was that I could see it. If the tunnel was a single, straight road, both Hatsu and I would proceed ahead toward this light. I didn't bother to ask but continued in, assuming that up ahead must be what he called the Main Street of Hell. Soon, the gentle slope gave out. The road curved ahead on a level. The light was shining where the road came to a wall. Before, the light had appeared somewhere below nose level, but now it was exactly at eye level and very close.

"We're here," said Hatsu. "Main Street."

Now the tunnel broadened into an area about ten feet square, and there was a small shed not much bigger than a police box. An electric lamp was shining inside. Seated on opposite sides of a table, their chairs facing each other, were two officials in Western suits. Over the door hung a sign, "Checkpoint No. 1." Later, I heard that this was where they checked the comings and goings of the miners, the length of time they put in at work, and such, but not knowing what this setup was for at the time, I simply found it unsettling the way half a dozen miners with blackish faces were standing wordlessly in front of the place. They were waiting for the change in shifts. I, too, had a chisel and hammer in my belt and carried a lantern, but Hatsu led me quickly past the checkpoint. Apparently, since I was just a job applicant come to inspect the mine and not even a newly hired trainee, there was no need for me to wait with the others. Hatsu paused for a moment to stick his head in the shed window and say something to the officials, neither of whom bothered to look at me. Instead, the assembled miners looked. But, perhaps because of the presence of the officials, none of them said a word.

As soon as we passed the assembly point, the appearance of the mine changed suddenly. Up until now, the ceiling of the tunnel had been high enough so that you could walk upright—you could stretch if you wanted to—without touching it, but suddenly it dipped down and gave you the feeling that your head might graze it now and then if you walked upright. Another inch or two, I thought, and I'd probably slam into the rock and have blood gushing out of my forehead, which meant I couldn't walk along imperiously, stretched to my full height, as in the pine grove. Frightened, I ducked my head down as far as possible between my shoulders and followed close behind Hatsu. Of course, I had lit my lantern earlier.

Just three feet ahead of me, Hatsu suddenly went down on all fours. Shocked to see that he had tripped, I planted my feet to keep myself from stumbling into him. This required a real effort since the slope of the road threatened to send me tumbling forward. I leaned the upper part of my body back, waiting for Hatsu to regain his footing, but this he made no move to do. He stayed down on all fours.

"Is something wrong?" I asked from behind.

He did not reply. I was sure he must have hurt himself and I was about to ask again if he was all right when he coolly began to move off.

"Are you sure you're all right?"

"Crawl!"

"What's that?"

"Crawl, I said!"

His voice was moving slowly away from me. And the sound of it I found puzzling. Granted, Hatsu was facing the other way, but his voice was still emerging from a point close enough so that it should have been perfectly audible. Instead, it was suddenly being swallowed up. And not because the voice itself was thin. It was Hatsu's normal voice made vague, as if it had been sealed in a bag. Something out of the ordinary was going on, I realized, peering into the darkness. Then I understood. At this point the tunnel, in which it had been possible to walk in the usual upright position, narrowed down so suddenly that crawling was the only way you could make it through. Hatsu's legs were sticking out of the narrow opening. His upper body was inside. Then one of his legs went in. And, almost immediately, the other leg went in. Now I resigned myself to having to go down on all fours. No wonder Hatsu had ordered me to crawl. I did as I was told. Or at least I tried to. I was holding the lantern in my right hand. When I plastered my wide-open left hand on the ice-cold mud (or rock, or clay, or whatever it was), the cold seemed to leap up my arm through my shoulder and into my heart. Trying not to set the lantern down, I had to bring my right hand up close to my face until it was almost touching—a very inconvenient arrangement. I froze in this position, wondering what to do. I looked at the lantern dangling from my right hand. Just then something dripped from the tunnel ceiling. The lantern flame hissed. A wisp of soot grazed my chin and cheek. It went into my eye, too. But I continued staring at the flame. Far off, I heard a clanging sound. There were miners at work somewhere, no doubt, but how far away and in what direction, I couldn't tell. It was not a sound from a world where north, south, east, or west meant anything. I made myself crawl ahead two or three "paces" in this position. True, it was inconvenient, but not impossible to move. The one thing that concerned me was the occasional drip from the ceiling and hiss of the lantern. Hatsu had left me behind with nothing but the lantern to rely on—a lantern that was hissing and threatening to go out. Each time it happened, though, the flame would grow bright again. And as soon as I began feeling reassured, another drop of water would fall. Hiss. Flicker. Now I was sure it was going to go out. In fact, water had been dripping from the tunnel ceiling all along, but with the lantern hanging down below waist level, I had probably not noticed the problem. It was only after I had brought the lamp close to my ear and heard the hissing that it made me nervous. Which slowed down my crawling even more. I had still gone no more than three paces when Hatsu's voice rang out.

"What the hell are you doing in there? Come on out! Hurry up or the sun's gonna set!"

No, I hadn't misheard him. Down here in the darkness, Hatsu had actually said the sun was going to set.

Crawling along, I looked in Hatsu's direction, thrusting my chin out so hard my Adam's apple was ready to pop. Six feet ahead there was something like the opening to a bear's den, from which protruded Hatsu's face—or what seemed to be his face. He was bent over and peering into this passage where I was taking too much time. I don't recall how I managed to get through the remaining six feet. I crawled to the hole as quickly as possible and poked my head out, by which time Hatsu had withdrawn his face and was standing outside the hole, his legs now in front of my nose. Overjoyed, I crawled the rest of the way out.

"What were you doin' in there?"

"It was so narrow."

"If you're gonna let narrow places scare you, keep outa the mine. Any dope knows there's no ground to stand on down here like on the land."

No, I hadn't misheard him this time, either. Hatsu had actually said that there was no ground to stand on in the mine as there is on the land. I'm making such a point of assuring you that he actually said these things because Hatsu was a man who often came up with wholly unexpected remarks.

Since Hatsu would come down hard on me every time I tried to make excuses for myself, I mostly kept quiet, but this time I let slip with, "I was worried the lantern was going to go out."

Hatsu thrust his lantern at me and began to examine my face in great detail. Then he gave me an order.

"Put it out."

"But why?"

"Because I said so. Put it out."

"Blow it?"

Hatsu burst out laughing.

I looked at him in amazement.

"Look, don't be stupid. Whaddya think is in these things? Rape-seed oil! It takes more than a drop of water to put 'em out!"

This finally set my mind at ease.

"Feel better? Ha ha ha ha!"

Every time Hatsu laughed, the whole tunnel shook. And when the sound died, the place seemed twice as quiet as before. Just then there came the clanging of hammers and chisels.

"Hear that?" Hatsu asked, flicking his chin toward the sound.

"Yes, I do," I said. I stood there listening for more, but Hatsu urged me ahead.

"Let's get goin' now. And stick close to me this time."

Hatsu was in a very good mood, probably because I was entirely at his mercy. It didn't matter how harshly he might criticize me, as long as he was in a good mood. In this sense, "not mattering" means making things work to your own advantage. Having fallen so low, I went shamelessly sniffing after Hatsu's tail. The road took a sharp turn to the left and sloped down again steeply.

"Watch it, now, time to go down," Hatsu called to me without turning around. The way he did this reminded me somehow of the way Tokyo rickshaw pullers warn their passengers about steep hills, which, despite the agony, made me want to laugh. Hatsu, quite unaware of this, started down. I followed, not to be outdone. The way proceeded down in terraces cut out of the earth. It turned every twenty-five or thirty feet, but altogether the descent must have been as much as at Atago Shrine.* With a tremendous effort, I stayed with Hatsu on the way down. At the bottom, I heaved a great sigh, which seemed to give me some pain. I assumed it must be the bad ventilation deep down in the mine, but in fact my health was suffering even then. After another fifty or sixty yards of painful breaths, the look of the place changed again.

Now Hatsu lay on his back with his hands on the ground and inserted everything from the waist down into a hole. The passage

---

*A Shintō shrine atop a steep hill in downtown Tokyo known for its flight of eighty-six stone steps.

was so low and narrow that the only way to negotiate it was with this special bottom-first technique.

"Look how I get through here. You do the same."

Almost before Hatsu had finished speaking, his trunk and head slipped out of sight. Oh, to be a master of one's craft! I stuck one foot through the opening, groping for a foothold with my sandal but encountering only empty space. The other side of the hole had to be a sheer cliff or a very steep slope. Meaning that if you went through headfirst, you'd also fall headfirst and injure yourself, and if you just shoved your feet through, you'd stumble. Realizing this, I stretched my legs out stiffly and set my hands on the ground behind me. I did this so clumsily, however, that the moment my hands hit the ground, my buttocks did, too—and with a loud slap. The impact must have been pretty strong because it hurt a little even through the seat-pad strapped across my buttocks. While cursing myself for having made a mess of it, I stretched both legs through the hole. They dangled down a foot or so, but still encountered nothing. All I could do now was move my hands and bottom forward, stretching my legs out farther. This caused me to slide down as far as my thighs, when at last the bottoms of my sandals landed on something hard. Just to make sure, I tapped the hard thing with my feet, figuring that if it felt all right, I would let go with my hands and stand on it.

"What's this with the feet?" growled Hatsu from below. "Don't be scared. Just put your weight on it and stand up."

The moment he said this, the upper part of my body slipped through the hole and came upright.

"Just like an umbrella with legs," said Hatsu, looking at me.

Having no idea what that was supposed to mean, I couldn't smile. Instead, I answered gravely, "Who? Me?"

Hatsu seemed to find this very funny for some inexplicable reason, and he laughed out loud. His attitude toward me changed after this; he treated me somewhat more kindly. You never know when some chance occurrence is going to win someone over to your side. Meanwhile, artful attempts to curry another's favor rarely seem to have their intended effect. I have yet to witness an act of flattery that managed to work as well as sheer good luck. Over the years I've tried to ingratiate myself with many different people in pursuit of some personal advantage, but virtually without success. It's a scary business because eventually you're going to be found out, however stupid the other person may be. Rarely has a planned response succeeded as well as my answer did to the "umbrella with legs" remark. Having realized how absurd it is to exert yourself and fail, I have lately come to deal with others from a purely fatalistic standpoint. The two areas of difficulty here, though, are speechmaking and writing. Both of these are bound to fail unless I take great pains in preparing for them. And even then I fail. The results may be the same, but even if I don't win anyone over with a painstaking failure, at least my weak points don't show, so I always do that much. Sometime I'd like to give a speech or write something that would make Hatsu like me, but he'd probably just laugh at me. That's why I haven't done it yet. (None of this has anything to do with anything. Let me get back to the story of Hatsu.)

Still laughing, Hatsu said from below, "Hey, stop lookin' so serious and come down here. And hurry up, a day doesn't last forever!"

Yes, he actually said this, too, down here in the mine with his lantern.

Climbing ten or fifteen feet down terraces cut in the earth, I came to where Hatsu was standing. He turned to the right. Another set of terraces went down twenty-five or thirty feet. At the bottom of those, Hatsu turned to the left. There were more terraces. Turning right, left, right, left, we zigzagged like a bolt of lightning down one level after another—how far down into the earth, I have no idea. It was my first time along this route, of course, and in the darkness of the mine it felt awfully long to me. When we had climbed down to the lowest level, where, it seemed, almost all ties with the world had been lost, we suddenly entered a room perhaps twelve feet by twelve. This "room," of course, was simply a place where the tunnel had been dug out more broadly, the walls of which swelled outward beyond the limits set by the floor and ceiling. It was as if we had fallen into a huge earthenware sake jar. I found out later that this place was called a work site. They would widen the tunnel like this when an engineer had concluded that a vein of ore was present. The work sites were thus naturally broader than the passages, and each would be worked by a team of three miners, on a piecework basis. Sometimes a work site estimated to require two weeks would be finished in four days, and others judged to need no more than five days they'd dig for half a month or more. In this way, roads would be dug in the mine, and if by a road they found a vein, they would dig out that spot, following wherever the vein led. Thus, the entrance where the trains ran might be level and the tunnel there a single straight line, but once the mine turned down and came to Checkpoint No. 1, branch roads ran off to the right and left with work sites established at scattered points. After a work site was finished, they would find more veins and dig wherever those led, as a result of which the mine was a mass of narrow passages and dark holes—probably something like an ants' nest. Or it might be compared to the way worms tunnel through a book. Human beings would eat the copper in the earth, and when they were finished eating they would find more copper and go to eat that, as a result of which these roads had been dug every which way. You could go on and on through the mine without ever encountering a miner unless you came to a work site. You'd hear clanging sounds now and then, but by themselves these only made the place seem all the more deserted. True, I had come inside the mine, but Hatsu had been taking me on detours around the work sites, it seemed—probably because I was here mainly to see what the place looked like inside. I actually saw miners at work for the first time only after we came to the bottom of the long series of terraces. No matter how far we climbed down the lightning-bolt zigzag, it had never seemed to end and we never encountered a soul along the way, so when we entered a work site for the first time and met real, live human beings, I was overjoyed.

They were sitting on a log. There were three of them. The log had been stripped of its bark and polished. About the size of a railroad cross-tie, it was a big, heavy thing. I couldn't imagine how they had managed to transport it this far. I understand that these things are left in the work sites by the setters to shore up the ceilings, in order to prevent cave-ins when the dug-out areas expand. Two of the men were actually sitting on the log and the third was squatting down and facing it. In the space between them was a small wooden tub. It lay on the ground, inverted. The third man was pressing it down. All three men were emitting strange cries. The man suddenly lifted the tub, revealing a pair of dice. At that moment, Hatsu and I entered the room.

The three men raised their eyes in unison, looking at me and at Hatsu. A lantern had been fastened to the earthen wall. Its dark light shone on the three sets of flashing eyes. Nothing flashed but those eyes—really. The room, of course, was dark. The lantern, which by rights *had* to be bright, was dark. The way it smoldered, giving off murky smoke, it looked like a cloudy liquid that moved. No sooner did its cloudy tip blacken and turn into smoke than the smoke was sucked into the darkness. Thus, the interior of the room was hazy. And it moved.

The lantern was fastened above the three men's heads. Which is why the only parts of the men that could be seen with some clarity were their heads. But since the three heads were black, they were all but invisible. The effect was especially strange because the three heads had been clustered together, but the moment I entered the room they drew apart. The tub had appeared from among them. And the dice had appeared from beneath the tub. Having seen the tub and the dice and heard their strange cries, I had next seen their faces—faces I could hardly make out. Of one man's face, only the tip of a cheekbone and a wing of the nose caught the light. Half the brow of the next man shone through. The whole face of the third was dimly visible, but this was simply because of the light it received from my own lantern, some four or five feet away from him. In this pose, the three fixed their eyes with a flash—on *me*.

Filled with joy though I was at having met up with other human beings at long last, the moment I saw these three sets of eyeballs, I stopped dead in my tracks.

"Who the hell . . . ," one man started to say, then cut himself short. The other two kept silent. Nor, still frozen in my tracks, did I attempt to speak. I could not speak. Hatsu answered for me:

"It's a new guy," he said energetically. To be quite honest, the moment those three sets of eyes shone and I was asked "Who the hell . . . ," I forgot that Hatsu was next to me and I was aware of nothing but my own fear. Surely what happened to me is what is meant by the expression "to be rooted to the spot." Just as I became rooted to that spot and was going stiff all over, Hatsu spoke up. His voice emerged from behind my left ear, and as it passed by on its way to the three men, it reminded me that I was not alone. Oh, yes! Hatsu is here! As a result, my stiffening arms and legs returned to normal. I took one step sideways, intending to have Hatsu step out in front of me, which is exactly what he did.

"Don't you guys ever do anything else?" he asked, holding his lantern by his side and looking down at the tub and dice on the ground in the midst of the three men.

"You want in?"

"Not today. I'm showin' this guy around."

With a healthy grunt, Hatsu lowered himself onto the log. "How about a little break?" he asked, looking at me. I had been frightened stiff (literally), but his invitation made me very happy and restored my spirits. I sat down next to him, six feet from the nearest miner. Now, for the first time, I saw how the seat-pad worked. It was positioned exactly right to cushion your buttocks. And it kept off the chill. Earlier, I had been feeling a little dizzy and had lost my bearings—if it was possible to *have* bearings down here in the mine. Let's just say I wasn't feeling too good. But sitting down and relaxing like this was a great relief. The four men had all kinds of things to talk about.

"Know about the new girl in the Hiromoto?"

"Yup."

"Buy her yet?"

"Nope. You?"

"Me? I'm—ha ha ha!"

This was the man whose face had been dimly visible in its entirety. It was still visible—dimly. For example, its shape seemed to stay pretty much the same whether the man laughed or not.

"You get around, don't you?" said Hatsu, and he gave a little laugh, too.

"I'm not the only one. You could die any time in this hole."

"That goes for all of us," said one of the other men, his voice strangely full of feeling. This took me completely off guard.

Suddenly my nearest neighbor on the log spoke to me.

"Where you from?"

"Tokyo."

"Well, you won't make any money here," said one of the others.

I had been amazed at the persistence with which Chōzō had showered me with promises of money-making, and I had been taken aback at the harshness with which the men in the boiler had warned me that I would never make any money here. I had come this far assuming that, at the bottom of the earth, at least, I would be spared such talk, but now the first words spoken to me by the first human beings I had encountered in the mine were about money. It was ridiculous and I wanted to say as much, but I decided to hold off. I knew I'd be beaten to a pulp if I didn't watch my step. Of course, I'd be beaten to a pulp if I said nothing, so I asked, "Why not?"

"There're gods in this mine. You can save your money, but they won't let you take it out of here. It always comes back to them."

"What gods?" I asked.

"Let's call 'em goddesses," he replied, and the four men enjoyed a good laugh among themselves. I kept silent. Ignoring me, the others launched into a discussion of the "goddesses." It must have gone on for ten minutes or more while I thought about other things. What most interested me were my thoughts about how Tsuyako and Sumie would react if they could see me squatting down in this dark mine wearing these mud-stained clothes. Would they feel sorry for me? Would they cry? Or would they think I had fallen so low they could no longer love me? I had no difficulty in arriving at the con- clusion that they would, indeed, feel sorry for me and cry, which made me want to give them at least a glimpse of me like this. Next I thought about the ridicule I had suffered by the fire last night and how Tsuyako and Sumie would have reacted if they had seen that. My conclusion here was quite the opposite of the earlier one. I was glad that neither had been at my side. When I imagined to myself what the scene would have looked like—the two stylish women there with me as I submitted spinelessly to my tormenters—I thought my armpits would start streaming from the embarrassment I felt. In other words, the sheer fact of my having descended to the ranks of the miners didn't bother me so much. I even felt a touch of pride in it. But what I didn't want the women to see was my lack of standing as a new miner. We always want to conceal a loss of dignity from anyone, but we especially want to conceal it from women. Women are helpless creatures who depend on us, and the more we are depended on, the more we want to demonstrate that we are men of dignity. This feeling would seem to be especially strong in un- married men. There's a bit of the showman in every human being, however dire his straits. As I sat there resting in the depths of the mine, seat-pad beneath my buttocks, lantern in hand, my thoughts took on precisely this dramatic quality—which was, in a sense, a respite from my suffering. The theater, which may be called a pub- licly sanctioned respite, must certainly have developed from this kind of experience. Playing the protagonist in an undeveloped drama deep inside me, I was feeling both defeated and triumphant at the same time.

Suddenly there came a huge sound that seemed to slam through my lungs. I couldn't tell whether it had occurred underfoot or overhead. Both the log I was sitting on and the black ceiling above me gave a jump. My head and arms and legs moved. Sometimes, if you're dangling your legs over the edge of the veranda and something hits your knee, the lower part of your leg twitches up. That's just how my whole body moved, but much more violently. And not just my body. My mind did the same. Turning a somersault in the midst of my private "drama," I came back to myself all at once. The sound lingered on, as if a thunderbolt had been buried in the earth, its free reverberations chained down until, frustrated, writhing with pent-up energy, it could only smash against the rocks, be enveloped again, rage once more only to be hurled back, and, all hope of escape closed off, go on roaring and roaring.

"Don't let it scare you," said Hatsu. He stood up.

I stood up.

The three miners stood up. "There's not much left," said one of them, picking up his chisel. "Let's get it over with."

Hatsu and I started out of the work site. Then the smoke hit us. With the smell of gunpowder, it entered my eyes, my nose, my mouth. Choking, I whirled around. A clanging sound in the work site told me the miners had begun their job.

"What *is* this?" I asked Hatsu in my misery. When I had first heard the roaring sound, I had been convinced that a huge explosion had occurred in the mine and that our lives would be in danger if we didn't get out of there fast. Hatsu, meanwhile, seemed to be burrowing deeper into the mine. Though frightened, I followed after him, being neither physically capable of doing as I pleased nor psychologically independent, and calming myself with the thought that, for all his seniority, when the time came to flee, I could count on him to flee. That was when the choking cloud of smoke blew in. I whirled around, partly out of fear of going too far into this place, when the clanging sound of the three miners smashing ore in the smoke moved me to ask my question out of sheer amazement that we might be safe after all.

"Don't be scared," said Hatsu, coughing a few times. "It's just dynamite."

"Is it OK?"

"Maybe it's not OK, but there's nothin' you can do about it. If you're gonna be scared of dynamite, you can't spend one day in the hole."

I kept silent. Hatsu forged on ahead as if elbowing his way through the smoke. I couldn't believe that he was totally free of discomfort; rather, I thought, he must be putting on a bold front for me, the newcomer. Either that or the smoke had already passed from one tunnel into another and, had we been on the surface, I would have seen that it was gone by now, but because of the darkness here below I might have just *thought* that the smoke was hanging in the tunnel and that I was choking, in which case it was not Hatsu who was to blame but me.

At any rate, I followed after him, enduring the discomfort. When we had passed through another womb-like opening and descended another set of twenty-five-foot terraces, turning right and left, we came to a fork in the road. A clattering sound came from the far end of the branch road. It sounded like the noise a rock makes when you throw it down a deep well, but the "well" in this case seemed much deeper than the ordinary well. By which I mean that the sound of the rock hitting the sides as it fell was particularly sharp and clear. And it lasted a very long time. The final clatter came from the absolute bottom and it took a long time to reach us. But reach us it always did in the end. It had only to travel in a straight line where there were no escape routes. Though it might be on the verge of dying halfway home, every bit of sound produced at the bottom, however far away and faint it might be, would be sent up by the reverberating walls without loss. That, roughly, was what it sounded like.

Hatsu came to a halt.

"Hear that?"

"Yes."

"They're throwin' ore down the pit."

"Oh, I see . . ."

"As long as we're here, I'll give you a look at the pit."

He said this as if it had occurred to him unexpectedly. With a vigorous backward step, Hatsu turned the heels of his sandals in a new direction. He cut to the right before I could answer, so completely was I absorbed in listening to the sounds. I followed him into the darkness.

The side road ran up against a wall just four feet past the entrance. A sharp turn to the right, and six feet ahead a dull glow filled the tunnel, which broadened and rose in height. In the glow were two black shadows. When we approached them, one of the black shadows thrust his left foot forward and, with a powerful scooping motion, flipped a large winnowing basket behind him at an angle. The basket landed upside-down atop the planks on which he was standing, the contents falling far below with that clattering sound. A foot beyond him was a large hole, maybe six feet across. The man was a digger, and he had just thrown in a basketful of loose ore. A sheer rock wall rose above the far side of the hole. The glow of the lanterns was too dim to bring out the color of the rock, but the entire wet surface of the wall shone in their light.

"Take a peek," said Hatsu.

The planking extended some three feet out over the lip of the hole. I stepped about a third of the way onto the planks.

"More," Hatsu urged me from behind.

I hesitated. Even at this point, there was no telling how far I'd fall if the planks gave way. And if I went out a foot farther, I'd have to jump one more foot to solid ground in an emergency. A foot may not seem like much, but down here it's the same as sixty feet on the surface. And so I hesitated.

"Go ahead, you can do better than that. How're you ever gonna be a digger?"

This was not Hatsu's voice. It probably belonged to one of the black shadows. I did not look back. But neither did my feet move forward. Only my eyes moved—slowly, down the wet, dimly shining wall at the far side of the pit, as far as they could see, maybe six feet altogether, beyond which there was only perfect darkness. And because it was so perfectly dark, I did not know how much my eyes were taking in. But it was deep. Infinitely deep. Nerves on edge at the awful prospect of falling in, I began to feel as if I were being nudged from behind. My feet remained planted where they were.

"Hey, get outa the way," said a voice.

I turned to see one of the diggers standing there with a heavy-looking straw bag in his arms. The bag itself was no more than half as big as a bale of rice, but I could tell it was heavy from the way he clutched the bottom with both hands and supported some of its weight on his hip, holding his breath with the effort. I moved aside

119

immediately, drawing back to a relatively safe spot, from which, if the planks were to break, I could leap to solid ground. I assumed the digger would proceed with caution since the bag was blocking his view, but much to my surprise he continued to move forward with heavy steps. Some two feet from the edge, he brought his legs together, and I assumed he was going to stop. But then he took another step. Now he had only one foot to go. This he cut in half with another step. Then he brought his feet into perfect alignment. And then he gave a grunt. His chest and hips moved forward simultaneously. Certain he was going over the edge, I was about to cry out when the heavy bale somersaulted from his hands and he remained rooted to his spot on the planks. Of the fallen bale, nothing more was to be heard. Or so I was thinking when there came a distant thud. The bale had apparently fallen all the way to the bottom.

"Neat trick, huh? Think you can do it?" asked Hatsu.

"I don't know," I said, cocking my head in all-too-obvious bewilderment. Hatsu and the diggers laughed out loud. I simply went on with my bewilderment, resigned to being laughed at. Hatsu then delivered the following speech to me:

"It's like anything else. You gotta have training. It looks easy till you try it. Say they make you a digger and you're scared to go near the edge. You try throwing stuff in at arm's length. Everything'll fall on the planks and miss the pit. It's even *more* dangerous that way 'cause the weight of the ore pulls you in. If you don't throw it from the chest like these guys—"

The other man interrupted Hatsu, laughing. "You gotta fall into the pit a few times. It's good for you. Ha ha ha ha."

Retracing our steps to the earlier tunnel, we walked with the diggers, who turned right after fifty yards. Hatsu and I continued straight down an incline. At the bottom, we wove our way twenty-five or thirty feet to the end of a level passage, where Hatsu came to a stop.

"Ready to climb down more?" he asked.

No, of course not, I had ceased being "ready" a long time ago. But while, on the one hand, it would seem that I had endured one hardship after another to come this far because I was sure I'd fail the test if I gave up partway, I had also been figuring that we would reach the bottom before too long. If, after all we'd been through, Hatsu now had to stop and make a point of asking me whether I was ready for more, that meant we had more than a couple of blocks left to go. I looked at his face in the darkness as I pondered this question. Maybe I ought to say I'd had enough, I thought. One's course of action at a time like this is determined entirely by the other person's whim. Idiot or genius, it's the same for everybody. Which is why it was faster to decide by studying Hatsu's face than by consulting my own heart's desire. This was one of those cases in which my surroundings rather than my character were to decide my fate, in which the worth of my character would sink far below the norm. Among all such cases in which the character I was so confident I had established for myself simply crumbled to pieces, this was one of the most vivid examples. It was also one of the sources of my theory of the non-existence of character.

As I mentioned earlier, I studied Hatsu's face. I saw in it no friendly invitation to join him in continued descent. Neither did I find there sage counsel to climb down for my own good, nor a threat to make me go down whether I wanted to or not. Of course there was no hint that he was daring me to take the plunge. I saw in Hatsu's face only contempt—a firm conviction that I could never make it. That in itself was all right, too. But beyond the look of contempt there lurked the urgent question of failure. Failure to pass the test now would be far more important than my honor, my dignity, or anything else. I would have to continue on down, even if it meant suffocating to death.

"Let's go," I declared.

Hatsu looked as if I had taken him off guard. "OK, then," he said gently. "But don't forget, it's gonna be a little risky."

And no wonder. We had to climb straight down a perfectly perpendicular shaft like a couple of monkeys. A ladder hung there against one wall of the shaft, though it seemed more like a pole dangling in midair, the lower end of which could not be seen from above. How far down it went, and where it was fastened to the wall, there was no way of telling.

"OK, I'll go first, and you follow. But be careful."

I had never expected to hear such considerate language from Hatsu. Probably he was feeling a little sorry for me, the way I had offered so docilely to climb down. He did an about-face, precisely aiming his hindquarters toward the opening. Then he knelt down. And, without a moment's delay, he began to sink into the hole, step by step, feet first, until only his face was left. Eventually, even his face disappeared. As long as his face was visible, I felt reasonably confident, but of course as soon as the top of his black head slipped down into the hole, anxiety and helplessness made it impossible for me to stand still and, on tiptoe, I peered down from above. Hatsu continued his downward climb. All I could see were his black head and the light of the lantern. Unnerving as this was, I still found it possible to think, "If I don't get down there while Hatsu is still visible, I might never make it." This would result in total humiliation. Concluding that the only thing to do was to get down there as quickly as possible, I spun around and set my knees on the ground as Hatsu had done. Sliding my hands along the ground, I felt for the rungs of the ladder with the bottoms of my sandals.

Grasping the top rung with both hands, back curled like a shrimp's, I lowered my feet to where I guessed there might be something to stand on. Slowly, I stretched my legs out. When I was standing straight, the flame of the lantern came close to my chest. If I didn't move, I'd be smoked to death. All I could do was lower one foot. And to accomplish that, I had to bring one hand down to the next rung. As I lowered the lantern, it began to move in unpredictable ways. When I let it swing freely, it seemed it was going to set my clothes on fire. But when I tried to be extra careful, it smashed against the rock wall and almost went out. Back when I had thrust my thumb in the cup and let the lantern dangle like a pendulum, I had thought it was a very handy device, but now it was a pain in the neck. Besides, the ladder was narrow. And the distance from one rung to the next was awfully long. It took at least twice the effort of the ordinary ladder to go down a rung. My fear only made matters worse. And each new rung I grasped felt slimy. All but pressing my nose against one to peer at it in the feeble light, I saw it was coated with clay—smeared on, no doubt, by the sandals going up and down. Partway down the ladder, I craned my neck and looked down. I never should have done that. My head started to spin and my desperate grasp began to loosen. "I might be killed! No! No!" I clung to the ladder, shutting my eyes tightly. Through a swirling mass of large soap bubbles, I saw Hatsu climbing down. Strictly speaking, if I *could* have seen Hatsu, it would have been when I looked down. There was no way he could have been there amid soap bubbles whirling before my closed eyes. And yet he was.

Climbing down. It was very strange. Now that I think of it, I must have glanced at Hatsu the moment before the dizziness hit me, but what with the reeling and the fumbling and the sudden fear of dying, I forgot about the image of Hatsu impressed on my retinas until it revived itself when I closed my eyes and grabbed onto the rung of the ladder. Whether there is any scientific basis for such an event, I don't know. I was in a dream state. I was in the dark, in fear for my life, and in mental chaos, unsure whether I was alive or dead. When I saw Hatsu climbing down, I was too far gone to know whether he was doing it inside my eyes or beneath my feet. Strange to say, though, I opened my eyes and looked down again. And yes, there he was again. But now he seemed to be climbing down the opposite wall. Maybe because this was my second glance down, it didn't make me dizzy enough to let go. Instead, I focused my eyes on Hatsu, who was, in fact, climbing down the opposite wall. How in the world . . . ? But just then the lantern started to hiss again. This was upsetting. The thing was supposed to be failure-proof. Meanwhile, Hatsu seemed to be zooming down. In this situation, that would be the best thing for me to do, too, I realized. Grabbing one slimy rung after another, I eventually made it down another twenty feet or so, where my feet came to rest on earth. Yes, it was earth, I found with a tentative step. Just in case, I kept my hands on the ladder while inspecting underfoot, and there was no doubt about it: the ladder ended there. But so did the foot-deep shelf of earth I was standing on. Below was more vertical shaft. On the opposite wall, though, was another ladder, positioned so you could reach out from here and grasp it. Which is what I did, since there was nothing else I could do. Then I went down as quickly as I could. This ladder was the same length as the first one. And where it ended, there was another one on the opposite wall, as before. Having no choice in the matter, I switched again. And when I managed, with what seemed to be my last breath, to reach the bottom of this one, another new one hung on the opposite wall. There was virtually no end to them. By the time I came to the sixth ladder, the strength had gone out of my hands, my legs were beginning to tremble, and I was breathing in a very odd manner. Below, all trace of Hatsu had disappeared long before. The harder I looked, the deeper became the darkness. My lantern kept hissing with the drops that hit it. Cold water seeped into the straw of my sandals.

When I rested a moment, it felt as if my hands were going to drop off. I worried that I might miss my footing if I started down again. But I had no choice. I had to climb as far down as there was a shaft to climb, or else I'd tumble headfirst and split my skull open. Such thoughts gave me strength, somehow, to climb to the bottom. I still can't figure out where that strength came from. It didn't arrive all at once, but gradually, seeping into my arms and belly and legs, so that I was clearly aware of its coming. The same sort of thing happens when you're studying all night for an exam. Exhausted, you doze for a few seconds, and when you suddenly wake up, you're good for another five or six pages. Studying like this, you may not know what you've read, but you manage to read through it. In the same way, I couldn't have declared with certainty that I had climbed down, but I was definitely there. And just as you know for sure how many pages of a book you have prepared even though you may have forgotten its contents, I knew precisely how many ladders I had come down. Fifteen. I had reached the bottom of a fifteen-ladder climb, and still there was no sign of Hatsu, I was shocked to discover. Fortunately, however, there was only one way to go. I scrambled through the narrow opening and there, at last, was Hatsu. Without indulging in his usual tough talk, he asked simply, "How you doin'? Rough, huh?"

It had, indeed, been rough, and I told him so. He then encouraged me to make a further effort.

"We're almost there. Whaddya say?"

"More ladders?" I asked.

He laughed. "No, no more ladders. Don't worry." And he gave me a kindly smile.

As long as I had made it this far, I might as well press onward, I decided, falling in behind Hatsu—downward again. The farther down we went, the more water there was on the tunnel floor. Each step made a splash. The lanterns revealed a sheet of grayish water on the path, as when the sewage ditches in Shitaya overflow. And the water was *cold*. The skin between my toes felt as if it were being cut. It was a relief each time I lifted a foot, but then I had to plunge it down into the unbroken waters again. With one foot up, I wanted to go on standing there like a heron. I had to put it down, of course, and when I did, the splash of my sandal bottom against the water raised waves like fish scales. No sooner did they sparkle in the light of the lantern than they disappeared. The calm surface was broken again with my next step. More glittering fish scales. As I advanced deeper and deeper into the earth like this, the water level rose. Telling myself—with no justification whatever—that all I had to do was make it through this spot and I'd be on dry land, I rounded a bend and the water suddenly rose from my ankles to my shins. I forged on, hoping the next curve would do it, but, turning to the right, there was a sudden drop and I was up to my knees. Every move made a big sloshing sound. My knees left wakes of whirling eddies, and these rose gradually higher up my thighs. I knew my life was in danger. Something was wrong. Something was causing the water to rise like this, and any minute now the whole mine was going to fill up. Such thoughts sent a chill from my hips to my belly. But Hatsu plowed on through the muddy water, absolutely unperturbed.

"Are we all right?" I asked from behind, but Hatsu went on sloshing through the water without answering. To me, it seemed impossible for anyone to work in water like this, copper mine or otherwise. This water sloshing around could only mean that something had gone wrong or that I had been led into an abandoned tunnel—a disaster in either case, I feared, and I was about to ask Hatsu about it again when the water came up to my hips. This was more than I could take.

"Are we going on?" I called out to Hatsu. My voice did not sound as it would have in asking an ordinary question. My very life had practically come flying out of my mouth from an excess of fear for my own well-being. Since I was still enough in possession of myself to worry what Hatsu would think of me, though, my voice had come out not as a simple, amorphous scream, but disguised as a fearful question. Not even Hatsu could ignore such a sound. Hip-deep in water, he stopped and turned toward me, holding his lantern aloft. Peering through the darkness, I saw that his brows were knit with concern and his lips were smiling.

"What's the matter?" he said. "Give up?"

"No, it's just this water . . ." I looked down fearfully, but he was not the least bit impressed. He was still smiling, like a man happily lifting up his kimono skirts to cross a flooded street. This did much to clear up my doubts, but the fundamental cowardice remained, and just to make sure, I asked again, "Are we all right, do you think?"

Hatsu looked more amused than ever, but finally he became serious. "This is Tunnel 8. The bottom. There's always water here, nothing to be scared of. Come on, follow me."

He was not going to humor me. All I could do was follow after him, wet to the crotch. In this dark tunnel, I was (to use a daring metaphor) soaked in darkness from head to foot. Which was bad enough in itself, but in addition I was soaked in real water—water the color of the tunnel, which made me feel twice as bad. And the water had been rising slowly from ankle depth. Now it was up to my hips, and every move I made kicked up waves that wet me higher than the actual water level. Not only did the wet spots not dry, the waves sometimes leapt higher still, sending chills through me higher and higher until they reached my belly. Chilled from the top down by the tunnel and from the bottom up by the water, I trailed after my guide through this unfamiliar territory like a slug. Then, from the right, more water came flowing from a deep, cave-like opening. Inside the cave there echoed a clanging sound. A work site, no doubt.

Standing before the opening, Hatsu said, "Hear that? Somebody's working way down here at the bottom. Think you can do it?"

Bending over until my chest touched the water, I peered into the cave. Over everything hung a dull glow—if I can call it a glow. Actually, it was more like a vague smudge of something that was left after a weak, tiny little light had been stretched and pulled and pulled and stretched so far beyond its power to illuminate that whatever light it had to give off was overwhelmed by the darkness. The clanging sound came from a point where an object somewhat blacker than its surroundings clung to the rock wall at an angle. The sound scattered against the walls of the cave in a futile search for an escape route, rebounded from the surface of the water and, coalescing, emerged from the mouth of the cave. Water, too, emerged from the cave. There was a degree of brightness to the water, in contrast to the absolute darkness of the cave ceiling.

"Want to go in?" asked Hatsu.

The cold sent a shudder through me.

"Not really," I said.

"All right. Never mind. *Today.*"

Adding this proviso, he looked hard at me. I, of course, was hooked.

"You mean I have to start working here tomorrow? How long do I—how long do you have to stay in the water when you work here?"

"Hmmm," replied Hatsu, thinking. "There's three shifts goin' 'round the clock . . ."

Which meant that each shift lasted eight hours. I turned my gaze on the black water.

"It's all right," he said. "Don't worry."

Now, all of a sudden, he was trying to comfort me. He was probably feeling sorry for me.

"But," I protested, "you have to work eight hours in this place."

"Well, sure, you've got to put your time in. But *you* don't have to worry."

"Why's that?"

"Look, I'm tellin' you it's all right."

He started walking. I followed him in silence. After a few sloshes, he suddenly whirled around.

"New guys only work in Tunnel 2 or 3. The ones who come down here are the guys who really know their way around."

He flashed me a grin and I grinned back.

"Feel better?"

The best I could do was say that I did. He seemed very pleased with himself. Suddenly the water receded to knee level. With my toes, I could feel that there were steps in the earth. I started counting them, and by the time I reached three, the water had come down to my ankles. Then the ground leveled out. I was overjoyed that we had reached high ground so quickly. My happiness increased by leaps and bounds as each turn led to drier land. Finally, after all the sloshing and splashing, we reached a spot where there was not so much as a drip. Hatsu asked if I wanted to see some machinery. When he explained that he was talking about the contraptions that collected the ore thrown down the several pits, sent it up to Tunnel 1, and hauled it out of the mine in electric cars, I begged off. No doubt this machinery moved in fascinating ways, but I had no desire to look at things that I would have nothing to do with after today. If I was not going to look at the machinery, that meant my tour of the mine was pretty much over. My guide Hatsu then informed me that it was time to go back. He chose a relatively dry route for our return trip. Not even he needed more than one soaking to the waist, it seemed. Still, there was a fifty-foot stretch in which the water reached

our calves. At this point I began to fear that we had come to the
deep spot again, and I dragged my frozen feet along, recalling how,
the first time through, I had felt as if my navel were turning to ice,
and expecting it to happen again at any moment. Instead, the farther we went, the shallower the water became—and the lighter my
steps. Finally we reached another dry passage.

"Is that all?" I asked, but Hatsu only laughed. I was in good spirits, too, at that point, but soon we came to the bottom of those endless ladders. I could have stood anything else—even water up to the
chest. But those ladders! At least on the way back, if I could, I
wanted to avoid them. And yet, undeniably, there we were, in that
very spot. Someone had once told me the story of the plank road of
Szechwan.* These ladders were those planks dangling in space, all
hint of the original incline having been snatched away. At this point
my legs refused to move. It felt like a sudden attack of beriberi, and
when that happened, something pulled at the seat of my pants.
Some readers might think that it was Hatsu who pulled me, but
they'd be wrong. It was just a feeling I had. If forced to describe it, I
might say I was like an old man bent over with lumbago. I just
couldn't straighten up. Of course, I wasn't ready to declare that I
was under the spell of the dangling plank road, though it's true that
I had been gradually relaxing the intensity of my efforts in response
to Hatsu's sympathetic attitude. Whatever. I just couldn't walk
anymore.

Observing my condition, Hatsu said, "Can't walk, huh? Better
take a break till you straighten out. I'll be back soon. Gonna go see
somebody."

With that, he slipped into the darkness and was gone.

Now I was alone. I plopped down on my backside. The advan-
tages of a seat-pad become obvious at times like this. At least I
didn't have to worry about hurting myself on the rocks or dirtying
my clothes in the mud—one ray of happiness amid the darkness of
despair. I leaned my stiffly bent back against the rock wall. This was
the most I was willing to do by way of making the horizontal vertical. In this posture, I stared at the opposite wall. Either my mind
stopped working because my body wasn't moving or my body took

---

*A notoriously steep road located in a mountainous province of western China
bordering on Tibet. Ladder-like planks were installed to assist travelers over the
worst terrain.

it easy because my mind was relaxed, or maybe a little of both, but in any case everything went fuzzy for a while, during which I seem to have been drifting between life and death. At first I had a strong desire to breathe the daylight air, if only a single cubic foot of it, but gradually my mind went dark. With that, I became oblivious to the darkness of the mine. The darkness of the mine, the darkness of my mind: the two became one and indivisible. I did not sleep, however. Of that I'm sure. In the stillness, my consciousness became highly attenuated, that's all. But even this attenuated consciousness was one part real world in ten parts water. As diluted as it became, it never quite disappeared. It was like talking to someone on the telephone instead of face-to-face, or possibly a little less distinct than that. For me, in whose eyes the sun of the world of men had become too intense; for me, who could stay neither in Tokyo nor the countryside; for me, who sorely needed a dose of something that would break the fever of my agony; for me, who had above all to disperse the excessive stimuli that had swarmed through the strands of my nervous system to their outermost ends; for me, having my consciousness sink beneath the surface like this was an overwhelming need, a desire, an ideal. It was a far more elevated paradise than the miner's life I had imagined to myself as I had tramped along the road behind Chōzō. If fleeing was the first stop on the way toward letting myself die, this realm I had entered was the—I don't know which stop, but it was a station not far from the end of the line. Having been thrust so unexpectedly to the verge of death in the brief interval during which I was left alone by Hatsu, I felt—well, how do you think I felt? Frankly, I was happy. Set adrift, however, amidst a consciousness that had been diluted in ten parts water, this sense of happiness did not strike me with the same intensity as other emotional ties with the real world. It, too, was extremely diluted. But it was definitely there. No one who has not lost consciousness can miss an awareness that he is happy. My mental state was different from impaired psychological phenomena in which the range of mental activity has been narrowed down. My mind was still free to pursue the full range of its activities at will. Only the intensity of those activities had diminished, the single difference between my usual self and myself at this time being one of degree. In this palest interval of life, there continued to exist a pale happiness.

Had this state continued for an hour, I would have been satisfied for an hour. Had it gone on for a day, I'm sure I would have been satisfied for a day. Indeed, I probably would have been happy if it had continued for a hundred years. But—and here I encountered yet another new mental activity.

By which I mean that this state did not remain stationary as I would have wished. It began to move, like the flame of a lantern that is running out of oil. Expressing levels of consciousness in terms of numbers, I might say that what normally functioned at a level of ten had come down to five. After a short while, it had dropped to four. Then three. Eventually, it would have to go to zero. I was aware of the gradual dilution of happiness that accompanied this process, but only with the gradually diminishing degree of awareness that also accompanied this process. The happiness itself was doubtless still happiness. Thus, logically speaking, however much my consciousness might decrease, I should not have been capable of thinking myself anything other than happy and satisfied. Nevertheless, the moment my descending consciousness was about to strike zero, something leapt out of the darkness. What leapt out was the thought, "You're going to die!" This was followed closely by another thought: "You can't let that happen!" The moment it struck me, I yanked my eyes open.

My feet were ready to drop off. The blood between my knees and hips was starting to freeze. My belly felt as if it were full of cold water or something. Only from the chest up did I feel human. When I opened my eyes and thought about what had just happened, there seemed to be an orderly connection until "You're going to die! You can't let that happen!" following which there was a sudden break. After the break had come the act of opening my eyes. In other words, I had reached a turning point in my life with "You're going to die!" the very first act I followed it with being the opening of my eyes, and the two things were totally unconnected. Yet they were totally connected, the proof of which was the fact that, when I opened my eyes and looked at my surroundings, the shout "You're going to die!" and so forth was echoing in my ears. I could still hear it. I say there was a "shout" in my "ears," but only because there is no other way to describe it. Not that this was something that needed describing. I was convinced that there really was someone who had warned me, "You're going to die," etc. Of course there was no one there, nor could there have been. Not a person, at least. By which I am not pointing to a god. I hate gods. I suppose what happened was I panicked and cried out to myself in my own mind, but I had never dreamed that human beings were so worried about death. This should make suicide an impossibility. The soul works differently at such times. You're controlled by your instincts but you're completely unaware of it. This is something we ought to be on guard against. One interpretation of an experience like mine might be that I had been saved by a god. Another might be that the spirit of someone—most often a lover, in these cases—had been watching over me. Considering how young I was (and in love with myself), I'm rather impressed that I didn't interpret the voice as having come from Tsuyako or Sumie. I was born without that poetic streak, I guess.

All of a sudden, Hatsu was back. The moment I looked at him, my consciousness at last returned to clarity. Everything came back to me at once: that I had now to climb the dangling plank road, that tomorrow I would have to begin clanging with hammer and chisel, that there would be those other things to deal with—the mud-rice, the bedbugs, the jangle, the "goddesses," and, last of all, the fact of my own degeneracy.

"Feelin' better?" Hatsu asked.

"Yes. A little, I think."

"Let's get you up, then."

I thanked him and, standing there, watched Hatsu latch onto a rung and vigorously set one foot on the ladder.

"Don't forget," he said, looking back at me, "the climb's gonna be a little tough." With that, he started up.

A chill of desolation ran through me as I watched him go. He climbed like a monkey. There was no sign that he would be taking it easy for me. Afraid that I'd be abandoned again if I didn't follow quickly, I forced myself up. Two or three steps were all it took for me to appreciate the truth of Hatsu's warning. The climb was very tough. And not just because I was exhausted. On the way down, you leaned a little forward, which allowed the ladder to support some of the weight of your upper body. Climbing up, however, it was just the opposite. You tended to lean back. Since you had to support the extra weight entirely with your hands, each rung took its toll on the upper arms and shoulders, the sum total falling upon the hands and fingers. As I mentioned earlier, the rungs were slippery. Climbing up even one ladder was no mean feat. And there were fifteen of them. Hatsu had disappeared long before. All I had to do was let go, and I would tumble headfirst through the pitch darkness. If I hung on with all my might, my arms would simply pull out of their sockets. Midway up the seventh ladder, I was breathing flames and feeling the immense hardships of manual labor. My eyes were full of hot tears.

I tried bringing my upper and lower eyelids together two or three times, but my vision remained blurred. I couldn't even manage a clear view of the rock wall, less than six inches from my face. I thought of rubbing my eyes with the backs of my hands, but unfortunately both were occupied at the time. I became angry and frustrated. How had I ever sunk so low as to be playing these monkey games, I wondered. Resisting the backward pull, I slumped against the ladder as best I could and let it take as much of my weight as possible. In this position, I began to think. (Or to rest, it might be more accurate to say.) Maybe I just stopped climbing. In any case, I didn't move. I *couldn't* move. I stood there, rigid. I was unaware of the hissing of the lantern or the seeping of water into my sandals. I had no sense of how many minutes passed by. Then my eyes filled again with hot tears. Unusually clear though my mind was, my eyes were clouded over. No amount of blinking seemed to help. It was as if my eyes were wide open in hot water. A sodden gloom had come over me, which rose to frustration and then to rage, increasing in fury but incapable of being translated into action. Gritting my teeth, I gave the rung I was holding several shakes. Or tried to. It didn't move, of course. Maybe I should let go, I thought. The best thing would be to end this quickly—plunge down headfirst and smash myself to bits. The urge to die was overwhelming. The very same person who, at the bottom of the ladders, had been determined to avoid death at all cost, now, halfway up, was ready to die without question. Of all the psychological shifts I have experienced in my life, this one was the most memorable. Since I'm not a psychologist, I don't know how best to explain this kind of change, but it seems to me that the psychologists are the very ones who are short on practical experience, so I'd just like to set down my own humble view of the matter, with all its inaccuracies, for what it's worth.

When I had first sat down to rest on my seat-pad, my only thought had been just that—to rest. My mind had been at ease. Stimuli were at a minimum. As I remained leaning against the tunnel wall in such a state, that state had progressed smoothly, and in the natural course of things, my consciousness had begun to drift away. My soul had begun to sink. The course of mental activity in such cases is fixed. Normally, it will take off from the positive and proceed gradually toward the negative. When this normal course has been exhausted, however, and the soul is on the verge of the dead end, it can function in one of two ways. The first is to raise its sail into the wind and slip straight into the depths. That's it: you die. The second is to leap back before the final curtain. Having advanced toward the negative, the soul suddenly reverses itself and returns toward the positive. Then your grasp on life becomes suddenly firm. What I had experienced beneath the ladders was this second possibility. Having approached the nearer shore of the Three-Channeled River,* unperturbed by the nearness of death, my soul had eliminated the bother of retracing its steps by leaping directly into the midst of the real world. I call this the Experience of Turning from Death and Returning to Life.

On my way up the ladders, however, I encountered precisely the opposite phenomenon. I had to climb in pursuit of Hatsu, but he had long since disappeared. My head urged me upward, my heart screamed danger, and my hands would not let go. I was lower than a monkey. Miserable. In pain. The whole thing was torture. The intensity of my self-awareness was gradually approaching fever pitch. In this case, the course of mental activity was to rise from negative to positive. When such a state goes on to develop to the fullest intensity, again you have two functions as a result, one of which I find especially interesting—namely, that miraculous somersault taken by the soul from the zenith of the positive to the nadir of the negative. What I'm talking about here, to put it more plainly, is that phenomenon of resolving to discard one's life at the very moment it reaches its greatest clarity. I call this the Function of Entering Death through Life. This may sound like a contradiction, but in actual practice, as an inherent function of the soul, it occurs with surprising natural-

---

*Buddhism's River Styx. The departed soul crossed this river on the way to hell, his actions on earth determining which of the three crossings, from shallow to deep, was the appropriate one for him.

ness. Enough theory, here's proof. Those who die in a burst of passion go cleanly to their deaths, but those who cower in the face of death never seem to accept it fully. Nor do I have to look to others for a good example. There's me. When, on the ladder, I was feeling angry and ready to die, I was not the least bit afraid of releasing my grip. And no, of course the usual pang of fear did *not* occur. But the moment I was about to let go and die, I became aware of yet another strange psychological phenomenon.

By nature, I'm not the sort of person you'd encounter in a novel, but I was still young back then, and whenever the thought of suicide popped into my head, it was always as a kind of spectacle to be staged for others. I would use a pistol or dagger and die magnificently, in a manner that would elicit praise. I often thought of taking the famous suicide leap at Kegon Falls. But quietly hanging myself in a toilet or storage shed? No, this I rejected as beneath me. As I stood on the ladder, this same old vanity suddenly poked its head out. Don't ask me where it poked its head out *from*, but it did— probably because there was room enough for it to do so. Which means that, as solemn as my determination may have been, it was still not all that urgent. On the other hand, if my vanity could put in an appearance at the very moment of firmest resolve, when my hands were beginning to leave the rungs, it must have had pretty deep roots. Not that there was such a great difference between my vanity and the desire to be enshrined in bronze after death. It was not so amazing as to set me apart from ordinary human beings. Given the particular time and place, however, it does seem to have been something of a luxury. Thanks to this little extravagance, to this weakness that surfaced at the decisive moment, I abandoned my impulsive rush to death and have prolonged my life (such as it is) to this day.

Here, then, is how it went. Having decided to die, I let my body drop back slightly and was loosening my grip when it occurred to me that, as long as I was going to die anyway, I could do better than to die in this place. A command (which sounds funny, but it was just like a command) echoed in my head: "Wait! Wait! Get out of here and go to Kegon Falls!" My loosening grip tightened. My clouded eyes grew suddenly clear. My lantern was burning. Above me, the mud-smeared ladders continued up into the darkness. I had to climb them. If I failed partway up, my death would be pointless. To tumble down like a piece of ore in the dark hole, where there was not another creature, shut off from the light of day, never to be missed (not even by my guide, Hatsu), or, if found, to be reviled by those half-beast–half-human miners—no, I could not let that happen! I must complete the climb! My lantern was burning. The ladders continued up. Beyond the ladders were the long tunnels of the mine. Beyond the mine, the sun was shining. Open fields; high mountains; and, beyond them, Kegon Falls. I had to climb, no matter what!

I stretched my left hand out above my head, gripping the slimy rung so hard my fingers left their imprint on it. I straightened my soggy torso and, simultaneously, lifted my right foot. The light of the lantern began to move upward through the dark shaft, illuminating layer after layer. Each rung my feet left behind slowly fell away into the darkness. Each breath I expelled struck the black wall in front of me. My breath was hot, and at times it shone white. I clamped my mouth shut, and the air rushed noisily through my nostrils. Still the ladders did not end. Water dripped down from the lip above. I would give the lantern a shake, and as an arc of light grazed the cliff wall, the flame would hiss and flicker, sending up a ribbon of smoke once again when the lantern came to rest. Again I would shake it, and again the light would move at an angle, falling on the blank wall beside the foot-wide ladder. The sight of its emptiness sent a shiver through me. My eyes spun. I closed them and climbed. No flame, no wall—just darkness. Hands and legs moving. Groping to live. Living to climb. To live was to climb, to climb was to live. And still the ladders were there above me.

After that, I was all but in a trance. Whether I managed to climb on my own or through some divine assistance, I can't really say. When I suddenly realized that I had climbed as far as I could and there were no more rungs for me to grasp, I plopped down on the tunnel floor.

Hatsu, who had been nervously awaiting my arrival, welcomed me joyfully. "What happened? You made it! You took so long, I thought maybe you got killed. I was thinkin' about goin' to check, but it woulda been too creepy alone. Anyhow, you made it. Good boy!" He seemed pretty worried, waiting up here.

I simply replied, "I felt a little sick, so I rested halfway up."

"Sick? You musta had a tough time. Whaddya mean, 'halfway up?' Halfway up the ladders?"

"That's it."

"Well, I guess you can't work tomorrow."

When I heard that, I thought to myself: "To hell with you! I'm finished crawling through mole holes. I may not look it, but beautiful girls have fallen in love with me. When I get out of this place, I'm going straight to Kegon Falls. And I'll die like a hero. I can't stand to spend another minute with an animal like you!"

But when I spoke to Hatsu, I said simply, "If you're ready, let's go."

He looked at me suspiciously. "Go?" he said. "You're feelin' spunky!"

"What the hell do you think I am, a stupid animal like you?" I wanted to say, but all that came out was "Yes, I am."

Hatsu continued to dawdle about. And he did it in a way that implied more contempt for me than surprise.

"You sure you're OK?" he asked. "This is nothin' to joke about. You look pale."

"All right, then," I said, "I'll go first." And I started off in a huff.

"Hey, wait up, you can't do that!" he cried. "You come after me!"

"Oh, really?"

"Sure, you know what I mean, wise guy. *I'm* guiding *you*. You don't go ahead of me."

All but pushing me aside, he took the lead. As soon as he was in front, he sped up. Bending at the waist, crawling on all fours, twisting sideways, ducking just his head—the shape of the tunnel had him moving every which way. And he did it with tremendous speed, as if he had been born in the earth and educated in a copper vein. Not to be outdone, I took off after him, cursing him to myself for charging ahead in such a fit of temper, but mere determination was not enough. I clattered along after him, left, right, up, down, but after five or six bends in the tunnel, I lost sight of him. Then he started singing some kind of song, but all I could catch was "la la la la la." The man himself was nowhere to be seen, but his voice reverberated throughout the tunnel, bouncing back as if trapped in the earth. "He's just doing it out of spite," I thought. "I'll show him! I'll catch up with him!" I gave it all I had at first, stooping and crawling along, but Hatsu's song drew farther and farther away. I gave up any hope of catching him and decided, instead, to continue on with the "la la la la la" as my guide. That worked fairly well at first, but I began to lose track of the song, too, and by the time it faded out completely, I was, of course, lost. Had there been only one path to follow, I would have damn well found my own way to the sunlight, and to hell with Hatsu, but they'd been scraping this mine out of the earth for so many years now it had tunnels opening every which way like some ground-spider's stronghold. All I had to do was walk into the wrong one and I'd be up to my waist in water again or come out to the hanging planks. I had to be careful.

I stood still in the darkness, thinking, and staring at the lantern flame. I had gone all the way down to Tunnel 8; to get back I'd have to climb up to where the electric train ran. Any tunnel would be all right, I assumed, as long as it went up. I would turn back if I entered one that went down. And if I wandered around, I'd eventually come to one of the work sites. Then I'd ask a miner the way. Having decided this much, I went stumbling along at random, unable to tell north from south, east from west. In my frenzy, I grew short of breath, but at least, with all the rushing around, my legs were no longer cold. Still, I couldn't find my way out. I seemed to be tracing the same route back and forth. In my frustration, I felt like smashing my head against the wall and splitting it wide open. Which "it" would split—my head or the wall? My head, of course, but I was in such a rage that I think the wall might have split open a little, too. The more I walked, the more the ceiling became a pain. The walls on either side of me were a pain. The terraces beneath my straw sandals were a pain. The greatest pain of all was this whole damn mine that had me trapped and wouldn't let me go. I'd slam my head against one part of this great pain and at least put a crack in it. And though I didn't actually do it, I kept thinking about doing it because I wanted to go to Kegon Falls as quickly as possible. I was still in the midst of these gyrations when a lone digger appeared up ahead. He was holding one of those straw winnowing baskets in his arms and tottering in my direction, lantern swaying, apparently on his way to the pit with chunks of ore. My heart leapt with joy when I saw his light. Certain now that I'd be all right, I approached him with new courage—not that I had to go very far to approach him, since he was also moving toward me. When our two lanterns came within

137

six feet of each other, I looked at the digger in anticipation. He was an absolute paleface—extreme even down here in the mine, let alone if you got him up in the light. I refused to speak to him. To think that a person like this might try to rib me or embarrass me, I could never accept the idea of asking him the way. I'd get out of here alone if it killed me. I passed him by, declaring to him deep in my guts, "I haven't fallen so low that I'd talk to a piece of shit like you!" Unaware of all this, of course, he passed me by in silence. The way ahead became dark now that there was only one lantern. My frustration mounted, but that didn't help me find the way. I was surrounded by paths that led only to more paths. Left, right, straight ahead: I tried them all without success. I was ready to give up any hope of ever finding my way out when, just ahead of me, I heard clanging. Half a dozen paces later the tunnel ran into a wall and turned left. There I found a small work site with a single miner hammering away at his chisel. Each blow brought a shower of ore from the wall. Beside him stood a bale. It was the same size as the one I had seen earlier being thrown into the pit, and it was crammed full of ore, ready for a digger to come and lug it off. I was not going to miss this chance to ask the way, I decided, but the man was completely absorbed in his hammering, and I couldn't really see his face. This seemed like a good chance for a rest, and the bale would make a perfect stool. I dropped down onto it, seat-pad first. Suddenly the hammering stopped. The miner's shadow grew long and tall. He was still holding the chisel in place.

"What the hell are you doing?"

His penetrating voice echoed through the tunnel and slammed into my ears. The tall shadow came toward me with great strides.

He was a long-legged, barrel-chested, solidly built man. His face was small in proportion to his height. At a point where I could make him out fairly clearly, he came to a halt, looking down at me, his jaw set, his large eyes staring at me from beneath double-folded lids. He had a strong, straight nose and a dark, ruddy complexion. This was no ordinary miner. His words shot out at me.

"You're a new one."

"That's right."

By the time I spoke, my buttocks had risen from the bale. The closer he came, the more he frightened me. Until this moment, I had been despising the whole ten-thousand-plus of them as a pack of animals; I had sworn an oath to myself to die and leave the world behind. But neither of these truths prevented me from being frightened when this miner approached me with his big strides. Still, when he spoke to me again, it reassured me somewhat.

"What're you doing wandering around here? You lost?"

I could tell from his tone of voice that he had looked me over and knew I had not intended anything by sitting on his bale of ore.

"Well, actually, I arrived yesterday and I'm down here looking at the mine."

"Alone?"

"No, the boss sent somebody with me . . ."

"I thought so. You can't get in here alone. Where is he, this guide of yours?"

"He went out ahead of me."

"Just like that? He left you by yourself?"

"Well, I guess so."

"That's a hell of a thing to do to somebody! Anyway, don't worry, I'll show you how to get out of here. Just wait."

With that, he started clanging the hammer and chisel again. I did as I was told and waited. Having met this man, I no longer felt like finding the way out by myself. My determination to show them I could get out alone if it killed me had suddenly evaporated. I was aware of the change, but I didn't feel particularly ashamed. It didn't matter, I thought, because I had never announced my intention to anyone. Since then, I have always done things that I need not have done or should not have done simply because I have announced my intention of doing them to others. There's a big difference between saying and not saying what you're going to do. After a while the clanging stopped. The miner came over to me and sat down cross-legged.

"Just wait," he said, taking out a tobacco pouch, "I'm going to have a smoke."

The pouch was a brownish thing, made of some kind of leather or paper. He carried it tucked in the waistband of his pants under his jacket. With obvious relish, he inhaled the smoke to the bottom of his lungs, and while he was releasing it through his nose, he tapped the short stem of his pipe with his pipe holder. I saw a tiny shower of sparks leap from the metal pipe bowl and fall to the toe of his sandal, where the sparks were extinguished. The miner blew into his empty pipe. From the bowl emerged a puff of smoke that had been trapped in the stem. Only now did he speak to me.

"Where are you from? What'd you come to a place like this for? You look kind of frail—I'll bet you've never worked before. Why are you here?"

"It's true, I've never had a job. I came here because . . . something happened . . ."

That was as far as I wanted to go. I was annoyed by all his questions and didn't bother to tell him that I'd be leaving the mine, much less that I intended to die. But talking with him was different from talking with the others. I wasn't keeping up a respectful front while inwardly despising him as an animal. I simply didn't spill out everything that was on my mind. What I did tell him, I said with sincerity and honesty. The respect came from within. The miner stared silently for a while at the bowl of his pipe. Then he pressed in another wad of tobacco. When the smoke started streaming from his nose, he opened his mouth.

What most surprised me when he began to speak was the extent of his education—the refined sentiments, the insight, the intensity, the superior vocabulary. He employed difficult expressions of a sort that a miner could never hope to know, and he did so with the ease and naturalness of one who had been using such words as an everyday part of his home life until the day before. Even now the sight of him comes back to me vividly. With his big eyes wide open and fixed on me, his head thrust a little forward, the knuckles of one hand pressing against his knee, left shoulder slightly cocked, he spoke to me, grasping his pipe in the fingers of his right hand, his handsome teeth showing now and then from between thin lips. I recall the exact words he chose, the order in which he spoke them, and I have recorded them here without alteration (though there's nothing I can do about his tone of voice):

"You know what they say, 'The older the wiser.' I may be engaged in this lowly profession, but I want you to take what I have to say as good advice from someone older and wiser. Youth is an emotional time of life—how well I remember! And in that time of life, a young man tends to make mistakes. It's true for you, I'm sure. It certainly was for me. It's true for everybody. I understand what you're going through. I don't know how much your circumstances differ from mine, but believe me, I understand. I'm not going to criticize you. I

sympathize with you. I know you've got your reasons. If I were in a
position to offer you advice, I'd listen to your story, but I'll never be
able to leave this hole. It wouldn't do you any good to tell me. You
know, I was a—"

When he cut himself short at this point, I noticed that his eyes
were shining a little strangely. Some powerful feeling had obviously
taken hold of him. Whether this was because of what he had just
told me—that he would "never be able to leave this hole"—or because of what he was about to say, I couldn't tell. But his eyes were
undeniably strange. And they were focused on me with penetrating
intensity. Beneath that intensity, there was something—call it nostalgia, call it melancholy—something warm and appealing. Now, in
this black hole, humanity was this miner, and this miner was his
eyes. Suddenly my entire spirit was drawn into them, and I absorbed his every word. He began again, as he had before the pause:

"I was a student once, too. I've been educated beyond high school.
But when I was twenty-three, I became involved with a woman
and—I'm not going to go into detail, but because of this I committed a terrible crime. By the time I realized what I had done, it
was too late. There was no place left for me in society. I hadn't committed this crime lightly. Circumstances had forced me into it. But
society is a coldhearted master. Keep your sins hidden and it for-
gives you, but bring them out into the open and it will never let you
go. I'm an honest, straightforward sort of person. I don't like the
twisted and false. So, yes, I had sinned, but having done so, there
was nothing I could do but face the fact. I had to abandon my studies, cast aside all hope of distinguishing myself. My life was ruined.
It was a painful truth, but an immovable one. And in addition, the
hand of justice was reaching out for me."

(I don't know how consciously he employed this literate phrase-
ology, but he expressly referred to "the hand of justice.")

"Still, I was not convinced that I was the guilty one. I couldn't
blindly accept punishment. That kind of thing is just not in my nature. So I ran. As far as I could. I ended up here and buried myself in
the hole. For six years now, I haven't seen the light of the sun. Every
day I spend swinging the hammer. Six whole years of nothing but
hammering. Next year will be the seventh, and it'll be safe for me to
leave the hole. But I won't leave. I can't leave. The hand of justice
can't touch me, but I won't leave. What would be the use? Even if I

141

could go back to the world, the deeds I committed there wouldn't go away. I still carry the past around in my guts. And you—it's the same with you, isn't it? You still carry the past around in your guts, don't you?"

His question took me off guard. I had no ready-made answer for him. Inside my guts was anything but the "past." It was more like the present, including everything from over a year ago to the day before yesterday. I strongly considered confessing all my secrets to this man, opening myself up to him. But he seemed almost determined to prevent that as he continued his story.

"I've seen every dirty thing there is to see about men in the six years I've lived here. But still I don't feel like getting out. No matter how angry it makes me, how sick to my stomach, I don't want to leave. Back in society—that place where the sun shines—there are far more painful things than what I have here. That's what keeps me going. I know this place is dark and cramped, and that's enough for me. Now my body stinks of copper and it can't go a day without the smell of an oil lamp. But—but that's *me* I'm talking about, not you. We mustn't let this happen to you. It's a terrible thing for a living human being to take on the smell of copper. We can't let that happen. I don't care what great decision brought you here, what your purpose in coming here may be. All it takes is a couple of days here for decisions and purposes to be snuffed out. That's where the real pity lies, the shame—which may be all right for some bastard without ideals who doesn't know how to do anything else but use a hammer and chisel. But somebody like you—you were in school, I suppose. Where was that? Oh, never mind, it doesn't really matter. And you're young. Too young for the hole. This is a place for human trash. It's a cemetery. A place where human beings are buried alive. A trap. And once you're caught in it, you never get out, no matter how fine a man you are. You didn't know that, I'm sure, and you probably let some procurer talk you into coming here. This makes me very sad for your sake. It's a terrible thing to cause the degeneracy of an individual human being. Just killing him would be less of a crime. The degenerate goes on to cause harm, to hurt others. I know what I'm talking about because that's just what I have done. It's the only thing I *can* do—now. And all the screaming and crying in the world isn't going to change that. Which is why you have to get out of here fast. For the others. It's not just you who'll suffer if you become degenerate . . . Tell me, are your parents living?"

I answered simply that they were.

"All the more reason for you to get out. And you're a Japanese, aren't you?"

I did not reply.

"If you're a Japanese, you should take a profession that will benefit Japan. For a man of learning to become a miner is a great loss to the nation. That's why you should get out now. If you're from Tokyo, go back to Tokyo. And do something decent—something that's right for you and good for the country. You simply must not stay here. If you don't have the fare, I'll give it to you. So get out. Go home. You understand what I'm trying to tell you. I'm in the Yamanaka Gang. Just come to the Yamanaka Gang and ask for Yasu. Be sure to come. I'll see to it that you have your fare."

With that, Yasu finished speaking. I had been told that there were ten thousand miners in this place, and I had come to the conclusion that every last one of them was a monster, an animal without the slightest trace of intelligence or human feeling. For me to have met Yasu at a time like this was something right out of a novel. Snow in midsummer would have seemed less of a miracle to me than my having been the recipient of Yasu's lecture in the mine. Sure, I had heard "It's always darkest before the dawn," and I knew the old sayings about Buddha swooping down to save you from hell, and adversity being the surest guide to salvation, and these had left me with the vague impression that, if I were in deep trouble, someone would show up to save me, thus adding a touch of drama to situations in which I *had* been in trouble. But this was totally different. I was all the more amazed by this encounter with Yasu because it occurred at the precise moment when seething flames of indignation had permanently branded my heart with the overpowering certainty not only that ten thousand men were brute beasts but that every single one of them was my mortal enemy. Yasu's admonishments struck me with such force that they turned my original intention on its head.

Both of us kept silent for a time. Having said all there was for him to say, Yasu had no further need to speak, but now I had an obligation to make some sort of reply. No. Describing my position as an "obligation" is an affront to Yasu. I wanted desperately to express the gratitude I felt in my heart, and I wanted him to hear some of the thoughts that were going through my head. My nose was stuffed, however, making it impossible for me to speak. Had I tried to force the words out, I felt, they would have come through my nose instead of my mouth. As I struggled with my feelings, the corners of my mouth began to tingle and my nostrils to twitch. Soon, denied an exit, the emotion that clogged my nose and mouth coalesced in my eyes. The lashes became heavy and the lids began to burn. It was a difficult moment for me, and Yasu, too, wore an odd expression on his face. The awkward silence continued as we sat cross-legged on the ground, facing each other. Then, from the neighboring work site, there came the clanging sound of ore being chipped from the rock. Thinking back on it now, I wish I had learned the exact distance beneath the surface of the earth of the place in which Yasu and I faced each other without speaking. Even in the city such chance encounters are rare, let alone in the depths of a mine. Down there two men sat upon a stage, wordlessly gazing into each other's eyes, one bestowing sacred teachings, the other shedding precious tears, both forgotten by the world, by other men, by history, and even by the sun. Of this, who was there to know?

Yasu lit another pipeful. One after another, thick puffs of smoke floated up and melted into the darkness, and before long my voice came back to me.

"I want to thank you for everything you've said. And I agree: this is no place for human beings. Until I met you, I was sure that today would be my first and last day in the mine . . ."

I cut myself short here, unable, of course, to say that I had planned to leave the mine and die.

"All the better," he said with enthusiasm. "You should leave as soon as possible." When I kept silent, he went on, "And don't worry about the money for your fare. I'll raise that."

His repeated offers to pay my fare I took as a sign of good will, but I had not the slightest intention of accepting his money. Nor was this the same as my having declined the boss's offer of charity the day before. I had badly wanted to accept that—so badly that I would have bowed down to the ground for it. But I had forced myself to refuse it when I calculated that it was more to my advantage to become a miner than to accept travel money. No such calcula-

144

tions were involved with Yasu. I simply didn't want to take his money. I ought to have taken it, of course, if I was not going to negate his goodwill, and it would certainly come in handy if I was going to quit the mine, but still I didn't want to accept it. Now that I think the matter over, this feeling seems to have sprung from a sense that it would have been a shameful thing to accept money from a man of such fine character—that my character would stand in a position inferior to his. Since he was such a gentleman, I wanted to be as much of a gentleman as possible, fearing that if I weren't I'd lose face. To accept another's goodwill is gratifying to both parties, but one who accepts money when he has no reason to do so, merely to put himself in an advantageous position, is no better than a beggar. The thought of demonstrating to a man so worthy of respect as Yasu that I was a beggar, that I was in no way superior to a beggar, I found intolerable. The stupidity of youth is counterbalanced by a surprising cleanness.

"I can't accept your money," I said.

Yasu had taken a few more puffs and was just putting his pipe back in its case. "Sorry if I insulted you," he replied, glancing up.

I felt terrible. If he had insisted that I take the money then, I'm sure I would have. Since that time, I have noticed that, when people accept money, they tend to refuse it at first and pocket it later. This is probably just a social form that developed from the psychological state I was then actually experiencing. Being the man he was, Yasu merely apologized, thus saving me from being trapped into following the form.

Yasu immediately turned from the question of my fare to ask, "You *will* be going back to Tokyo, though, won't you?"

My determination to die had dulled somewhat by then, and I felt there was some possibility of my returning home after I had saved enough to pay my way. "I'll give it serious thought," I replied. "I'd like to come to you for advice again soon."

"I see. Well, then, I'll show you the way out."

He thrust his tobacco pouch into his waistband and covered it with the skirt of his jacket. Holding my lantern, I stood up. Yasu led the way. The climb was surprisingly easy. After four or five of those terraced places and two stretches of crawling, we came out to a tunnel with a fairly high ceiling where you could walk upright. We followed the long, curving roadway, climbing to the right. At the top of the slope we suddenly came out to Checkpoint No. 1. When we could see the electric lights shining, Yasu came to a halt.

"I'll leave you here," he said. "That's the checkpoint. Climb to the right from there and you'll come to the tracks. After that, it's one tunnel all the way. I can't go out now, though. It's too early for me. I have to work some more. But I'll be back in the evening. Any time after five. Come and see me if you're free. Watch yourself, now— and goodbye."

Yasu's shadow slipped into the darkness. By the time I had turned to thank him, his lantern had rounded the corner. I found my way to the mine entrance alone and staggered as far as the boiler. Many thoughts crossed my mind on the way. This man called Yasu—what would he be doing now if he had developed his talents in society in the normal way? One thing was certain: he would have risen to far greater heights than a miner. Had society killed Yasu, or had Yasu done something that society could not forgive? It was unthinkable that such a man—so refreshingly honest and straightforward— could have committed some extreme outrage. Perhaps the fault lay not with Yasu but with society. Being so young, I had only the haziest notion of what "society" was in the first place, but I felt sure that any society that would expel a man like Yasu could not be worth very much. Maybe because I was standing in his corner, I could not bring myself to believe that Yasu had committed a crime for which he had had to run away. What I needed to believe was that society had been at fault; society had killed Yasu. But, as I say, I had no idea what society was. I just assumed it was people. And I had even less idea why people would have killed a good man like Yasu. I more or less concluded that society was at fault, though this didn't make me hate society. It simply caused me to take pity on Yasu. I wished I could take his place. I had come this far on my own initiative, planning to kill myself, and if I changed my mind there was nothing to prevent me from going home. Yasu had been killed by other people, and he had no choice but to live here. Even if he wanted to go home, there was nowhere for him to go. He was by far the more pitiful of the two.

Yasu had called himself a degenerate, and I suppose it is a form of degeneracy for a man who has been the recipient of higher education to become a miner. But it pained me to think that he seemed to mean not only a debasement of social position but a corruption of personal integrity as well. Was Yasu offering up his money to the "goddesses"? Was he shooting dice in the mine? Did he torment sick men by forcing them to watch funeral processions? Had he put up a wife for collateral? No, not Yasu. Of that I was sure. Not a single miner had failed to mock me from the moment of my arrival the day before. Alone among them, Yasu—in the deepest, darkest hole of all—had given full recognition to my individuality, my character. Yasu was doing the work of a miner, but he was not a miner deep in his heart. Despite this, he had said he had become a degenerate, that he would never be able to escape from this state as long as he lived, that his was a living death in the depths of degeneracy. Fully aware of this, he yet continued to live and to work. To live and wield his hammer. To live—and try to save *me*! As long as Yasu was alive, I could not die. To die would be a form of weakness . . .

I had made up my mind. Now, whatever I did, it would be *after* becoming a miner. Hurrying back as quickly as I could, I found Hatsu sitting on a rock, waiting for me, some fifty yards from the boiler. The rain had stopped. The sky was still overcast, but I didn't have to worry anymore about getting wet. There was a breeze blowing down from the mountain. I felt cold but tremendously happy to see the bright, daylight world. As I rushed toward Hatsu in my joy (though still dragging my tired feet), he fixed me with an odd stare and said, "Hey, you found your way out! Pretty good!"

Pretty good, indeed! How could he sit there playing dumb? Assigned to be my guide, he had not only abandoned me but purposely taunted me with that "la la la la la" of his, after which I had run around in circles until I was ready to bash my head against the rocks, when I was saved in the nick of time by Yasu, through whose kindness I had found my way out, only to hear this nonsense from Hatsu. In spite of what he had done, though, he was afraid of the boss, which is why he had been clever enough to wait for me so that we could arrive at the boiler together. When I saw him on his rock, smiling his lame smile, I wanted to let him have it on the head with a gob of spit. I had decided against dying, however, only moments before. For a while, at least, I would have to stay in this place. If I spit on him, we'd have a fight. If we had a fight, I'd lose. And not only that, I'd be thrown into the pit, and my decision against death would be wasted. Which is why I replied, "Oh, I managed one way or another."

This only seemed to increase his puzzlement.

"Good goin'! Did you make it alone?"

Considering my age, I think I handled the answer to this pretty well. All I mean is that my answer didn't work to my disadvantage, nothing more praiseworthy than that. For a nineteen-year-old, though, I think I was rather sly. What I'm proud of is the fact that, while Yasu's name was on the tip of my tongue, I managed to stop myself from saying it. That's a ridiculous thing to be proud of, I know, but here is what was on my mind. Yasu of the Yamanaka Gang was undoubtedly one of the more important miners. If word got around that such a man had kindly taken the trouble to bring me all the way to Checkpoint No. 1, then my assigned guide would lose face. Once it was proven that he had not only abandoned his responsibilities by hurrying out ahead of me but had actually done so with malicious intent, there would be no way for him to maintain his innocence with the boss. And if that happened, he would take his revenge. I would have loved to have the truth come out (I'm no Christian hypocrite restrained by some notion of forgiveness), but revenge would have caused me a lot of trouble. To tell the truth, it was this notion of trouble that restrained me.

"Yes, by asking directions along the way," I replied peaceably.

Hatsu looked both disappointed and relieved. Eventually, he lifted himself from the rock and said, "Let's go see the boss."

He started off, and I followed him without a word. I had met the boss in the boiler the day before, but he lived in another place. It was a two-story house on a patch of land that had been leveled out and stabilized at the corners with rock walls, some fifty feet above the boiler. The house itself was not bad-looking, but it had no trees, no yard, nothing. As with the other buildings, it had a devil thrusting its head out a second-story window. We approached the front door and Hatsu called his greetings. A downstairs window rattled open and the boss showed his face. He had obviously been lounging around in his dotera and knit undershirt, which he didn't bother to change for us.

"Oh, you're back, I see. Thanks, Hatsu. Go take a load off."

Hatsu disappeared without a moment's delay, leaving me alone with the boss, who spoke to me from the window while I stood outside.

"How was it?"

"I got a good look."

"How far down did you go?"

"Tunnel 8."

"Tunnel 8?! Well, now! See how awful the mine is? I don't suppose—" he began to say, leaning toward me just a bit.

"I'd like to stay," I said. "Even so."

"Even so," he echoed, looking hard at me for some time as I stood before him without speaking. The head in the upstairs window was still there. In fact, it had been joined by two others. I could hardly stand to look at them. A shudder ran through me to think that I would be surrounded by such faces when I got back to the boiler. For all that, I was determined to stay. I would stay no matter what I had to put up with—though this didn't prevent me from feeling sorry for myself when I glanced upstairs after making my declaration to the boss. "Have I fallen so low that I must beg on hands and knees to be kept with animals like that?" I thought, feeling as helpless in body and soul as a slug doused with salt. Finally, the boss began to speak again, crisply and clearly.

"All right. You're hired. But the doctor'll have to look you over first. It's a rule. You need a health certificate. Today . . . never mind, it's too late today. Go tomorrow morning. What? His office? It's south of here. You must have seen it on your way up. The blue house. Anyhow, that's it for today. You must be tired. Go back to the boiler and have a good night's sleep."

With that, he closed the window. I dipped my head to him slightly just before he closed it, then I went back to the boiler. The boss's kind suggestion that I have a good night's sleep was a welcome one, but if that had been a real possibility, I wouldn't have been in such agony in the first place. Awake, I had the savages to contend with; asleep, it was the bedbugs. If I happened to open the lid of a rice tub, what would come out was wall mud that couldn't pass through my throat. But I would stay here. Having decided to stay, I was determined to show them I could do just that. I would stay at least as long as Yasu was alive. As long as Yasu was alive and working, I, too, would stay alive and working, even if every last human being in the hole turned into a bedbug. With such thoughts in my head, I retraced the fifty yards to the boiler and went upstairs. There they were, sitting around the hearths, waiting for me. My heart sank, but I tried to look as indifferent as possible, taking my seat in an unobtrusive place. Then it started—the digs, the jeers, the taunts, the jokes—without a let-up. I remember each and every one of them. They pricked my tender mind with such ferocity that I'll remember them for the rest of my life. But there's no need for me to repeat them here. You can assume they were pretty much the same as those of the day before. Now I wanted to see Yasu. I forced myself to eat another one of those suppers, including two bowls of rice, and then I quietly slipped out of the boiler.

To reach the boiler of the Yamanaka Gang, I walked up the stone-walled road where the jangle had passed, climbing to the right at the top of the gradual slope, where some large pagoda trees leaned overhead. The boiler was in behind the trees. Peering into the front entrance in the dusk, I saw one digger cleaning his jacket in the light of a lantern. Inside, the place was surprisingly quiet.

"Excuse me," I asked the digger politely, "would Yasu be back from work by any chance?"

The man looked up, glanced at me, then turned to the interior. "Hey, Yasu!" he called. "Somebody here to see you!"

I heard footsteps, and Yasu came out without a moment's delay, almost as if he had been waiting for me. "You're here!" he cried. "Good! Come in."

He wore a navy blue kimono with bright vertical stripes of red and yellow and a sash of some sort of speckled toweling—the kind of thing a Tokyo stableman might wear. I was a little taken aback at this. Meanwhile, Yasu was studying my outfit. Cocking his head, he said, "I see what you mean—nothing but the clothes you ran away from Tokyo in. Brings back memories. I used to dress like that. Now, I'm like this." He held his arms out wide. "What do I look like? A rickshaw puller?"

Unable to answer honestly, I forced a grin.

Yasu laughed aloud. "Deep inside, I'm even more degenerate than this! Don't be shocked!"

I went on grinning, at a loss for words. This was how I handled embarrassing situations at that stage of my life. When it came to such things, Yasu was far more worldly than I. He saw what was troubling me and came to the rescue with a few simple words. "I've been waiting for you," he said. "Come in, come in!" I felt a surge of admiration. Here was a man who exploited his experience of the world in order to help those less experienced than himself. Having suffered only the opposite here—the endless ridicule—I was all the more appreciative of Yasu. Now I followed him inside. Like my boiler, this one had a large, open room, though it was not quite as large. Here, too, electric lights were burning, and there were hearths in the floor. The number of men was smaller, maybe five or six all together. And since they were gathered in a group at the far end of the room, Yasu and I could talk in private.

"When are you going home?" he asked.

"I've decided not to go," I replied.

The look of disgust on his face all but branded me a fool.

"Everything you said to me made perfect sense," I explained, "but I didn't come here on a whim. Even if I wanted to go home, I've got no place to go home to."

"What do you mean?" he asked sharply. "What did you do? Can't you show your face in the world, either?" He seemed more shocked to be asking the question than I was to hear it.

"No, it's not that I *can't* show my face. I don't want to."

When I said this, Yasu, who had been observing my every gesture and expression and my tone of voice, suddenly burst out laughing.

"Not a whim, huh? Stop your joking! You don't *want* to show your face? What's that mean? I wish *I* could afford such a luxury— even for a day!"

"I know," I said gravely. "I would trade places with you if I could."

Yasu burst out laughing again.

"You're hopeless! Think about it for a minute. How can someone who doesn't *want* to show his face in the world *want* to show his face in this hole?"

"I don't. Not at all. They badgered the hell out of me last night and today. But what else can I do?"

Yasu laughed again.

"The bastards," he said. "Who did it? Taking advantage of a kid . . . Anyhow, I'll get even for you—if you'll go home."

I found his words tremendously reassuring. Now I was all the more determined to stay. With Yasu on my side, I wouldn't have any need to fear even those savages. Eventually I'd have the guts to curse out the whole bunch of them. Then, I said to Yasu, I wouldn't have to rely on him to get even for me, and I pleaded with him to let me stay. The sheer stupidity of this brought a look of disgust and pity to his face.

"All right," he said. "Stay. It's entirely up to you. You don't have to ask my permission—or my advice."

"But I can't stay unless you say it's all right."

"Well, if that's how you feel about it, all right. Stay for a while. But only for a short while."

I solemnly swore to heed his counsel. Nor was I simply being polite. This was exactly what I had been planning to do. We talked a lot after that, but most of what he had to say was on the order of his effusions in the mine. I was especially moved to hear that his elder brother was a senior civil official stationed in Nagasaki. The whole affair must have been very painful for both of them, I thought, which set me to thinking, with a touch of sadness, about my parents and myself. When it came time for me to leave, Yasu saw me to the door and encouraged me to come and see him anytime I needed advice.

Outside, I found that the overcast sky had cleared and a partial moon had risen. The road was surprisingly bright, but there was a deep chill in the air. The moon was shaped like the mine entrance— rounded at the top, flat at the bottom, and I felt as if its clear, cold light were seeping through my kimono, through my undershirt, and into my skin. I folded my arms across my chest and set off down the road, burrowing my nose and chin into my arms and raising my shoulders as high as I could manage. My flesh was stiff with the cold, but deep inside I felt far richer than I had before. A short while, hell! Once you get used to this place, there's nothing to it. Over ten thousand men had come together here, working together, eating together, sleeping together day after day. With a week's practice, I, too, should be able to become as degenerate as any of them. The word "degenerate" came into my head at that moment just like this. At the time, however, it was nothing but a verbal convenience, representing none of the word's concrete meaning, so it was not particularly frightening to me. I arrived at my boiler in a fairly good mood. Some thirty feet from the entrance, I heard voices raised in a commotion. Here, outside, the solitary moon hung in the sky. I stood for a time, listening to the voices and looking up at the moon. I no longer wanted to go inside. But standing outside, bathed in the moonlight, was also hard to bear. I thought of going back to Yasu and asking him to put me up for the night. I stepped back a pace but reconsidered. No, that would be asking too much. I wandered into the boiler. To one side of the entrance was a large room cut off from the entryway by shoji doors. The electric lights hanging from the ceiling inside cast no shadows on the paper, but the commotion was definitely coming from in there. Stepping out of my geta, I tiptoed past the shoji and up the stairs. At the top, I surveyed the big room and breathed a sigh of relief. No one else was there.

The only exception was old Kin, stretched out flat as a rice cracker. And the man dangling in his canvas sling. Both, however, were so quiet they might just as well have not been there; the room was simply big and empty. Arriving at the very center of the room, I stood still, thinking. Should I spread a quilt and go to sleep? Or should I just stretch out in my kimono? Or, yet again, should I spend another night propped against a pillar? Without a quilt, I'd be cold. The pillar would be painful. I really did want to have a quilt under me if possible. Perhaps I was so tired I would be able to sleep even with the bedbugs. And if I chose a clean quilt, there shouldn't be any problem. Maybe the number of bedbugs changed from day to day and this was a light day. Grasping at such frail straws, I pulled out a couple of quilts and eased myself in between them.

If I were to write down that night's experience exactly as I recall it, it would be of no interest to anyone and would serve no purpose other than to promulgate my own stupidity. Suffice it to say that I suffered the same kind of torture as the night before—only worse. Almost as soon as I was down, I leapt up. After all the bedbug bites I had suffered the night before, I asked myself, how could I have been so stupid as to sleep on those quilts again? I know they say you have to lie in the bed you've made, but this was ridiculous! Anybody with an ounce of common sense could—and should—have avoided making such a bed. I was sitting cross-legged on the quilts, fuming at myself, when I felt another violent stab. Buttocks, thighs, and knees all shot up. I stood atop the quilts on one leg, like a heron. Then I looked at my surroundings. Then I burst into tears. All I could do was untie my blue sash, fold it four layers thick, and use it to smash every square inch of flesh on my naked body. Then I put my kimono back on. Then I went to the pillar where I had slept the night before. I leaned against it. I thought about home. What I missed most of all—more than my father, more than my mother, more than either Tsuyako or Sumie—was our six-mat room. I hungered for that room—the muslin quilt in the closet, the quilt and its handsome sleeved coverlet with the black velvet collar attached. Oh, I thought, what I would give for half an hour of warm, comfortable sleep on that quilt and under that coverlet! Who's sleeping in the six-mat room now? Or could it be that, since my departure, the room has been left empty, the only furniture in place my low writing desk? The quilt, the coverlet remain folded in the closet, unused. What a waste! And how I envy my father, my mother, Sumie, and Tsuyako, sleeping soundly one and all, unbitten! Or are they tossing and turning, unable to sleep? Father especially. Whenever he can't sleep, he throws a fit and loudly knocks the ashes from his pipe in the middle of the night. He says he's up for a smoke, but I sometimes think the smoking is an excuse. The knocking is what he really wants, as a way to deal with his anger. He's probably knocking his pipe against the ashtray right now. But what is he thinking as he knocks? Is he disgusted with his son, or is he too worried about me to sleep? Poor Father! On the other hand, since I'm not thinking about him all that much, maybe he's not all that worried about me. Then there's Mother. Whenever she can't sleep, she goes to the toilet. Then she opens the little window to the garden and washes her hands. But she forgets to lock it and receives a scolding from Father the next morning. I'm sure that's what happened last night, and it'll happen again tonight. Sumie is another matter. She's sound asleep. Of that I have no doubt. But that's all right. It's just the way she is. When she had me nearby, she'd make herself round and square and use every trick she knew to trap me, but I'm sure she forgot about me as soon as I left. She's eating three meals a day and sleeping just fine. It's true, and I can prove it, though at first she seemed so mysterious to me because I had never encountered anyone like her in a newspaper novel. Some pretty powerful destiny must be at work if I had to fall for a woman like that. I know damned well what she's up to, but I guess I'm still crazy about her. What a bind! Damn her, I can still see that white face of hers hovering before my eyes! Meanwhile, Tsuyako is awake. And she's probably crying, poor girl. But what can I do? I've never been in love with her, never tried to make her fall in love with me. I can feel sorry for her, but that won't change anything. I'll just have to stop caring. Finally, though, what I want more than anything is to be given some unbroken sleep. Sure, I'd like to stuff myself with ordinary white rice, but even more than that, I'd like a bed without bugs. I want to fall fast asleep, if only for half an hour. If I could have that, I could do anything . . . slit my stomach open . . .

While thoughts like this were going through my head, the morning came. I guess I must have fallen asleep while thinking, and when I woke up I wasn't thinking any more. I won't go into detail about what happened after that—wandering downstairs, washing my face, eating wall mud—since it was the same as the day before. I waited impatiently for nine o'clock, when the infirmary would open, then left the boiler. Having been told that the infirmary was the blue-painted building I had seen two days before on my way up, there was no mistaking the road or the place. I found it a couple hundred yards from the boiler, right next to the road—a wood frame house, but an imposing building nonetheless, certainly far too grand for the savages. That such primitive men became sick at all was amazing in itself, but to think that the mine supplied the sick with the instruments, the medicines, the doctors, and the building to make them well again, I could not help feeling what a strange and wonderful place the world is. It was as if thieves had pooled their spoils to erect a grammar school and regularly sent their children to it. The two extremes of civilization and barbarism came together in this painted house of blue, and when one had finished influencing the other, it was the barbarism that emerged fitter than ever. Badly matched opposites yield strange results. Such were my thoughts as I approached the infirmary, though from windows along the way, the usual monsters were poking their heads out and staring down at me. The sight of these grotesque faces was enough to blot out my hard-won thoughts. If there had been even one among them with a face like Yasu's, I would have been revitalized with joy, but every single one of them, as if in a conspiracy, strove to bring savagery to new heights. Men like that didn't need an infirmary, I concluded.

The weather, at least, was beautifully clear and bright. Against the mountain walls, which seemed to have been torn out of the red earth, the sun was shining. Saturated with two days of rain, the earth in the eastern sun evidenced no signs of drying out. Instead, it was absorbing all the rays the sun could give it. The showy scene was tempered by the moist softness within. Viewed from between one boiler and the next, the mountains below thickly overlay one another in a burst of blue. The wind had died. The air felt a good fifteen degrees warmer than the night before. By the side of the road, a single dandelion was in flower, its lovely color almost wasted here. This, too, was more than the savages deserved.

I came to the infirmary. At the end of a ground-level, concrete-floored corridor some thirty feet in length hung a sign: "Examination Room." Just before it on the right was another: "Waiting Room." I turned from the six-foot-wide corridor and entered the waiting room. The floor here, too, was concrete, and on it were two long benches. A small glass window bore a sign in bold, square characters: "Reception." I went to the window holding a piece of paper with my name on it. A young man of twenty-two or -three seated behind the window took the paper from me and proceeded to study it very closely, knitting together his almost non-existent eyebrows.

"This you?" he demanded.

I was not too pleased with his insolent manner. What need did he have to treat me with such contempt? "Yeah," I said, answering him as brusquely as possible. He glared at me a while, as if waiting for some polite phrases, but I had nothing more to add and stood there with my mouth shut tight.

"Wait here," he said at last, slamming the window closed and going out. I heard his sandals flapping. What the hell did he have to make so much noise for?

I sat on a bench. The receptionist was taking forever to come back. My mind wandered until the jangle appeared before me. I could see Kin being dragged to the window. And still they needed an infirmary? What was the point of prescribing medicine and giving treatment to patients here? What absolute hypocrisy! They torment the sick, they jeer at funerals, and still they send men to doctors? That's taking civility to a new extreme.

"Hey, you! Go around there." The voice of the receptionist intruded on my thoughts. The arrogant young man had resumed his overbearing stance in the window and was glaring down at me.

I left the waiting room. Turning right into the corridor, I stepped into the examination room, where I was struck by the odor of medicine. With the smell came the realization that I was going to die soon. How strange if I were to die and become part of the earth here! I suppose that's what they call destiny. I knew about "destiny" as a word, but I had never grasped its meaning—not really. I had been satisfied with knowing its definition, just as a Westerner might have to imagine what a bamboo shoot is. But bring together death, one of the great realities of man, and the hole, where the human animals known as miners live, and in the space between them dangle a pampered youngster who has lived without want until a few days before. Now, for the first time, the young man can see that destiny is a thing that uses its magical powers to toy with an innocent youth. What was until now a mountain becomes no longer just a mountain. What was until now the dust of the earth becomes no longer mere dust of the earth. The sky, which had seemed merely blue to me, is no longer just blue. This infirmary, this room, this medicine, this odor: everything takes on the mystery of a dream. Everything. Who—or what—is the person sitting here in this chair? I can scarcely tell. He sees the world outside himself with clarity, but he has no idea what meaning that world might have. Seated in this room used both as examination room and pharmacy, I surveyed the things around me—the rug, the table, the medicine bottles, the window, the mountains outside the window. My eyes apprehended them with perfect clarity, but as nothing more than images in a picture scroll.

Just then the door opened and the doctor appeared. His face was of the miner type. He wore a black morning coat and striped pants. Thrusting his chin out above his collar, he asked, "You the one?"

His tone of voice to me resounded with all the esteem one might reserve in one's heart for a horse or a dog.

"Yes," I replied, leaving my chair.

"Occupation?"

"No particular occupation."

"No occupation. How have you supported yourself till now?"

"My parents have done that."

"Your parents. You've been sponging off them?"

"Yes, I guess so."

"So you're a sponge."

I didn't reply to this.

"Take your clothes off."

I took my clothes off. After briefly checking my chest and back with a stethoscope, the doctor suddenly grabbed my nose.

"Breathe."

I breathed through my mouth. The doctor brought his hand near my mouth.

"Now I'm going to cover your mouth."

He placed his hand beneath my nose.

"What do you think, Doctor? Can I become a miner?"

"Absolutely not."

"Is there something wrong with me?"

"I'll write it out for you."

He wrote something on a square piece of paper, which he all but threw at me. "Bronchitis," it said.

Bronchitis. The first step toward consumption. And once you had that, you were finished. No wonder I had had a premonition of death when I smelled the medicine. So I was going to die, after all. Another couple of weeks and I'd be dragged to the window like Kin and forced to look at a jangle. Then I'd have my own jangle, complete with the chanting and the smashing of the wash basins. Of course, as a newcomer, there might not be anyone who'd chant and smash for me, but . . . well, finally, I didn't know what was going to happen. And that was all right, too. Even now, as I go on living and working, I don't know what's going to become of me. As long as the world continues in an unbroken flow, the bright colors will go streaming by. I had always felt a miner to be the filthiest thing in the world, but if you looked at everything as a series of constantly changing colors, questions of filthy or not filthy simply didn't enter in. Since nothing mattered, you could do as you liked. If I kept my hands in my pockets, destiny would take care of things one way or another. I could die or I could live. It didn't make any difference. Going to Kegon Falls would be too much trouble. Go home to Tokyo? Why bother? Two or three coughs and my life would be over. Destiny had blown me this far, and until destiny blew me away, just staying here would be the least troublesome, the most convenient, the best way to let things run their natural course. I could wait for death as long as I stayed here training in degeneracy. Other kinds of training might be difficult for a consumptive, but degeneracy . . .

I came upon the dandelion I had noticed on my way down. Before, its color had struck me as too beautiful for this place, but now it made no impression on me at all. I stood there a while, looking at it and wondering why it had seemed so beautiful, but still it was not beautiful. Then I started walking again. Climbing the gradual slope, I naturally turned my face upward. As always, there were miners looking down at me from the barracks, chin on hand. Their faces, which on the way in had filled me with such loathing, now seemed like clay dolls' heads. They were not ugly, not frightening, not hateful. They were just faces, as the face of the most beautiful woman in Japan is just a face. And I was exactly like these men, a human being of flesh and bone, entirely ordinary and entirely meaningless.

In this state, feeling as if I were crossing a desert island, I came to the boss's house. When I called out to announce my presence, the shoji door clattered open and a girl of fifteen or sixteen appeared. Ordinarily, I would have been amazed to see a girl like that in a place like this, but now I felt nothing. Like a machine, I stated my business, and she, with one hand on the shoji, turned to call into the house, "Father! Someone to see you!"

I grasped the fact that she was the boss's daughter, but, having grasped the fact, my mind did nothing with it. Even though she went on standing there, I forgot all about her. Then the boss came out.

"What's up?"

"I went to the infirmary."

"Did you bring your health certificate? Let's see."

I had forgotten about the certificate in my right hand and now began to wonder where I had put it.

"Look. You're holding it," said the boss.

He was right. I smoothed out the wrinkles and handed it to him.

"Bronchitis. You're sick."

"Yes, I've been rejected."

"That's too bad. What're you going to do?"

"Please hire me anyway."

"You know I can't do that."

"Yes, I know. But I can't go home anymore. Please hire me. Please. I'll do anything—run errands, keep the place clean . . ."

"'Do anything'? What can you do if you're sick? This is a tough one, but since you dragged yourself all the way up here, let me think about it a while. I'll know pretty much what's happening by tomorrow. Come and see me again."

Having turned to stone, I made my way back to the boiler.

That night, I was calm when I joined the circle around the hearth. No matter what the miners said to me, I ignored them. Nor did I feel any need to do otherwise. Let them raise all the commotion they liked; let them pester me and treat me cruelly. They and I were nothing more than images in a group portrait carved upon a single plank of wood. When it came time to sleep, I did not put out a quilt but remained sitting cross-legged by the hearth. After the others had dropped off, I dozed a little, too. Since there was no one to feed charcoal to the fire, it gradually weakened, and with the increasing cold, I woke up. The chill seeping in around my collar gave me shivers. I went outside and looked at the sky. It was filled with stars. Why were they shining like that? What were they trying to accomplish? I went back inside. Old Kin was there, stretched out as flat as ever. When would he be given his jangle? Which of us would die first, Kin or I? Yasu had supposedly been in the hole for six years, but how many more years would he go on hammering ore? In the end, he, too, would be stretched out flat in the corner of the boiler. He, too, would die. Sitting by the fireless hearth, I went on thinking until dawn. The thoughts came one after another in an endless stream, but all were dry and desiccated—no tears, no passion, no color, no scent. No fear, no terror, no ties, no regrets.

When the sun came up, I had the usual breakfast and went to see the boss.

"Oh, you're here," he said cheerfully. "I found just the right job for you. It took a little doing. At first I couldn't think of anything, but then it occurred to me—you can be the boiler bookkeeper. We can get along fine without a bookkeeper, of course. The old lady's been doing it till now. But I know how bad you want a job. What do you say? If you want it, I think I can get it for you."

"I'm very grateful," I said. "I'll take anything. What does a bookkeeper do?"

"It's easy. You just keep the books. We've got a lot of men here, and they're always buying things—sandals, beans, seaweed, whatever. You just write down what they buy every day. The old lady's the one that hands out the stuff. All you do is keep a record of who took how much of what. Then I just look at the ledger and deduct what they owe from their pay. It's not exactly what you'd call hard labor. Anybody can do it. But we've got a bunch of illiterates here, you know. If you'll do the job for me it'll be a big help. What do you say?"

"Sounds fine. I'll do it."

"It's not going to pay much, I'm sorry to say. Four yen a month. Minus food."

"That's plenty for me," I replied, though I was not especially over-joyed. Nor, of course, was this any great relief. Finally, though, my position at the mine was set.

The next day, I took my place in the corner of the kitchen and started keeping the books in the time-honored fashion. Suddenly the miners began treating me differently. Now, instead of despising me, they went out of their way to butter me up. And I wasted no time in practicing to be a degenerate. I ate the mine's rice and was eaten by the bedbugs. Every day, procurers would show up from the towns with new pigeons. And every day they'd bring more kids. I used part of my monthly four yen to buy the kids sweets. Later, though, after I had decided to go back to Tokyo, I stopped doing that. I performed my duties as bookkeeper for five months. Then I went back to Tokyo. That's all there is to my experience as a miner. And every bit of it is true, which you can tell from the fact that this book never did turn into a novel.

AFTERWORD

Afterword

IN THE OPENING paragraph of *The Miner* (*Kōfu*), Sōseki suggests what the reader is in for: "Just pine trees and pine trees and more pine trees that don't add up to anything." Like the trees, which are never seen as constituting a fully comprehended forest, the events of the book are not going to "develop," he hints in an odd locution. Abandoning any hope of forcing either the trees or the events into a preconceived framework, he will play games with them, hoping for some sense of mastery—and perhaps some fun.

Experience for the protagonist turns out to be a long, often funny series of discreet thoughts and sense impressions that constitutes neither a conclusive picture of the world nor a finished portrait of himself. Life, for him, is merely "a series of constantly changing colors . . . images in a picture scroll" (pp. 157, 158),[1] and a literary work that remains true to life (and, most important, true to the indeterminate nature of human personality) will never "turn into a novel" (p. 161).

A sophisticated student of Western—primarily English—literature and a lover of traditional Japanese (and Chinese) poetry and humor, Natsume Sōseki (1867–1916) had been experimenting in fiction for three years, writing works of humor, fantasy, and melodrama, when he began serializing *The Miner* in the *Asahi* newspaper on January 1, 1908. *The Miner* was his second novel as a professional writer. Sōseki had caused an uproar the previous year when he abandoned a teaching post at the University of Tokyo, the nation's premier educational institution, to join the staff of the *Asahi* for the sole purpose of writing fiction, a genre associated with the world of the geisha and prostitute and far beneath the dignity of anyone with his own unimpeachable scholarly credentials. But "if being a newspaperman is a trade, then being a university-man is also a trade," he had declared, plunging wholeheartedly into the creative writing that would occupy the final decade of his life.[2]

The plunge was perhaps a bit too exuberant in the case of the first novel he serialized in the *Asahi,* from June to October 1907. Everything about *The Poppy* (*Gubijinsō*) shows that Sōseki was trying too hard. The language is labored and ornate, the characters painted in intense monochromes and acting out a convoluted plot with conflicting loves and obligations, chance encounters, sly machinations, and dramatic confrontations. The novel was a hit even before it reached the newsstands, thanks in part to the success of Sōseki's earlier works and a lingering curiosity about his highly publicized resignation from the University. One department store sold "Poppy" robes, and a jewelry firm came out with "Poppy" rings. Once the novel reached the pages of the *Asahi,* the enthusiasm spilled over into a warm public reception, if not universal critical acclaim.³ The shortcomings of the book were clear to Sōseki himself, again even before serialization. On June 17, 1907, he wrote to a friend that he was already finding his manuscript unpleasant to read, and by July he confessed that he wanted to kill off his heroine. A few years later he rejected another friend's suggestion that the novel be translated into German, saying that he would just as soon see the book go out of print in Japan, if it weren't for the occasional royalty payment; still less did he want to compound the embarrassment by having Germans read the thing, too.⁴

If the few brief mentions of *The Poppy* in his correspondence show Sōseki's dissatisfaction with that novel, *The Miner* demonstrates conclusively his absolute rejection of it. No two books from a single hand could have been more starkly different. Both novels begin with their central characters walking through the countryside, but there the similarity ends.

In *The Miner,* the elaborate locutions and circumlocutions have given way to a tough, telegraphic, colloquial prose—language that may suggest an unstoppable flow of thought but never invites the reader to linger over a well-turned phrase, as is so painfully true of *The Poppy.* And as different as the prose styles are the landscapes through which Sōseki's characters walk. The squarely built aspiring diplomat Munechika and his tall, thin friend, the philosopher Kōno, who appear in the opening scene of *The Poppy,* are climbing the flanks of Mt. Hiei outside of Kyoto, gazing at the peak towering above them, its very name reverberating with the rich history of Japan's traditional political and cultural center. Not only do we not know the name of the pine grove in which the protagonist of *The*

Miner is walking, we never get to see what he looks like, so firmly are we locked inside his brain (or his text), and he is known to us only as "I" (*jibun*). Far from being rich with historical associations, the landscape is almost phantasmagorical—dark and abstract. And from it, inexplicably, materializes a series of Bosch grotesques: the fat-lipped Chōzō with his protruding bones and crooked, tobacco-stained teeth; the urinating tea-stand woman with her twisted mouth; men with suppurating eyes and sloping foreheads, pale skins and wasted flesh; a bland, faceless bumpkin eternally swathed in his stinking red blanket; a disturbingly bat-like boy who swoops down alone from the hills.

Ironically, *The Poppy*, with its roots firmly planted in nineteenth-century realism, was entirely fictional, whereas the abstractly modernist *Miner* was based in part on the experience of a young man who visited Sōseki with the express purpose of selling his "story" as material for a novel. We know from the notes Sōseki took at the time that the young man spent his first night on the road in Ōmiya, that the procurer took him to Maebashi to board the train for Utsunomiya, and that he went to work in the famous (or, for its pollution, notorious) Ashio copper mine, but Sōseki has removed nearly all such identifiable labels from his narrative.[5] Whereas it is possible to learn something about the scenery east of Kyoto or about wealthy Tokyo life-styles from *The Poppy*, *The Miner* is worthless as travel literature, and it gives us hardly more than a glimpse of the life of the miners, for Sōseki has done everything he can to make the excursion of his protagonist a psychological one. He is clearly speaking of himself when he has his narrator say, "Thank goodness, I *do* have this great gift . . . the ability to dissect my experience with an open mind and to evaluate every little piece of it" (p. 53). This is the foundation of all Sōseki's mature fiction, and it is the direction in which he decisively turned, beginning with *The Miner.*

Natsume Sōseki is two writers: the popular comedian of *I Am a Cat* (*Wagahai wa neko de aru*, 1905–6) and *Botchan* (1906), and the intellectual's tragedian of *The Wayfarer* (*Kōjin*, 1912–13) and *The Heart* (*Kokoro*, 1914).[6] The comedian makes us laugh at greed, dishonesty, and affectation; the tragedian reveals only "betrayal, guilt and loneliness," the theme that Sōseki was "obsessed with throughout his later career," in the words of Edwin McClellan.[7] Although the contrast between the two Sōsekis is clear, the precise timing and nature of the change in Sōseki's writing have been less well defined.

Howard Hibbett has traced a parallel between periods of mental suffering that Sōseki experienced and the deepening darkness of the novels. "If [Sōseki's] early novels reflect more clearly the surface changes of his society," observes Hibbett, "it is in the later novels, in which he probes his own darkest psychological problems, that he symbolizes the widespread anxiety beneath those exciting changes." [8]

The key here is self-analysis. In *The Heart*, the Sōseki novel most widely read in the West and surely one of the author's finest works, the protagonist's misanthropy comes less from what he sees in others than what he discovers in himself.

When I was cheated by my uncle I felt very strongly the unreliableness of men. I learned to judge others harshly, but of my own integrity I knew I could be certain. I thought that in the midst of a corrupt world I had managed to remain virtuous. [When I caused K to commit suicide,] however, my self-confidence was shattered. With a shock, I realized that I was just as human as my uncle. I became as disgusted with myself as I had been with the rest of the world. [9]

Likewise, Hibbett observes, as Sōseki's "courageous efforts toward self-discovery continued, he found in himself an aggressive element which he shared with those 'others' whom he had feared and despised." [10]

Whether or not we follow Hibbett in his use of the term "aggressive," there can be little doubt that the change in the novels has much to do with the degree to which Sōseki's protagonists are willing to recognize undesirable traits in themselves that they share with others. As long as they are confident of their own superiority, they can afford to stand back and ridicule, but as the gulf diminishes, the intellectual distancing of humor becomes increasingly difficult to maintain. The laughter becomes muted in *Sanshirō* (1908), and in *And Then* (*Sore kara*, 1909) it finally dies.

Rather than their capacity for "aggression," I would like to emphasize Sōseki's later protagonists' growing awareness of their own vulnerability to change. For all their misanthropy, the later characters condemn man not as inherently evil but as "unreliable." [11]

Sensei, the protagonist of *The Heart*, sees in the uncle who cheated him of his inheritance "the personification of all those things in this world that make it unworthy of trust."[12] In *And Then*, the protagonist Daisuke sees his entire nation tempted by money. But Daisuke understands and sympathizes with his harried countrymen, for introspection has taught him to doubt the honesty of his own motives and hardened his resolve to absent himself from the social battlefield.[13] Someone as simpleminded as the hero of the early *Botchan*, of course, cannot plumb such complexities and has no capacity for sympathy. When he says "there's nothing so unreliable as people," he sees himself surrounded by liars and cheats.[14]

Much of the humor in Sōseki's earlier fiction springs from the difficulties faced by simple characters who classify people as either good or bad. One particularly amusing example can be seen in *The Autumn Wind* (*Nowaki*, 1907) when the idealistic philosopher Dōya is telling a young admirer how few readers have responded to his essays. A notable exception, Dōya says, was a patent medicine salesman who came to ask him to use his writing skills to compose an advertisement for a new brand of eye drops. This Dōya refused to do, but the man proceeded to ask for Dōya's help with some advertising balloons. Dōya's job, had he taken it, would have been to get people to look up at the balloons.

"How were you supposed to do that?"

"All I'd have to do was walk along or ride the streetcar, and whenever I saw a balloon I was supposed to say, 'Look! Look! A balloon! It must be an ad for Tenmeisui Eye Drops!'"

"What a laugh! So he wanted you to fool people. You have to admire his nerve."

"Yes, it was very funny—if a little ridiculous. I told him he didn't need me to do a job like that. All he'd have to do was hire some rickshaw puller. But that wouldn't work, he said. Nobody would listen to a rickshaw puller. It would have to be a serious-looking person, preferably a man with a moustache, or no one would be taken in."

"Now that's going too far! Who was this fellow, anyway?"

"Who was he? Just an ordinary human, out to fool the world and looking for someone to help him do it. What did he care? Ha ha ha."

"But this is shocking! I would have beaten the stuffing out of him!"

"Start beating up one and you have to beat them all up. It won't do any good to get so angry. The whole world is made up of men like him."[15]

Dōya does not seem to include himself among the "ordinary humans," which places him with the earlier Sōseki characters who see people in terms of stereotypes or categories. Kiyo, the old woman so devoted to Botchan, warns him of the evils of country people, while in her letters from rural Kyushu, Sanshirō's mother warns him to beware of city people.[16] Instead of making for humor, a dialogue on the relative merits of country versus city people in *The Heart* is what leads to Sensei's dark observation that "there is no such thing as a stereotype bad man in this world. Under normal conditions, everybody is more or less good, or, at least, ordinary. But tempt them, and they may suddenly change. That is what is so frightening about men." [17]

The problem for Sōseki's later protagonists, then, is that introspection has taught them the fragility of "ordinary" human nature (including their own), the ease with which good becomes evil, the difficulty of observing the change, and the consequent insecurity that underlies all human relationships.

This is the stuff of modern tragedy, but it is far from what Sōseki's contemporaries were expecting from him as late as March 1908. In that month, the journal *Chūō kōron* carried a symposium in which thirteen prominent writers and intellectuals gave their views of Sōseki. They saw him as an original stylist, a pioneer in humor, a writer attempting to transcend the real world, and a man "incapable of writing tragedy" whose works "are finally not modern fiction." [18]

Sōseki was serializing *The Miner* in the *Asahi* at the time, and receiving universally negative reviews. Yet this novel, still so little appreciated even today, was the very work in which Sōseki formulated the view of human nature that underlies his late masterpieces.

So full of passion and anxiety are Sōseki's later novels that it would seem to be an error to search for the source of their tragic insights in a work so cool and detached as *The Miner*, yet this oddly humorous book, in which the laughter is provoked less by human foibles than by the thinking process itself, served as an indispensable test-tube for Sōseki in his search for an appropriate fictional medium. And with all the clarity of a test-tube, *The Miner* yields up the results of the experiment with maximum visibility, even if, in its vitreous starkness, the vessel itself is not immediately appealing.

The story of a young man whose love life has fallen to pieces, *The Miner* simply shows the nineteen-year-old protagonist fleeing from Tokyo, being picked up by a procurer of cheap labor for a copper mine, then traveling toward—and finally burrowing into the depths of—the mine where he hopes to find oblivion. The unusual setting was suggested to Sōseki by a young man who suddenly showed up on his doorstep in November 1907 and insisted on selling the story of his disastrous love affairs and subsequent experience in the Ashio copper mine as material for a novel. The young fellow, known to posterity only by his surname, Arai, needed the money for train fare, he said. Sōseki had no time to listen to his story just then but gave him the fare and told him to come back that evening, never expecting to see him again. Surprisingly, Arai returned as promised and told Sōseki his story for three hours, concentrating on the events leading to his departure from Tokyo. Not wishing to reveal another's personal affairs, Sōseki suggested that Arai write his own story and Sōseki would try to have it published, but this never happened.

Sōseki was not scheduled to begin another serialization for some months, but when the writer Shimazaki Tōson reported to the *Asahi* that he could not have his manuscript of *Spring (Haru)* ready to begin appearing on New Year's day, the paper turned to its staff novelist. Sōseki obtained Arai's permission to use only the details of the life of the miners, then set about writing his own entirely original novel, which began appearing on January 1, 1908.[19]

Sōseki stripped away all the melodramatic elements from Arai's story, leaving only the bare bones of the journey and the descent into the mine. He then turned this virtually non-existent plot material into a 250-page novel by having the protagonist reflect at length on his every thought and perception, in terms both of what he noticed at the time and of what the experience means to him now as a mature adult. This prolix analysis of non-events (such as a split-second of visual clarity that requires three pages of description and commentary) drove some readers to distraction. "You'd think Sōseki was some kind of antique dealer, the way he attaches a certificate of authenticity to everything in the novel," fumed one critic who had read about half the installments.[20]

These remarks appeared in the March 1908 symposium on Sōseki cited earlier. Not one of the contributors had a good word for *The*

Miner. Even one enthusiastic fan who claimed to have hungrily devoured everything Sōseki had ever written admitted to reservations about that one novel. After a year of spectacular popularity with *I Am a Cat*, *Botchan*, and *Pillow of Grass* (*Kusamakura*, translated as *The Three-Cornered World*) in 1906, Sōseki had disappointed critics (if not the general public) with *Autumn Wind* and *The Poppy* in 1907. He was not living up to his early promise, it was felt, and *The Miner* seemed to confirm his decline.[21] The editor of the magazine feature concluded that while Sōseki's decreasing popularity was being interpreted by some as merely a reaction to the excessive early praise, the inferiority of *The Miner* was undeniable.[22]

One can hardly blame critics in 1908 for reacting negatively to a work that discarded all the conventions of modern fiction—conventions that were still being learned by a relatively unsophisticated readership. Instead of plot and character, Sōseki gave them perceptions and analyses of perceptions, and neither his lively colloquial tone of voice nor the eccentricity of his focus seemed to compensate for the loss of familiar elements. The opening passage, in which the protagonist first sees the procurer Chōzō and analyzes the situation before turning and walking back to him, truly comprises a "certificate of authenticity" to tax the patience of any plot-hungry reader.

Sōseki himself was aware of the difficulties many readers would have in identifying with the novel. Some, he told an interviewer, would object to the retrospective narration for its cooling and distancing effect, but he had chosen it for the opportunity it gave him to dissect the character's every action and analyze his motives. This was an extremely complicated business, he noted, for we ourselves are not aware of many of our own motives. A precise analysis of motives would be virtually impossible to set down on paper in any case, and an attempt to do so would involve a lot of maddening hairsplitting and would not be very interesting to read. That was why not many writers were attempting to do it—and why Sōseki himself wanted to give it a try. "I am not so much interested in events themselves as in laying bare the truth behind them." He did not want to investigate cause-and-effect relationships that link events, he said, but rather to analyze the elements that compose events, each discreet from the other. The interest here lay in satisfying a certain kind of intellectual curiosity about how events in life are constituted, but "people lacking such intellectual curiosity will not find it much fun."²³

To be sure, despite its snatches of lively dialogue and its comically obsessive pursuit of trivia, few readers have found *The Miner* to be fun, and this includes the scholarly world. The novel is never included in "selected" works of Sōseki, only the complete works. One self-proclaimed "indispensable" Sōseki handbook has no article on *The Miner*.²⁴ Many of the numerous collections of scholarly essays on Sōseki omit studies of the book.²⁵ Etō Jun's famous 1965 study of Sōseki, which did much to shape all subsequent scholarship, devotes less than a page to *The Miner*, concluding only that it was an étude leading toward the more accomplished characterizations in *And Then*.²⁶ Miyoshi Yukio reluctantly grants that *The Miner* was "one door" that Sōseki had to pass through on the way toward the later works, but he sees the novel as "merely a product of chance" owing to the journalistic exigencies that led Sōseki to fabricate it from materials lying at hand.²⁷ Edwin McClellan's pioneering introduction of Sōseki to Western readers does not even suggest that *The Miner* exists.²⁸ Beongcheon Yu's later book-length study devotes five pages to *The Miner* and credits it with being an anti-novel, but it negates the book's thematic connection with Sōseki's other works and contains factual misstatements that suggest a less-than-careful reading.²⁹

Some commentators, however, have recognized the experimental value of *The Miner*. One writer has labeled it a "prophetic" stream-of-consciousness novel, and Sōseki's indebtedness to William James has often been pointed out.³⁰ Donald Keene is the first to have provided a balanced account in English of the novel's reception and pioneering significance (questioning the accuracy of the "stream-of-consciousness" label, for example), but there is little in his commentary to contradict Beongcheon Yu's earlier assertion that *The Miner* has "no thematic relationship to the rest of [Sōseki's] works."³¹ It is important to recognize, however, that *The Miner* was not merely an experiment in technique but a turning point in Sōseki's own grasp of the human condition. For in *The Miner*, Sōseki's "ordinary human being" ceases to be an evil "other" and becomes instead an untrustworthy "self."

Sōseki may have obtained the story material for *The Miner* from an informant, but the novel was the direct result of his continuing exploration of his own internal landscape, and it marked a new depth of psychological observation in his fiction.[32] In *The Miner*, the narrator-hero's haphazard descent into the dark bowels of the earth parallels his descent into himself. The experience leads him to the familiar Sōseki conclusion that "there is nothing so unreliable as man" (p. 16), but this he supports by spelling out at great length what he calls at one point "my theory of the non-existence of character" (p. 121).[33] What we mistakenly call personality is "nothing but a bunch of memories," he insists (p. 16). "In fact, there is no such thing as character, something fixed and final. The real thing is something that novelists don't know how to write about—or, if they tried, the end result would never be a novel" (p. 7).

Not only with regard to style, as mentioned earlier, but here, at the book's philosophical core, Sōseki was no doubt reacting to the weaknesses of his own just-completed melodrama, *The Poppy*, with its all-too-clearly defined characters and its unambiguous moral center. Kumasaka Atsuko has noted that the character Kōno in *The Poppy*, a philosopher, is presented as a man who understands life and humankind and who knows how one should live. He can distinguish the moral from the immoral; he can see inside people and sense their fates; and he can criticize the schemers in life without implicating himself. Senuma Shigeki has pointed out that the death of the head schemer in *The Poppy* is not an inevitable development of a tragic plot but merely a punishment dealt out to her by the author from an elevated moral plane. In its critique of modern egoism, Kumasaka concludes, the novel is as self-righteous as any didactic piece written under the Tokugawa shōguns with their officially enforced moralism.[34]

Shortly before he began serializing *The Poppy* in the *Asahi*, Sōseki delivered a lecture in which he defined the novelist as one who must "provide an interpretation of how we ought to live and teach the common people the meaning of existence."[35] The tone of voice that Sōseki adopted here was reminiscent of the confident, self-righteous preaching that readers had heard from Dōya Sensei in *Autumn Wind*, and clearly, when Sōseki launched into *The Poppy*, he still saw himself as standing on a lectern several steps above the ordinary man.

In *The Miner*, however, all such certitude crumbled away. Not only is there no center of righteousness in the book, the very form of the novel is lost. The two developments are inseparable. When, nearly halfway through the work, two such seemingly important characters as the boy and the red blanket disappear, never to re-enter the action, the narrator observes, "At this rate, my book will never turn into a novel" (p. 70). *The Miner* contains many such passages in which the novelist thinks out loud to inform the reader that the view of human changeability set forth in the book—the view that, six years later, would cause Sensei to withdraw from the world entirely—is responsible for the novel's odd shapelessness. Through his narrator's mouth, the author has the last word concerning his literary experiment: "That's all there is to my experience as a miner. And every bit of it is true, which you can tell from the fact that this book never did turn into a novel" (p. 16).

Not only does *The Miner* reject novelistic form but it even sacrifices narrative certainty. Observing his own inconsistencies, the ease with which he has changed, the narrator concludes with comical scrupulousness that he can only speculate (he must use "probably") on what his past motives might have been (p. 10).

Most of the passages that spell out the "theory of the non-existence of character" appear in the first two-fifths of the book, which derive their story material from only the first half-page of the twelve pages of notes that Sōseki took from his young informant. The "story" in question is the description of the protagonist's trip to the mine. The rest of the novel, set in the mine and its environs, draws heavily—and faithfully—on the factual information that Sōseki recorded in his notes, and it is in every way more conventionally realistic.[36] Tamai Takayuki speaks of a "dislocation between the first and second halves of the book which many people have noted," and he agrees with still more commentators that Sōseki became overly "dependent on his materials" in the latter part of the book.[37] Donald Keene echoes other scholars in suggesting that in this novel Sōseki "undoubtedly also wished to call attention to the inhuman conditions under which the miners worked."[38]

Virtually no one sees any continuity of purpose in Sōseki's approach, for the author himself seems to have forgotten his spirited remarks about the collapse of the novel. The distancing humor all but disappears. The descriptions of the various shafts and caves and pits within the mine are far more lengthy and detailed than called for in a book that was "never" supposed to "turn into a novel." Perhaps Sōseki the new professional writer became fascinated with the process of creating from notes a place he had never seen before. Whether intended as local color or as a symbolic journey through the frightening chaos of the psyche, there is more of this descriptive material than is thematically necessary—until the protagonist confronts both death and his own social conditioning in the dark "hell" (p. 104) of the mine.

Alone in the depths, the young protagonist seems ready to surrender himself to nothingness when he is momentarily saved by his instinct for survival and—perhaps more important—by his bourgeois preconceptions. "As long as I was going to die anyway," he thinks, "I could do better than to die in this place. A command . . . echoed in my head: 'Wait! Wait! Get out of here and go to Kegon Falls!'" He does not want his death to be "pointless." He wants to die in the conventionally romantic manner and not be "reviled by those half-beast–half-human miners" (p. 135). Suddenly arrogant, he is abandoned by his guide and he refuses to put himself in the inferior position of asking directions of the next man he meets, a particularly extreme example of a pasty-faced miner. He then encounters a more appealing miner called Yasu, an educated individual like himself who has been hiding in the mine to escape the consequences of a disastrous love affair. Yasu urges him to go back to the city, to get a decent job, to work for the sake of the family and the nation. This warmly compassionate Japanese superego even offers to pay his fare if need be (pp. 138–43).

Overcome with emotion, the boy vows to live up to the example of Yasu's admirable character. He is "saved"—or so it has seemed to many scholars who have overlooked the one unequivocal clue that Sōseki is by no means playing it straight here. Meeting Yasu by chance down in hell among the thousands of animalistic miners, says the narrator, is "something right out of a novel" (p. 143). Sōseki did not spend a hundred pages denouncing the "lies" of conventional novels to let a line like this slip in by accident. Here, in the climactic scene of the most conventionally novelistic part of *The Miner*, the protagonist has been deflected from the earlier-discovered truth of his own amorphousness by the socially conditioned illusions that hold novels together and keep individuals in their place. Yasu is none other than the young man's socialized self. After this meeting, with its rush of patriotic and familial fervor, he emerges from the mine with all his conventional values reconfirmed. The miners are ugly and disgusting savages; the "lovely color" of a flower he sees is "almost wasted here" (p. 156). In the clinic where he must go for an examination, however, a whiff of medicine reminds him of death and the vulnerability of humans to their fate, and once more he begins to see the world as alien, a meaningless succession of form and color. He passes the flower again, and it no longer seems beautiful to him (p. 158). The encounter with Yasu has had no more permanent effect on him than any other experience in the flow of consciousness.

Of all the studies I consulted in preparing this essay, only one, by Sasaki Masanobu, recognizes the significance of the Yasu episode as "something right out of a novel" and duly notes the subsequent return of the protagonist to his "characterless" state. Indeed, Sasaki goes so far as to assert that Sōseki constructed the entire episode for the sole purpose of demolishing it.[39] This directly contradicts earlier commentators, who invariably conclude that the protagonist has been "saved," but who do so only at the cost of ignoring the conclusion of the book, in which the narrator has come to accept his inconsistencies and his ordinariness as part of the meaningless succession of images. When the flower ceases to be beautiful, the miners' faces cease to be ugly: "They were just faces, as the face of the most beautiful woman in Japan is just a face. And I was exactly like these men, a human being of flesh and bone, entirely ordinary and entirely meaningless" (p. 159).

I can only marvel at how so many scholars could have read through such lines and still concluded that the narrator had been saved from his alienation. And all—including Sasaki—seem to have missed the simple fact that the protagonist could not possibly have been saved or cured (as one psychiatrist/critic would have it) because the protagonist is the narrator and his entire theory of characterlessness has been formulated in retrospect, "years" after his presumed salvation should have taken place (p. 48). Perhaps Sasaki's skeptical view of Yasu's patriotic ardor is a function of age. Having been born in 1940, he was spared the propaganda of the Japanese Empire, as most of the other scholars I read were not.[40]

In any case, it is important to recognize that Sōseki is being consistent to the very end of this book that "never did turn into a novel." His protagonist has discovered that he "was exactly like these men . . . entirely ordinary and entirely meaningless." Without this awareness of a shared, undependable humanity, the mature Sōseki might have continued to be a penetrating critic of his times, but he would never have attained the stature that certifies him as a major voice of the twentieth century.

Sōseki was, of course, not alone in his questioning of the validity of "character" in literature. To a theorist like Robbe-Grillet, writing in 1957, character is simply one of "several obsolete notions" hanging on from traditional criticism, despite its "fifty years of disease, the death notice signed many times over by the most serious essayists."[41]

But the death knell began sounding even earlier than he suggests. Dostoyevski was already tearing at the solidity of the ego in *The Double* of 1846. In 1888, August Strindberg prefaced his play *Miss Julie* with these remarks: "An event in real life—and this discovery is quite recent—springs generally from a whole series of more or less deep-lying motives." In attempting to account for the "multiplicity of motives" behind his characters' actions, Strindberg says, "I have tried to make my figures rather 'characterless.' . . . My souls (or characters) are conglomerates, made up of past and present stages of civilization, scraps of humanity, torn-off patches of Sunday clothing turned into rags—all patched together as is the human soul itself."[42]

The parallel between these observations and Sōseki's, both in and about *The Miner*, is remarkable.[43] Strindberg sounds even more like Sōseki when he discusses the small cast of characters he has presented in his play (a parallel to the simplicity of *The Miner*'s plot and small cast): "I have done this because I believe I have noticed that the psychological processes are what interest people of our own day more than anything else. Our souls, so eager for knowledge, cannot rest satisfied with seeing what happens, but must also learn how it comes to happen."[44]

In practice, however, Strindberg's characters are primarily symbols of social class and evidence none of the amorphous quality suggested by his theory, the mature fruits of which are probably to be found in Robbe-Grillet's time and the theater of the absurd. Here we find Ionesco's "Pseudo-Drama" (as he called it) *Victims of Duty* (1952), and here, too, we find a world congruent with *The Miner*. The protagonist Choubert is urged to burrow down "deeper, my love, deeper" into his own psyche, where "it's so dark," until the darkened stage itself seems to encompass the chaotic interior of a mind, one full of infantile drives and snatches of trivia. Toward the end, the poet (and drama theorist) Nicolas enters to explain what has been going on. Rejecting Aristotelian theater, he says, "We'll get rid of the principle of the identity and unity of character . . . personality doesn't exist. Within us there are only forces that are contradictory or not contradictory." The Detective, a walking superego (much as detectives are for Sōseki, in whose works they lurk as representatives of state and social repressiveness), declares, "As for me, I remain Aristotelically logical, true to myself, faithful to my duty and full of respect for my bosses. I don't believe in the absurd, everything hangs together, everything can be comprehended in time." [45] Nicolas kills this rationalist, but soon he is behaving just like him in spite of himself, becoming another "victim of duty." Likewise, the protagonist of *The Miner* insists that the fragmented nature of personality absolves individuals from responsibility but admits that he has never been able to free himself from a need to live up to commitments, concluding that "people are put together in a tremendously convenient way so as to become victims of society" (p. 16). A victim of society is precisely what Yasu, in the mine-hell, urges the young man to become—apparently without success. All we know of the narrator's later life is that he has been "wandering all over the country for years now" (p. 48).

Without an exacting comparative study of style and narrative technique, it would be difficult to place Sōseki precisely among those writers who, "from the end of the nineteenth century on, . . . produced narrative works which on the whole undertook to give us an extremely subjective, individualistic, and often eccentrically aberrant impression of reality, and which neither sought nor were able to ascertain anything objective or generally valid in regard to it." [46] Nakamura Shin'ichirō, the longtime proponent of *The Miner* as stream-of-consciousness fiction, suggests parallels to Dostoyevski, Proust, Joyce, Camus, and Faulkner. [47] But Sōseki is rarely attempting to convince the reader of the immediate reality of what passes through the protagonist's mind. By the sixth paragraph, it becomes clear that the narrator is writing, commenting on his own thought processes in retrospect, and we are reading his pages, not floating somewhere inside his brain. [48] There is an eccentric consciousness of consciousness here that is more reminiscent of Beckett's bedridden writer/narrators Molloy and Malone ("There's this man who comes every week . . . . He gives me money and takes away the pages. So many pages, so much money").[49] Hugh Kenner speaks of "Beckett's invincibly comic method, which locates comedy in the very movements of the human mind" in such works as *The Unnameable*, "from which Beckett has succeeded in abolishing all content save the gestures of the intellect: immaculate solipsism compelled (this is the comic twist) to talk, talk, talk,"[50] or in the case of the crippled Malone, who can do little more than move his pencil, to write, write, write:

> Ah yes, I have my little pastimes and they
> What a misfortune, the pencil must have slipped from my fingers, for I have only just succeeded in recovering it after forty-eight hours . . . of intermittent efforts.[51]

The same niggling precision of self-observation is at work when Sōseki's unnamed narrator recalls that he fell asleep and "what happened to me after that, not even I can write" (p. 98).

Donald Keene has noted that Sōseki, in following *The Poppy* with *The Miner*, "had moved from the world of George Meredith to that of modern literature."[52] Indeed, so far had Sōseki moved into the world of modern literature that *The Miner* remains to this day one of Japan's most innovative contributions to contemporary fiction.

In a lecture he delivered in 1911, Sōseki declared that if an artist cannot derive an income directly from the public, "then all he can do is starve to death," and that is probably what would have happened to Sōseki if he had continued writing novels like *The Miner*.[53] With his next novel, *Sanshirō* (serialized from September to December 1908), Sōseki returned to working with a more conventional cast of characters. Gone, however, were the moralistic certainties of the early works, and Sanshirō's own shifting, vacillating character shared much with that of the young miner. "Contradiction" is a key word of the book, and the otherworldly Hirota Sensei has given up Dōya Sensei's self-righteous ranting to deliver speeches like this: "There is one thing we ought to keep in mind in the study of man. Namely, that a human being placed in particular circumstances has the ability and the right to do just the opposite of what the circumstances dictate."[54]

As Edwin McClellan has noted, "Just as Sanshirō is only potentially a tragic figure, so is Sōseki at this point only potentially a tragic writer."[55] This is because he was still holding the insights of *The Miner* at arm's length, keeping the shadows at a distance with laughter. He finally let his guard down in *And Then*, after which Sōseki developed into an authentic modern tragedian, portraying man struggling hopelessly with "all those things in this world which make it unworthy of trust"—most notably, his own nature.

Of course, a critic like Robbe-Grillet would accuse Sōseki of having compromised with the reactionary forces of anthropocentrism, of having once faced the void without dizziness, then chosen to experience it as suffering, "tragedified" it.[56] And, to some extent, he would be right. Sōseki's novels lost the bold, stoically comic inventiveness of *The Miner* and came to an end with the omnisciently narrated *Light and Darkness* (*Meian*, 1916), one of the closest Japanese approximations to a nineteenth-century European novel and one of the most tedious exercises in the language, the neat little cliff-hangers at the end of each day's installment suggesting a jaded professionalism that Sōseki had never displayed before.

In a sense, then, Sōseki's later career moved backward, from the very forefront of the avant-garde in 1908 to a tired, old white elephant in 1916. All the great works in between, however, and *Light and Darkness*, too, shared the insights that Sōseki first presented in *The Miner*, and these above all were what established him as Japan's great modern novelist.

Notes

THE FOLLOWING abbreviation is used in the notes: SZ, for *Sōseki zenshū*, 17 vols. (Iwanami shoten, 1974). The place of publication for this and other Japanese works cited in the Notes is Tokyo.

1. Parenthetical figures refer to page numbers in the translation, which is based on the standard text of *Kōfu* found in SZ 3: 435–674. Checks of questionable passages revealed no discrepancies between this text and the original serialization in *Tokyo Asahi shimbun*, Jan. 1–Apr. 6, 1908. The original manuscript has been lost. For a detailed discussion of textual variations (all of the most insignificant sort), see Itō Sei and Ara Masahito, eds., *Sōseki bungaku zenshū*, 11 vols. (Shūeisha, 1970), 4: 855–67, 877–83.

2. "Nyūsha no ji," SZ 11: 494. For Sōseki's resignation and his ideas on the social role of the novelist, see Jay Rubin, *Injurious to Public Morals: Writers and the Meiji State* (Seattle: University of Washington Press, 1984), pp. 70–73. For an introduction to Sōseki's life and works, see Edwin McClellan, *Two Japanese Novelists: Sōseki and Tōson* (Chicago: University of Chicago Press, 1969). See also Donald Keene, *Dawn to the West*, 2 vols. (New York: Holt, Rinehart and Winston, 1984), 1: 305–54.

3. Komiya Toyotaka, *Natsume Sōseki*, 3 vols. (Iwanami shoten, 1973), 2: 261–62. A casual piece in the August 1907 *Chūō kōron* ("Bundan jigon," p. 135) suggested (ironically, in retrospect) that Sōseki might be able to recoup his earlier reputation with his next novel, and the New Year review of literary events in the January issues of both that journal ("Teibi bundan gaikan," p. 223) and *Nihon oyobi Nihonjin* ("Bungei jihyō," p. 55) spoke of his cooling critical reception. The newspaper *Kokumin shimbun* reported on October 24, 1907, that *The Poppy* was not well received, but also, on October 31, that two publishers had been competing fiercely for rights to the book. See Hirano Seisuke, *Shimbun shūsei Natsume Sōseki zō*, 4 vols. (Meiji-Taishō-Shōwa shimbun kenkyū kai, 1979), 1: 157.

4. SZ 14: 587, 15: 295–96. Komiya, 2: 263.

5. SZ 13: 274. The notes suggest that Sōseki's informant left Tokyo at nine o'clock, reaching Ōmiya (seventeen miles northwest of Tokyo on the old Nakasendō Highway) at two in the morning, where he slept on a Ka-

183

gura stage. He encountered the procurer in a tea house, though by an avenue of pine trees rather than in a seemingly endless grove. (It might also be mentioned that the model for Chōzō, whose name was Hayashi, wore a jacket with straight sleeves, not the ratty dotera.) This meeting must have occurred much farther out from Tokyo than Ōmiya, since it was in Maebashi, another thirty-five miles northwest of Ōmiya, that the young man boarded the train with the procurer. They traveled east and north on the train to Utsunomiya, then continued (on foot, presumably) to Nikkō, where they arrived at night, having picked up another man and two thirteen-year-old boys somewhere along the way. Walking upstream by the Daiya River (the river feeding the famous Kegon Falls, a favorite site for romantic suicides, as mentioned in the text), they came to a sandal maker's shop, where they spent the night, finally reaching the Ashio mine the next day. Sōseki is not very precise with his geography, however. He has the protagonist leave Tokyo by the Senju Bridge, which would have sent the fellow off straight north and made a distraught young man's detour to the Nakasendō most unlikely. (In fact, the correct route would have taken him across the Toda Bridge.) He also has the narrator call the Nakasendō by the informal name "Itabashi Highway," used only for the section of the highway extending out as far as Ōmiya, although the town where the protagonist and Chōzō board the train, within easy walking distance of the pine grove, is modeled on Maebashi, well beyond Ōmiya. None of this is of the least importance, of course, as far as an understanding of the novel is concerned. Sōseki expunges almost all place names and even has the narrator tell us pointedly that he chooses not to reveal the name of the town to which Chōzō brought him (p. 20). Indeed, we might even fault Sōseki for being so inconsistent as to have mentioned the name of the Itabashi Highway at all.

6. The following translations of Sōseki novels were reissued in 1982 by G. P. Putnam's Sons, New York, as Perigee Books: *I Am a Cat, The Three-Cornered World, Sanshiro, And Then, Mon (The Gate), The Wayfarer,* and *Light and Darkness.* For *Botchan* and *The Heart,* see notes 9 and 14 below.

7. McClellan, *Two Japanese Novelists,* p. 56.

8. Howard S. Hibbett, "Natsume Sōseki and the Psychological Novel," in Donald H. Shively, ed., *Tradition and Modernization in Japanese Culture* (Princeton: Princeton University Press, 1971), p. 346.

9. SZ 6: 278; quoted, slightly altered, from the translation by Edwin McClellan, *Kokoro* (Chicago: Henry Regnery, 1957), p. 238.

10. Hibbett, p. 346.

11. *Tanomi ni naranai, tayori ni naranai, ate ni naranai,* etc.

12. "*Yo no naka ni shin'yō-suru ni taru mono ga sonzai shi-enai rei.*" SZ 6: 169; McClellan, *Kokoro,* p. 141.

13. SZ 4: 536–37; cf. translation by Norma Moore Field, *And Then* (Baton Rouge: Louisiana State University Press, 1978), p. 186.

14. SZ 2: 324; quoted from the translation by Alan Turney, *Botchan* (Tokyo: Kodansha International, 1972), p. 108.

15. SZ 2: 721–22.

16. SZ 2: 318; Turney, p. 101. And SZ 4: 24; cf. translation by Jay Rubin, *Sanshiro* (Seattle: University of Washington Press, 1977), p. 18.

17. SZ 6: 77; McClellan, *Kokoro*, p. 61.

18. "Sōseki ron," *Chūō kōron* (Mar. 1908), pp. 34–56; quotations from pp. 53–54.

19. "*Kōfu* no sakui to shizen-ha denki-ha no kōshō," SZ 16: 578–80; Komiya, 3: 1–3. The detailed descriptions of mining activities not covered in the notes suggest that Sōseki was consulting Arai as he wrote. A postcard dated January 10 (the tenth day of serialization) mentions that "Mr. Miner" came to Sōseki's home "again" that day and corrected his misuse of some mine argot in a section of the manuscript that would not appear for another month (SZ 14: 670). Apparently Arai came to work for Sōseki as a houseboy after that, but he made a rapid departure in April, the month that serialization ended, when Sōseki heard he had been complaining to a journalist that Sōseki had shared none of the profits from *The Miner* with him (Komiya, 3: 8–9). No doubt some of the strains of this situation are echoed when Sōseki has his narrator speak of "hiring a student houseboy mainly to do chores for you while telling yourself that you're doing it primarily to help him out" (p. 73).

20. Katayama Koson, "Sōseki ron," *Chūō kōron* (Mar. 1908), p. 34.

21. "Bungeikai," *Taiyō* (Feb. 1, 1907), p. 245; Kōbōshi, "Bungei jihyō," *Nihon oyobi Nihonjin* (Jan. 1, 1908), p. 57; "Bundan," *Chūō kōron* (Feb. 1908), p. 161.

22. "Sōseki ron," *Chūō kōron* (Mar. 1908), pp. 45, 56. The editor was Takita Choin. See Sōseki's letter to this distinguished editor on the forthcoming feature, SZ 14: 676, in which he resignedly notes Choin's dislike of *The Miner*.

23. SZ 16: 578–80.

24. Yoshida Seiichi, ed., *Natsume Sōseki hikkei* (Gakutōsha, 1971).

25. See, for example, the important Nihon bungaku kenkyū shiryō kankōkai, ed., *Nihon bungaku kenkyū shiryō sōsho: Natsume Sōseki* (Yūseidō, 1970). There is one essay on *The Miner* in the following five-volume set, which contains essays on everything: Miyoshi Yukio, Hiraoka Toshio, Hirakawa Sukehiro, and Etō Jun, eds., *Kōza: Natsume Sōseki*, 5 vols. (Yūhikaku, 1981). Rare, too, is the literary journal with its "special Sōseki edition" that devotes any space to *The Miner*.

26. Etō Jun, *Natsume Sōseki* (Keisō shobō, 1965), pp. 85–86. Etō specifically negates Nakamura Shin'ichirō's "simplistic" identification of *The Miner* with Joycean stream-of-consciousness writing. In her monumental 665-page study, crammed with minutiae and lengthy essays, Kumasaka Atsuko quotes briefly from *The Miner* in her discussion of *Sanshirō*. See her *Natsume Sōseki no kenkyū* (Ōfūsha, 1973), p. 49 and *passim*.

27. Miyoshi Yukio, "Kaisetsu," *Kōfu* (Shinchōsha, 1976), pp. 226, 229.

28. Edwin McClellan, "Introduction to Sōseki," *Harvard Journal of Asiatic Studies*, 22 (Dec. 1959): 150–208; revised and expanded in his *Two Japanese Novelists*.

29. Beongcheon Yu, *Natsume Sōseki* (New York: Twayne, 1969), pp. 64–69.

30. Nakamura Shin'ichirō, "Kōfu no imi," in *Bungei dokuhon: Natsume Sōseki II* (Kawade shobō shinsha, 1977), pp. 167–69; Shimada Atsushi, "Sōseki no shisō," in Nihon bungaku kenkyū, pp. 113–17; Matsui Sakuko, *Natsume Sōseki as a Critic of English Literature* (Tokyo: Center for East Asian Cultural Studies, 1975), p. 120.

31. Keene, 1: 322–24; Yu, p. 64.

32. Senuma Shigeki has noted that Sōseki's examination of his internal depths continued in 1908 with "The Paddy Bird" (Bunchō) and "Ten Nights of Dream" (Yume jūya; translated by Aiko Itō and Graeme Wilson in *Ten Nights of Dream, Hearing Things, The Heredity of Taste* [Rutland: Tuttle, 1974]), and while he feels that Sōseki failed to meld theory and technique in *The Miner*, he does recognize it as a philosophical turning point for him. By the time Sōseki finished *The Miner*, says Senuma, he had come to see anxiety and terror as innate elements of human life. *Natsume Sōseki* (Tokyo Daigaku shuppan kai, 1970), pp. 139–43.

33. *Mu-seikaku ron*. I have used the word "character" for *seikaku* and also for *jinkaku* (pp. 145, 147), allowing the context to convey the greater ethical content of the latter. In a few instances, I have translated *jinkaku* as "individuality" (pp. 39, 40), and in one case as *both* "character" and "individuality" (p. 147). If anything, this narrowing of terminology in English only serves to enhance Sōseki's study of the interplay between psychological amorphousness and social and literary structure.

34. Kumasaka, pp. 29–45; Senuma cited therein, p. 38.

35. "Bungei no tetsugakuteki kiso," SZ 11: 94–95.

36. The notes include only the sketchiest details of the geographical setting. Some of the miners' dialogues with the newcomer are nearly identical with those in the notes, as are the boy's first encounters with the slippery rice and the bedbugs in the dormitory known as a "boiler" (*hanba*). Young Arai was led through the tunnels by an unnamed miner (the model for

Hatsu), following much the same route as in the book, and experienced a few emotional moments alone down in the dark, during which he had thoughts of suicide. Later, as in the novel, he became separated from his guide and encountered a miner named Kin (the same name as that of the sick old man in the boiler), who became the model for Yasu. Unlike the other miners, this Kin had a "normal" face, and he delivered the boy a moving speech concerning his own misspent youth, noting that although the statute of limitations on his crime would be running out the next year, the sin he had committed (apparently in the pleasure quarter) would never disappear. (This reference to the statute of limitations under the criminal code of 1880 provides only the vaguest hint as to the exact nature of Kin/Yasu's crime. SZ 3: 732, n644.2.) He offered to pay Arai's fare if only the boy would leave the mine. He "grieved," he said, both for the boy and for society if Arai should stay "buried" there (though, significantly, he did not engage in Yasu's appeal to patriotism). Arai's decision against suicide and against taking Kin's money was much as detailed in the book, and his visit to the infirmary, leading to the diagnosis of bronchitis, also included a whiff of medicine that reminded him of death, but the notes contain no mention of a flower seen before and after the examination, another important departure by Sōseki from his source. The subsequent action of the novel is very close to the notes, which also observe that Arai obeyed Kin's admonition never to write to him in the mine. SZ 13: 274–86.

37. Tamai Takayuki, *Natsume Sōseki ron* (Ōfūsha, 1976), pp. 79–80.

38. Keene, 1: 324. Tamai, pp. 72–73, has noted Sōseki's likely interest in the 1907 labor uprisings at Ashio and other mines, sparked by the oppressive "boiler" system that surfaces in the novel, but, like other scholars, he recognizes that Sōseki's purpose has nothing to do with social commentary. It might also be noted that, having decided to make his narrator a mature man looking back at events of his youth, Sōseki could hardly feature events that had made headlines only a few months earlier.

39. Sasaki Masanobu, "*Kōfu ron*," in Uchida Michio and Kubota Yoshitarō, eds., *Sakuhinron: Natsume Sōseki* (Sōbunsha, 1976), p. 129.

40. Komiya Toyotaka (1884–1966) buys the sentiment whole hog; see his "Kaisetsu," SZ 3: 693–94. Senuma Shigeki (b. 1904) notes the apparent contradiction between Yasu's solid character (*jinkaku*) and the theory of characterlessness (*mu-seikaku*), and he admits that "it is not entirely clear how" the protagonist is saved (*Natsume Sōseki*, p. 139). Doi Takeo (b. 1920), the psychiatrist, speaks of the Yasu encounter as "therapeutic in the truest sense of the word"; see *The Psychological World of Natsume Sōseki*, trans. William J. Tyler (Cambridge: Harvard University Press, 1976), p. 26. Tamai Takayuki (b. 1929) agrees with Doi and the others who speak of sal-

vation (*Natsume Sōseki ron*, p. 78). Ochi Haruo (1929–83) also sees the subterranean encounter as an affirmation of character (*jinkaku*), but he admits that "the structure of the novel does not seem to take this as a conclusion," and while the meeting with Yasu "is of course not entirely meaningless, it seems that we cannot quite call it a spiritual rebirth"; see *Sōseki shiron* (Kadokawa shoten, 1971), p. 145. Kamiyama Mutsumi (b. 1947) limits his discussion to viewing *The Miner* as a technical experiment, but he dismisses the Yasu episode as a "secondary element of the novel"; see *Natsume Sōseki ron—josetsu* (Kokubunsha, 1980), pp. 275–77. Satō Yasumasa (b. 1917) is the only member of the prewar generation to note the significance of the "right out of a novel" remark, and while he does not cite Sasaki's 1976 study, he has clearly benefited from it; see "*Kōfu* no kokoromi," in Miyoshi Yukio, et. al., eds., *Kōza: Natsume Sōseki*, 2: 232–55, esp. 247ff.

41. Alain Robbe-Grillet, *For a New Novel*, trans. Richard Howard (New York: Grove Press, 1965), p. 27.

42. August Strindberg, *Eight Famous Plays*, trans. Edwin Björkman and N. Erichsen (London: G. Duckworth, 1949), pp. 105–7.

43. The connection was made by Komiya Toyotaka in "Kaisetsu," SZ 3: 693.

44. Strindberg, p. 111. It is unlikely that Sōseki was aware of Strindberg's ideas. A letter he wrote in 1914 (six years after *The Miner*) mentioned that he was not familiar with *Miss Julie*, and other references to Strindberg appear only in his later correspondence. SZ 15: 319.

45. Eugene Ionesco, *Three Plays*, trans. Donald Watson (New York: Grove Press, 1958), pp. 156–57, 159.

46. Erich Auerbach, *Mimesis*, trans. Willard Trask (New York: Doubleday Anchor, 1957), p. 473.

47. Nakamura, "Kōfu no imi," pp. 167–69; see also his "'Ishiki no nagare' shōsetsu no dentō," *Gunzō* (Dec. 1951), pp. 40–45.

48. The opening passage may be mentioned as an exception. Sōseki uses the non-past *-ru* ending, at times unpredictably, to describe past events with an immediacy resembling the historical present. As the narrator occasionally reminds us, however, he is *writing*, and the style is "too coherent, too carefully ordered" to satisfy Edouard Dujardin's definition of the stream of consciousness, i.e., "discourse before any logical organization, reproducing thought in its original state and as it comes into the mind," as Donald Keene has noted in *Dawn to the West*, 1: 323.

49. *Molloy*, in *Three Novels by Samuel Beckett* (New York: Grove Press, 1959), p. 3.

50. Hugh Kenner, *Samuel Beckett* (New York: Grove Press, 1961), pp. 14, 15.

51. *Malone Dies,* in *Three Novels,* p. 304.
52. Keene, 1: 324.
53. "Dōraku to shokugyō," SZ 11: 317. In fact, Sōseki's arrangement with the *Asahi* gave him both security and complete artistic freedom.
54. SZ 4: 223; Rubin, p. 153.
55. McClellan, *Two Japanese Novelists,* p. 34.
56. Robbe-Grillet, pp. 59, 61, 67.